Nelson Mandela was born in Transkei, South Africa on 18 July 1918. He joined the African National Congress in 1944 and was engaged in resistance against the ruling National Party's apartheid policies for many years before being arrested in August 1962. Mandela was incarcerated for over twenty-seven years, during which his reputation as a potent symbol of resistance to the anti-apartheid movement grew steadily. Released from prison in 1990, Mandela won the Nobel Peace Prize in 1993 and was inaugurated as the first democratically elected president of South Africa in 1994. He is the author of the international bestseller *Long Walk to Freedom*. He passed away on 5 December 2013, aged ninety-five.

Praise for *Conversations With Myself*:

'Outstanding . . . Its collection of letters and meditations belongs on the shelf of anyone interested in the nature of power and resistance' *New York Times*

'Whereas all the previous works on the subject seemed controlled, contained and distant, *Conversations With Myself* reveals the man for what he is: extraordinarily self-disciplined and with a capacity to forgive his persecutors' *Daily Telegraph*

'Readers have been made to feel as if they were miraculously eavesdropping on a medley of Mandela's thoughts and emotions . . . Each carefully chosen paragraph and episode exudes closeness, the sense that the text has come to us unadulterated, just as the great man wrote or spoke it . . . One of the more chilling aspects of reading Mandela's Robben Island correspondence is that you can almost hear the overseers turning the page, skimming through the contents of what was not meant for their eyes, probing into what only his loved ones should be reading. And yet this correspondence also breathes a dignity so fierce that it's heartbreaking' Ariel Dorfman, *The Nation*

'This book will reduce the reader to both rapture and tears . . . We have had the grand autobiography *Long Walk to Freedom*. Now, we are introduced to the human side of Mandela . . . Deeply moving' *Financial Times*

To my lovely boy

Sid

NELSON MANDELA

Conversations with Myself

MACMILLAN

First published 2010 by Macmillan

This edition published in Great Britain 2011 by Macmillan
an imprint of Pan Macmillan, a division of Macmillan Publishers Limited
Pan Macmillan, 20 New Wharf Road, London N1 9RR
Basingstoke and Oxford
Associated companies throughout the world
www.panmacmillan.com

ISBN 978-0-230-74901-6 HB
ISBN 978-0-230-75594-9 TPB

5 7 9 8 6 HB
5 7 9 8 6 4 TPB

A CIP catalogue record for this book is available from
the British Library.

Produced and originated by PQ Blackwell Limited
116 Symonds Street, Auckland 1010, New Zealand

Printed and bound by CPI Group (UK) Ltd, Croydon, CR0 4YY

Visit **www.panmacmillan.com** to read more about all our books
and to buy them. You will also find features, author interviews and
news of any author events, and you can sign up for e-newsletters
so that you're always first to hear about our new releases.

....

Hardback front endpaper image: from the unpublished sequel to Mandela's autobiography. The top two
numerals in each sum are years and indicate (from left to right) the number of years he was imprisoned;
his age when he was first imprisoned; his age when he was released.

Back endpaper image: signature from a letter written in prison (466/64 was Mandela's prisoner number).

For Zenani Zanethemba Nomasonto Mandela,
who passed away tragically on 11 June 2010
at the age of thirteen

. . . the cell is an ideal place to learn to know yourself, to search realistically and regularly the process of your own mind and feelings. In judging our progress as individuals we tend to concentrate on external factors such as one's social position, influence and popularity, wealth and standard of education. These are, of course, important in measuring one's success in material matters and it is perfectly understandable if many people exert themselves mainly to achieve all these. But internal factors may be even more crucial in assessing one's development as a human being. Honesty, sincerity, simplicity, humility, pure generosity, absence of vanity, readiness to serve others – qualities which are within easy reach of every soul – are the foundation of one's spiritual life. Development in matters of this nature is inconceivable without serious introspection, without knowing yourself, your weaknesses and mistakes. At least, if for nothing else, the cell gives you the opportunity to look daily into your entire conduct, to overcome the bad and develop whatever is good in you. Regular meditation, say about 15 minutes a day before you turn in, can be very fruitful in this regard. You may find it difficult at first to pinpoint the negative features in your life, but the 10th attempt may yield rich rewards. Never forget that a saint is a sinner who keeps on trying.

From a letter to Winnie Mandela in Kroonstad Prison, dated 1 February 1975, see pages 211–212.

CONTENTS

FOREWORD

....

Like many people around the world, I came to know of Nelson Mandela from a distance, when he was imprisoned on Robben Island. To so many of us, he was more than just a man – he was a symbol of the struggle for justice, equality, and dignity in South Africa and around the globe. His sacrifice was so great that it called upon people everywhere to do what they could on behalf of human progress.

In the most modest of ways, I was one of those people who tried to answer his call. The first time that I became politically active was during my college years, when I joined a campaign on behalf of divestment, and the effort to end apartheid in South Africa. None of the personal obstacles that I faced as a young man could compare to what the victims of apartheid experienced every day, and I could only imagine the courage that had led Mandela to occupy that prison cell for so many years. But his example helped awaken me to the wider world, and the obligation that we all have to stand up for what is right. Through his choices, Mandela made it clear that we did not have to accept the world as it is – that we could do our part to seek the world as it should be.

Over the years, I continued to watch Nelson Mandela with a sense of admiration and humility, inspired by the sense of possibility that his own life demonstrated and awed by the sacrifices necessary to achieve his dream of justice and equality. Indeed, his life tells a story that stands in direct opposition to the cynicism and hopelessness that so often afflicts our world. A prisoner became a free man; a liberation figure became a passionate voice for reconciliation; a party leader became a president who advanced democracy and development. Out of formal office, Mandela continues to work for equality, opportunity and human dignity. He has done so much to change his country, and the world, that it is hard to imagine the history of the last several decades without him.

A little more than two decades after I made my first foray into political life and the divestment movement as a college student in California, I stood in Mandela's former cell in Robben Island. I was a newly elected United States Senator. By then, the cell had been transformed from a prison to a monument to the sacrifice that was made by so many on behalf of South Africa's peaceful transformation. Standing there in that cell, I tried to transport myself back to those days when President Mandela was still Prisoner 466/64 – a time when the success of his struggle was by no means a certainty. I tried to imagine Mandela – the legend who had changed history – as Mandela the man who had sacrificed so much for change.

Conversations with Myself does the world an extraordinary service in giving us that picture of Mandela the man. By offering us his journals, letters, speeches, interviews, and other papers from across so many decades, it gives us a glimpse into the life that Mandela lived – from the mundane routines that helped to pass the time in prison, to the decisions that he made as President. Here, we see him as a scholar and politician; as a family man and friend; as a visionary and pragmatic leader. Mandela titled his autobiography Long Walk to Freedom. Now, this volume helps us recreate the different steps – as well as the detours – that he took on that journey.

By offering us this full portrait, Nelson Mandela reminds us that he has not been a perfect man. Like all of us, he has his flaws. But it is precisely those imperfections that should inspire each and every one of us. For if we are honest with ourselves, we know that we all face struggles that are large and small, personal and political – to overcome fear and doubt; to keep working when the outcome of our struggle is not certain; to forgive others and to challenge ourselves. The story within this book – and the story told by Mandela's life – is not one of infallible human beings and inevitable triumph. It is the story of a man who was willing to risk his own life for what he believed in, and who worked hard to lead the kind of life that would make the world a better place.

In the end, that is Mandela's message to each of us. All of us face days when it can seem like change is hard – days when our opposition and our own imperfections may tempt us to take an easier path that avoids our responsibilities to one another. Mandela faced those days as well. But even when little sunlight shined into that Robben Island cell, he could see a better future – one worthy of sacrifice. Even when faced with the temptation to seek revenge, he saw the need for reconciliation, and the triumph of principle over mere power. Even when he had earned his rest, he still sought – and seeks – to inspire his fellow men and women to service.

Prior to my election as President of the United States, I had the great privilege of meeting Mandela, and since taking office I have spoken with him occasionally by phone. The conversations are usually brief – he is in the twilight of his years, and I am faced with the busy schedule that comes with my office. But always, in those conversations, there are moments when the kindness, and generosity, and wisdom of the man shines through. Those are the moments when I am reminded that underneath the history that has been made, there is a human being who chose hope over fear – progress over the prisons of the past. And I am reminded that even as he has become a legend, to know the man – Nelson Mandela – is to respect him even more.

President Barack Obama

INTRODUCTION

The name Nelson Mandela is one of the best known and most revered on earth. The person who carries that name is a hero of his age, one of the great figures in the history of the twentieth century. The story of his almost three-decade imprisonment with other political leaders of his generation has become the birth legend, or creation myth, of 'the new South Africa'. He has become an icon. His life has been represented in countless publications, from biographies to journal articles, from feature movies to made-for-television documentaries, from coffee-table tomes to newspaper supplements, freedom songs to praise poems, institutional websites to personal blogs. But who is he, really? What does he *really* think?

Nelson Rolihlahla Mandela himself has contributed fulsomely to the Mandela literature, publications industry and public discourse. His autobiography, Long Walk to Freedom, *has been a best-seller since its publication in 1994. Authorised work has flowed out of his office since his release from prison in 1990. He has given thousands of interviews, speeches, recorded messages and press conferences.*

Long Walk to Freedom *was fundamentally, and very deliberately, the work of a collective. The original manuscript was drafted on Robben Island by what Ahmed Kathrada – his longtime comrade, friend and fellow prisoner – describes as 'an editorial board'. In the early 1990s Mandela worked closely with author Richard Stengel to update and expand the manuscript, with Kathrada and other advisors forming another collective overseeing the editing process. The same is true of his speeches. Aside from rare moments of improvisation, these are formal presentations of carefully prepared texts. And, not surprisingly, the preparation is usually the work of collectives. Similarly, interviewers over the years have found it almost impossible to penetrate Mandela's very formal public persona. He is 'the leader', 'the president', 'the public representative', 'the icon'. Only glimpses of the person behind the persona have shone through. The questions remain: Who is he,* really*? What does he* really *think?*

* * *

Conversations with Myself *aims to give readers access to the Nelson Mandela behind the public figure, through his private archive. This archive represents Mandela writing and speaking privately, addressing either himself or his closest confidantes. This is him not geared primarily to the needs and expectations of an audience. Here he is drafting letters, speeches and memoirs. Here he is making notes (or doodling) during meetings, keeping a diary, recording his dreams, tracking his weight and blood pressure, maintaining to-do lists. Here he is meditating on his experience, interrogating his memory, conversing with a friend. Here he is not the icon or saint elevated far beyond the reach of ordinary mortals. Here he is like you and me. As he himself expresses it, 'In real life we deal, not with gods, but with ordinary humans like ourselves: men and women who are full of contradictions, who are stable and fickle, strong and weak, famous and infamous, people in whose bloodstream the muckworm battles daily with potent pesticides.'*

    For most of his adult life, Mandela has been a diligent maker of records and an obsessive record-keeper. How else to explain his collection of Methodist Church membership cards recording his annual membership between 1929 and 1934? How else to explain his daily diary entries while travelling through Africa in 1962, or his habit of drafting most letters in a notebook during the prison years? Of course the archive has been ravaged by his years of struggle, of life underground, of life in prison. Records were secreted away or given to others for safe keeping. Some were lost along the way. Records were confiscated by the state, then either destroyed or used in evidence. Today the Mandela private archive is scattered and fragmentary. The single biggest accumulation is to be found in the Nelson Mandela Centre of Memory and Dialogue. Significant collections are also held by South Africa's National Archives, the National Intelligence Agency, the Mandela House Museum, and the Liliesleaf Trust. Myriad fragments are located in the collections of private individuals, mainly in the form of correspondence.

* * *

Conversations with Myself, *as a book project, has its origins in the 2004 inauguration of the Nelson Mandela Centre of Memory and Dialogue as the core function of the Nelson Mandela Foundation. At the outset, the Centre's priority was to document the scattered and fragmented 'Mandela Archive', but very quickly the collecting of materials not yet in archival custody became equally important. Mandela himself made his first donation of private papers to the Centre in 2004, and continued through 2009 to add to the collection. Very early on it became apparent to me as the Centre's Memory Programme Head that an important book could be crafted from the materials, under the Centre's purview. In 2005 a team of archivists and researchers began the painstaking work of assembling, contextualising, arranging and describing materials. Simultaneously they undertook preliminary identification and selection of items, passages and extracts that* could be considered for the book. *The team comprised the following members: Sello Hatang, Anthea Josias, Ruth Muller, Boniswa Nyati, Lucia Raadschelders, Zanele Riba, Razia Saleh, Sahm Venter and myself.*

In 2008 I began discussing the book with publishers Geoff Blackwell and Ruth Hobday. These discussions crystallised the Centre's thinking about the book, and introduced the project's final phase. Mandela was briefed and gave his blessing, but indicated his wish not to be involved personally. Kathrada agreed to be the special advisor to the project. Senior Researcher Venter and Archivists Hatang, Raadschelders, Riba and Saleh were deployed under my direction as project leader for the final selection and compilation process. Crucially, historian and author Tim Couzens was drafted into the team to bring to bear both specialist expertise and the eye of a scholar not enmeshed in the Centre's daily work. Finally, Bill Phillips – who had worked as senior editor on the Long Walk to Freedom *project in the 1990s – came in during the project's final editing phase.*

* * *

In a real sense, Conversations with Myself *is Nelson Mandela's book. It gives us his own voice – direct, clear, private. But it's important to acknowledge the editorial role played by the team. The words in this book were winnowed from a mass of material, primarily on the basis of theme, importance and immediacy, and that mass was defined by what exists and what was accessible. While we are confident that the bulk of material in Mandela's private archive was scrutinised by the team, not everything in the custody of private individuals was located and made available to us. It was by chance, for example, that in the final months we stumbled across the archive kept by former warder Jack Swart, who was with Mandela during the last fourteen months of his incarceration in Victor Verster Prison. Also late in the game, the National Intelligence Agency disclosed to us the existence of a small Mandela collection, most of which was made available to the team. The Agency's caginess suggests the possibility of further disclosures.*

While all of the Mandela private archive was considered for this project, the final selection drew most heavily on four particular parts. Firstly: the prison letters. Some of the most poignant and painful writings are to be found in two hard-covered exercise books in which Mandela carefully drafted copies of letters he subsequently sent through the prison censors on Robben Island. They date from 1969 to 1971 and cover the very worst time of his imprisonment. Stolen from his cell by the authorities in 1971, they were returned to him by a former security policeman in 2004. Throughout his time in prison Mandela was never sure whether his correspondence would reach its destination due to the actions of what he called 'those remorseless fates', the censors. His prison files in the National Archives contain numerous letters the authorities wouldn't post. They are kept together with copies they made of every letter that they did post.

Secondly: two major collections of taped conversations. Here, the spoken voice, not the written word, is heard. These encounters are so intimate, so informal, that Mandela frequently moves into reverie, enters into a dialogue with himself. The first set is about fifty hours of conversations with Richard Stengel, made when the two men were working together on Long Walk to Freedom. *The second is a set of about twenty hours of conversations with Ahmed Kathrada, who was sentenced with Mandela and six others to life imprisonment on 12 June 1964. Kathrada was asked in the early 1990s to assist Mandela in reviewing the draft texts of both* Long Walk to Freedom *and Anthony Sampson's authorised biography. The behind-the-scenes interaction of these two old comrades is relaxed. They are often chuckling or laughing out loud. The conversations are interesting not only for what Mandela says, but for how he says it.*

Thirdly: the notebooks. Before his imprisonment in 1962, it was a habit of Mandela's to carry a notebook. He had one with him during his journey through Africa (and to England) in 1962 to learn about revolutionary strategies, to be trained in guerrilla warfare, and to secure support from leaders of newly independent countries and nationalist movements. He had one with him when he was captured shortly after his return to South Africa. He resumed this practice in the years after his release from prison, when he was negotiating South Africa's transition to democracy, and even, to some extent, during his presidency. These later notebooks contain notes to self, aide-mémoire, records of meetings and drafts of letters. There are also several extraordinary chunks of writing, each of many pages (not reproduced here for reasons of space and narrow interest), from meetings of the African National Congress Working Committee, during which he meticulously recorded the points each speaker made. Why he did this is not entirely clear. Probably it was a lawyer's habit of carefully taking down information from his clients. Perhaps, at over seventy years of age, he felt he could not entirely trust his memory.

And fourthly: the draft of an unfinished sequel to Long Walk to Freedom. *On 16 October 1998, he took a piece of blue notepaper and with a favoured pen he put down, in a strong and decisive hand, the date in Roman numerals. He followed this with what was his working title: 'The Presidential Years'. Underneath it he wrote 'Chapter One'. At some point, at the head of the page, he wrote the word 'Draft'. The final year of his presidency, his involvement in the Burundi negotiations, political distractions of the moment, the demands of his charitable work, and an endless stream of visitors thwarted the book's progress.*

His advisors suggested he get a professional writer to work with him, but he refused. He was very protective of the writing, wanting to do it himself. He did have a research assistant for a while, but he grew impatient with the arrangement. Ultimately, he simply ran out of steam.

* * *

Not surprisingly, the Mandela private archive has no inherent organising principle or system of arrangement. For Conversations with Myself *we have grouped our selections according to an underlying rationale based partly on the chronology of Mandela's life, and partly on the major themes of his meditations and reflections. The book comprises four parts, each with its own introduction and each carrying a title drawn from classical modes, forms and genres – pastoral, dramatic, epic and tragicomic. Mandela is steeped in the classics. He studied Latin at school and at university. He read widely in Greek literature, and acted in classics of the theatre while at university and in prison.*

The book's form is inspired most directly by Marcus Aurelius's Meditations, *a volume of thoughts, musings and aphorisms penned in the second century AD. Marcus Aurelius was a leader, a Roman emperor, a politician and man of action, a soldier. While not, perhaps, a great philosopher or writer, he knew the benefits of meditation, record-making and daily discipline. He wrote in the midst of action. His book is full of wisdom. Its original title translates literally as 'To Himself'. Its attributes, and those of its author, are not entirely unrelated to those of a man and a book appearing eighteen centuries later.*

Verne Harris
Project Leader
Nelson Mandela Centre of Memory and Dialogue
August 2010

PART ONE

Pastoral

A series of police raids on Nelson Mandela's home in Orlando, Soweto, and a fire in the same house in 1985 meant that many of the records of his early life in rural Thembuland have disappeared, probably forever. This includes a family memoir he took down from his mother. There are photographs of his mother, but none of his father.

Many of Mandela's distinctive habits were acquired early. One of the most important, from his traditional background in Thembuland, was listening carefully to his elders and to all who spoke at tribal gatherings, and watching a consensus gradually emerge under the guidance of the king, the chief or the 'headman'. Habits of discipline, order, self-control and respect for others were demanded by both traditional authority and the educational institutions at which Mandela studied.

From the age of seven, he attended a one-roomed school in Qunu near his birthplace of Mvezo. Later he schooled at Qokolweni, the Clarkebury Boarding Institute, and the Wesleyan College of Healdtown. He completed his first degree at the University College of Fort Hare, near the small town of Alice. Fort Hare attracted the children of prominent black families throughout southern Africa, and nourished the cohort who inhabited Mandela's world for many years to come.

Most notable were Kaiser (K D) Matanzima (his nephew, though actually his senior in age) and Oliver Tambo, who became his political comrade, his law partner and his lifelong friend.

In 1941, Mandela left Thembuland and the Eastern Cape for a different life and a larger destiny. He never cut himself off completely from the place or the tradition but his life choices and the policies of his organisation, the African National Congress, introduced profound tensions in the way he related to them. This was expressed at a deeply personal level in his relationship with Matanzima. Mandela liked and respected him but they parted ways on the question of cooperation with the apartheid state. While in prison, Mandela wanted to receive a visit from Matanzima but bowed to the wishes of his fellow prisoners, who felt that such a visit would be too compromising politically. Much later, in the final months of his imprisonment, Mandela did finally receive him.

After his release from prison, Mandela built a home in Qunu. When he stays there, he is visited and consulted by traditional leaders. He followed with interest his grand-son's appointment to the chieftainship of Mvezo. In 2007 he founded the Nelson Mandela Institute for Education and Rural Development at the University of Fort Hare.

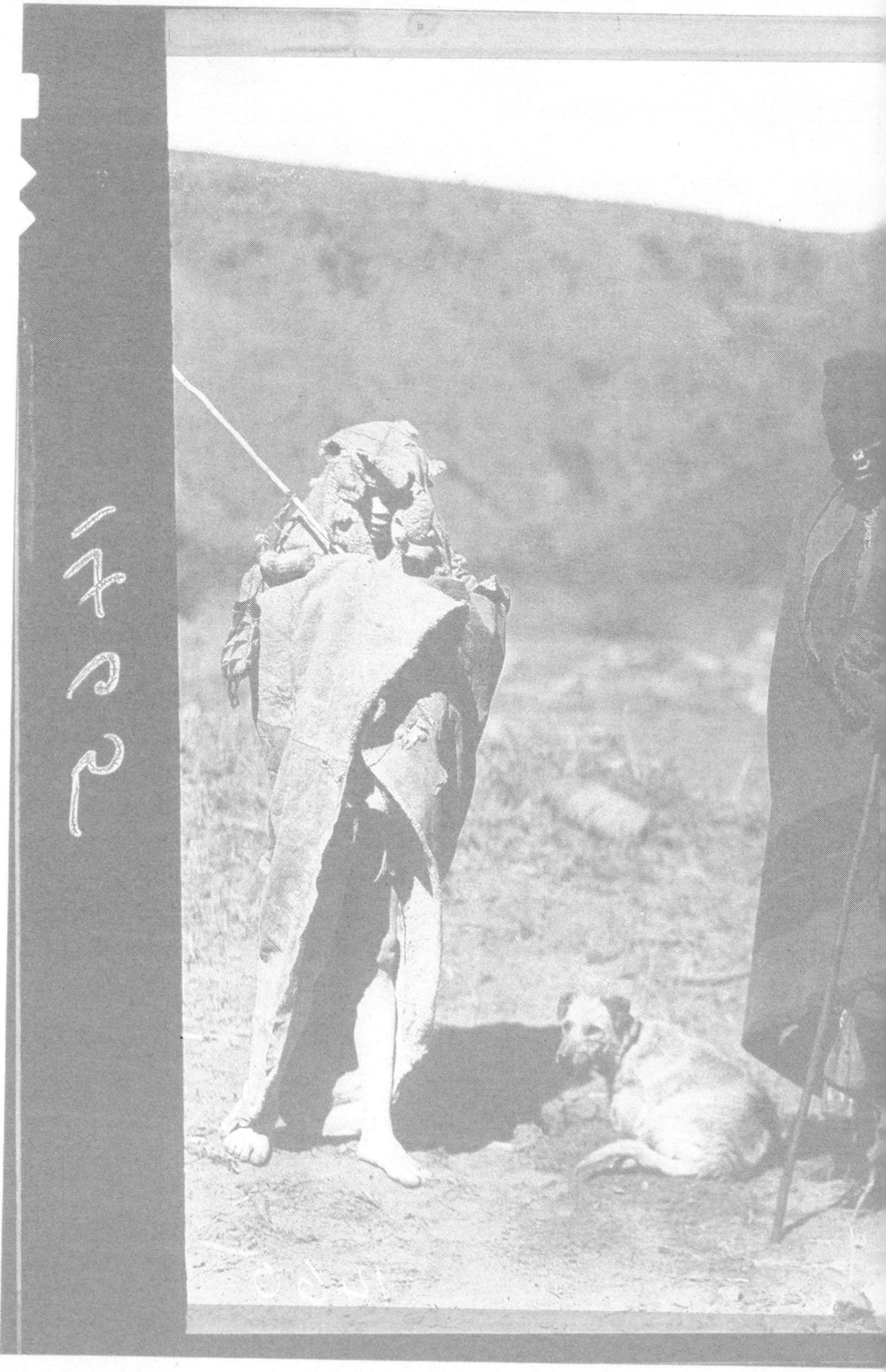

CHAPTER ONE

Deep Time

'I shall stick to our vow: never, never under any circumstances, to say anything unbecoming of the other . . . The trouble, of course, is that most successful men are prone to some form of vanity. There comes a stage in their lives when they consider it permissible to be egotistic and to brag to the public at large about their unique achievements. What a sweet euphemism for self-praise the English language has evolved! Autobiography . . .'

Excerpt from a letter to Fatima Meer, dated 1 March 1971, see page 7.

1. FROM A LETTER TO FATIMA MEER, DATED 1 MARCH 1971[1]

I shall stick to our vow: never, never under any circumstances, to say anything unbecoming of the other . . . The trouble, of course, is that most successful men are prone to some form of vanity. There comes a stage in their lives when they consider it permissible to be egotistic and to brag to the public at large about their unique achievements. What a sweet euphemism for self-praise the English language has evolved! Autobiography, they choose to call it, where the shortcomings of others are frequently exploited to highlight the praiseworthy accomplishments of the author. I am doubtful if I will ever sit down to sketch my background. I have neither the achievements of which I could boast nor the skill to do it. If I lived on cane spirit every day of my life, I still would not have had the courage to attempt it. I sometimes believe that through me Creation intended to give the world the example of a mediocre man in the proper sense of the term. Nothing could tempt me to advertise myself. Had I been in a position to write an autobiography, its publication would have been delayed until our bones had been laid, and perhaps I might have dropped hints not compatible with my vow. The dead have no worries, and if the truth and nothing but the whole truth about them emerged, [and] the image I have helped to maintain through my perpetual silence was ruined, that would be the affair of posterity, not ours . . . I'm one of those who possess scraps of superficial information on a variety of subjects, but who lacks depth and expert knowledge on the one thing in which I ought to have specialised, namely the history of my country and people.

....

1. Professor Fatima Meer, see People, Places and Events.

2. FROM A LETTER TO JOY MOSIELOA, DATED 17 FEBRUARY 1986

When a man commits himself to the type of life he has lived for 45 years, even though he may well have been aware from the outset of all the attendant hazards, the actual course of events and the precise manner in which they would influence his life could never have been clearly foreseeable in every respect. If I had been able to foresee all that has since happened, I would certainly have made the same decision, so I believe at least. But that decision would certainly have been far more daunting, and some of the tragedies which subsequently followed would have melted whatever traces of steel were inside me.

3. FROM A CONVERSATION WITH RICHARD STENGEL

I was being groomed for the position of chieftaincy . . . but then ran away, you know, from a forced marriage . . .[2] That changed my whole career. But if I had stayed at home I would have been a respected chief today, you know? And I would have had a big stomach, you know, and a lot of cattle and sheep.

4. FROM A CONVERSATION WITH RICHARD STENGEL

Most men, you know, are influenced by their background. I grew up in a country village until I was twenty-three, when I then left the village for Johannesburg. I was of course . . . going to school for the greater part of the year, come back during the June and December holidays – June was just a month and December about two months. And so all throughout the year I was at school . . . And then in [19]41 when I was twenty-three, I came to Johannesburg and learned . . . to absorb Western standards of living and so on. But . . . my opinions were already

---

2. Mandela is a Thembu and a member of the royal household, and was expected to marry a bride of the regent's choice.

formed from the countryside and . . . you'll therefore appreciate my enormous respect for my own culture – indigenous culture . . . Of course Western culture is something we cannot live without, so I have got these two strands of cultural influence. But I think it would be unfair to say this is peculiar to me because many of our men are influenced by that . . . I am now more comfortable in English because of the many years I spent here and I've spent in jail and I lost contact, you know, with Xhosa literature. One of the things which I am looking forward to when I retire is to be able to read literature as I want, [including] African literature. I can read both Xhosa and Sotho literature and I like doing that,[3] but the political activities have interfered . . . I just can't read anything now and it's one of the things I regret very much.

5. FROM HIS UNPUBLISHED AUTOBIOGRAPHICAL MANUSCRIPT
    WRITTEN IN PRISON

Nobody ever sat with me at regular intervals to give me a clear and connected account of the history of our country, of its geography, natural wealth and problems, of our culture, of how to count, to study weights and measures. Like all Xhosa children I acquired knowledge by asking questions to satisfy my curiosity as I grew up, learnt through experience, watched adults and tried to imitate what they did. In this process an important role is played by custom, ritual and taboo, and I came to possess a fair amount of information in this regard . . . In our home there were other dependents, boys mainly, and at an early age I drifted away from my parents and moved about, played and ate together with other boys. In fact I hardly remember any occasion when I was ever alone at home. There were always other children with whom I shared food and blankets at night. I must have been about five years old when I

----

3. Xhosa (isiXhosa) and Sotho (Sesotho) are two of South Africa's eleven officially recognised languages.

began going out with other boys to look after sheep and calves and when I was introduced to the exciting love of the veld. Later when I was a bit older I was able to look after cattle as well . . . [A] game I enjoyed very much was what I call Khetha (choose-the-one-you-like) . . . We would stop girls of our age group along the way and ask each one to choose the boy she loved. It was a rule that the girl's choice would be respected and, once she had selected her favourite, she was free to continue her journey escorted by the boy she had chosen. Nimble-witted girls used to combine and all choose one boy, usually the ugliest or dullest, and thereafter tease or bully him along the way . . . Finally, we used to sing and dance and fully enjoyed the perfect freedom we seemed to have far away from the old people. After supper we would listen enthralled to my mother and sometimes my aunt telling us stories, legends, myths and fables which have come down from countless generations, and all of which tended to stimulate the imagination and contained some valuable moral lesson. As I look back to those days I am inclined to believe that the type of life I led at my home, my experiences in the veld where we worked and played together in groups, introduced me at an early age to the ideas of collective effort. The little progress I made in this regard was later undermined by the type of formal education I received which tended to stress individual more than collective values. Nevertheless, in the mid 1940s when I was drawn into the political struggle, I could adjust myself to discipline without difficulty, perhaps because of my early upbringing.

6. FROM HIS UNPUBLISHED AUTOBIOGRAPHICAL MANUSCRIPT
   WRITTEN IN PRISON

The regent was not keen that I visit Qunu, lest I should fall into bad company and run away from school, so he reasoned.

Mandela's Methodist Church card, 1930.

He would allow me only a few days to go home. On other occasions he would arrange for my mother to be fetched so that she could see me at the royal residence. It was always an exciting moment for me to visit Qunu and see my mother and sisters and other members of the family. I was particularly happy in the company of my cousin, Alexander Mandela, who inspired and encouraged me on questions of education in those early days. He and my niece, Phathiwe Rhanugu (she was much older than me), were perhaps the first members of our clan to qualify as teachers. Were it not for their advice and patient persuasion I doubt if I would have succeeded in resisting the attractions offered by the easy life outside the classroom. The two influences that dominated my thoughts and actions during those days were chieftaincy and the church. After all, the only heroes I had heard of at that time had almost all been chiefs, and the respect enjoyed by the regent from both black and white tended to exaggerate the importance of this institution in my mind. I saw chieftaincy not only as the pivot around which community life turned, but as the key to positions of influence, power and status. Equally important was the position of the church, which I associated not so much with the body and doctrine contained in the Bible but with the person of Reverend Matyolo. In this circuit he was as popular as the regent, and the fact that in spiritual matters he was the regent's superior and leader, stressed the enormous power of the church. What was even more was that all the progress my people had made – the schools that I attended, the teachers who taught me, the clerks and interpreters in government offices, the agricultural demonstrators and policemen – were all the products of missionary schools. Later the dual position of the chiefs as representatives of their people and as government servants compelled me to assess their position more realistically, and not merely from the point of view of my own family background or of the exceptional chiefs who identified themselves with the struggle of their people. As descendants of the famous heroes that led us so well during the wars of dispossession and as the traditional leaders in their own right, chiefs are entitled to be treated with respect. But as agents of an oppressive government that is regarded as the enemy of the black man, the same chiefs are the objects of criticism and hostility. The institution of chieftaincy itself has been captured by the government and must now be seen as part of the machinery of oppression. My experiences also enable me to formulate a more balanced assessment of the role of the missionaries and to realise the folly of judging the issue simply in terms of relations with individual priests. Nevertheless, I have always considered it dangerous to underestimate the influence of both institutions amongst the people, and for this reason I have repeatedly urged caution in dealing with them.

Soon after returning from prison I travelled down to E.L. [East London] and met Comrade Silumko Sokupa and the Regional Committee of the ANC [African National Congress] to acquaint myself with the situation in that area. In their briefing they informed me that King Zanesizwe Sandile of the Ngqikas would visit me at the hotel. I was shocked because that was a breach of protocol to ask the king to visit me at a hotel.

I instructed the committee to phone and inform the king that he should remain at the Palace, I would later come and pay a courtesy visit there. At that moment the king walked in. I apologised and pointed out that many of today's youth were born and grew up in the urban areas. They know precious little about traditional leaders. It is not so much because of disrespect but ignorance which makes [them] unaware of protocol.

Heroes like the Khoi leader, Autshumayo,[4] Maqoma of the Rharhabe, Bambatha, Cetywayo of the Zulu, Mampuru of the Pedis, Tshivhase of the Vendas and a host of others, were in the forefront of the wars of resistance and we speak of them with respect and admiration . . . Even at the height of the severe repression by the apartheid regime there were courageous monarchs like Sabata of the Thembus and Cyprian of the Zulus who refused to betray their people . . . Many of our traditional leaders are also not aware of the lessons of history. They do not seem to know that there were once absolute monarchs in the world who did not share power with their subjects . . . It is monarchs . . . themselves or their predecessors, [who] decided to allow elected representatives of the people to govern, and who became constitutional monarchs who survived, like Queen Elizabeth II of Britain, King Carlos of Spain, Queen Beatrix of

---

4.   Autshumao (spelt by Mandela as 'Autshumayo'), see People, Places and Events.

the Netherlands, Queen Margrethe II of Denmark, King Harald of Norway and King Carl XVI Gustaf.

Had these monarchs clung stubbornly to their absolute powers they would long have disappeared from the scene.

But we must never forget that the institution of traditional leaders is sanctified by African law and custom, by our culture and tradition. No attempt must be made to abolish it. We must find an amicable solution based on democratic principles, and which allows traditional leaders to play a meaningful role in levels of government.

. . . I am not clear to what extent a significant initiative of the apartheid government . . . was available in other Bantustans. But in the Transkei there was a school for the sons of traditional leaders which gave them basic skills in the administration of areas under their jurisdiction. I would not urge that we should have such schools. But depending on the resources that the government has, it would be advisable to encourage sons of traditional leaders to get the best education. Although my own resources are very limited, I have sent a number of sons and daughters of traditional leaders to universities in South Africa, and to the United Kingdom and the United States of America. A literate corps of educated traditional leaders would in all probability accept the democratic process. The inferiority complex which makes many of them to cling desperately to feudal forms of administration would, in due course, disappear.

8. FROM A LETTER TO NOMABUTHO BHALA, DATED 1 JANUARY 1971

Your letter was one of the shortest I ever received, the entire contents consisting only of one compound sentence. Yet it is one of the best letters I had read for a long time. I had thought that our generation of rabble-rousers had vanished with the close of the fifties. I had also believed that with all the experience of almost 50 years behind me, in the course of which I attentively listened to many persuasive speakers, and read first-class biographies of some of the world's most prominent figures, it would not be easy for me to be carried away by mere beauty of prose or smooth flow of one's oratory. Yet the few lines that you scrawled carefully across that modest sheet of writing material moved me much more than all the classics I have read. Many of the personalities that featured in your remarkable dream lived, simply and without written records, some 3 centuries ago. Neither you nor I ever saw them plan the operations that were to make them famous in history, nor did we watch as they went into action. For most of them there is not even one authentic photograph which would at least give us a faint idea of their physical features or personality. Yet even a polished urbanite like yourself, who lives in the second half of the 20th century, with all the fantastic progress and achievement that mark it, and who is cut off from the influence of tribal life, cannot wipe away from your thoughts, plans and dreams the rugged and fierce heroes of the Neolithic age. They were unusual men – the exceptions that are found elsewhere in the world; in so far as their economy and implements were concerned they lived in the Stone Age, and yet they founded large and stable kingdoms by means of metal weapons. In the conflicts that were later to rock the country, they gave a good account of themselves, holding at bay for a continuous period of more than [one] hundred years, a community millennia in advance of themselves in economic organisation and technology, and which made full use of the scientific resources at their disposal.

I find the explanation for your dream in the simple fact that you read deeper lessons into our ancestry. You regard their heroic deeds during the deathless century of conflict as a model for the life we should lead today. When their country was threatened they showed the highest standard of patriotism.

Just as they refused to use the primitiveness of their economic system and ineffectiveness of their weapons as an excuse for shirking their sacred duty, so the present generation should not allow itself to be intimidated by the disparities current internal alignments seem to entail . . . But the full story of our past heritage remains incomplete if we forget that line of indigenous heroes who acted as curtain raisers to the major conflicts that subsequently flamed out, and who acquitted themselves just as magnificently. The Khoikhoi,[5] from whom the bulk of our Coloured folk is descended, were skilfully led by Autshumayo (S.A.'s [South Africa] first black political prisoner to be exiled to Robben Island), Odasoa and Gogosoa. During the Third Liberation War in 1799 Klaas Stuurman took the unprecedented step of joining forces with Cungwa, Chief of [the] Amagqunukhwebe. Many people, including freedom fighters with a long record of struggle and sacrifice, speak contemptuously of [the] Abatwa. Yet several S.A. historians have written objective and warm accounts on their unconquerable spirit and noble qualities. Those who have read reports of the Sneeuberg battles between [the] Abatwa and the Boers, and more especially that between [the] Abatwa, led by their chief, Karel, and a commando of more than 100 Boers around the great cave at Poshuli's Hoek, will have an idea of the important contribution made to S.A. history by a community that once were the sole occupants of our beautiful country.[6] In numerous engagements they showed unusual courage and daring and would continue to fight desperately even after the last arrow had been fired. These are the men who strove for a free South Africa long before we reached the field of battle. They blazed

5. The Khoikhoi make up one of the four groups who were the original inhabitants of South Africa, see People, Places and Events.
6. A description of the battle at Poshuli's Hoek appears in *The Native Races of South Africa: A History of the Intrusion of the Hottentots and Bantu into the Hunting Grounds of the Bushmen, the Aborigines of the Country,* George W Stow (published 1905), which Mandela read. (See his transcription from this book, pages 18–19.)

the trail and it is their joint efforts that supply the source of the vast stream of S.A. history. We are the heirs to a three-stream heritage; an inheritance that inspires us to fight and die for the loftiest ideals in life. The title 'African hero' embraces all these veterans. Years later, more articulate and sophisticated personalities were to follow and, in the process, the tableau of history was enriched a thousand times – the Selope Themas, Jabavus, Dubes, Abdurahmans, Gools, Asvats, Cachalias,[7] and now you and your generation have joined this legion of honour . . .

I am very fond of great dreams and I particularly liked yours; it was very close to my heart. Perhaps in your next dream, there will be something that will excite not only the sons [of] Zika Ntu, but the descendants of all the famous heroes of the past. At a time when some people are feverishly encouraging the growth of fractional forces, raising the tribe into the final and highest form of social organisation, setting one national group against the other, cosmopolitan dreams are not only desirable but a bounden duty; dreams that stress the special unity that hold the freedom forces together – [in] a bond that has been forged by common struggles, sacrifices and traditions.

---

7. For notes on these individuals, see People, Places and Events.

The Native Races of South Africa: George
W. Stow. P. 218.

Dr R. Rubidge who spent the greater portion of
his youth in wandering about the rocks & crags
of the Sneeuwberg mountains, stated that
after committing some depredations, the clan
was surrounded by a commando which had
pursued them and succeeded in cutting them off
among the rocks of a projecting shoulder of a great
precipice. Here the retreating Bushmen turned for
the last time at bay. Their untiring enemies were on
one side, a yawning gulf without any chance of
escape on the other. A dire but hopeless struggle for
life commenced. One after another they fell under the
storm of bullets with which their adversaries assailed
them. The dead and the dying were heaped upon the
dizzy projecting ledge, many in their death struggle
rolled and fell over among the crags and fissures
in the depths which environed them. Still they
resisted and still they fell, until one only remained;
and yet with the bloody heap of dead around him,
and the mangled bodies of his comrades on the rocks
below, he seemed as undaunted as when surrounded
by the entire band of his brave companions. Posting
himself on the very outermost point of the projecting
rocks, with sheer precipices of nearly a couple of
hundred feet on either side of him, a spot where no
man would have dared to follow him, he defied
his pursuers, and amid the bullets which showered
around him, he appeared to have a charmed life and
plied his arrows with unerring aim whenever
his enemies incautiously exposed themselves

....

Mandela transcribed portions of George W Stow's *The Native Races of South Africa: A History
of the Intrusion of the Hottentots and Bantu into the Hunting Grounds of the Bushmen, the
Aborigines of the Country*, see note 6, this chapter.

His last arrow was on the string. A slight feeling of surprise seemed at length to animate the hostile multitude which hemmed him in; they called to him that his life should be spared if he would surrender. He let fly his last arrow in scorn at the speaker, as he replied that "a chief knew how to die, but never to surrender to the race who had despoiled him!" Then with a loud shout of bitter defiance, he turned round, and leaping headlong into the deep abyss was dashed to pieces on the rocks beneath. Thus died with a Spartan-like intrepidity, the last of the clan, and with his death his tribe ceased to exist.

CHAPTER TWO

Cohort

'Western civilisation has not entirely rubbed off my African background and I have not forgotten the days of my childhood when we used to gather round community elders to listen to their wealth of wisdom and experience. That was the custom of our forefathers and the traditional school in which we were brought up. I still respect our elders and like to chat with them about olden times when we had our own government and lived freely.'

Excerpt from his unpublished autobiographical manuscript written in prison, see page 23.

1. FROM HIS UNPUBLISHED AUTOBIOGRAPHICAL MANUSCRIPT
   WRITTEN IN PRISON

Western civilisation has not entirely rubbed off my African background and I have not forgotten the days of my childhood when we used to gather round community elders to listen to their wealth of wisdom and experience. That was the custom of our forefathers and the traditional school in which we were brought up. I still respect our elders and like to chat with them about olden times when we had our own government and lived freely. It is always a great moment when I listen to an expert on our true history, culture, legends and traditions. We used to pester men like Mweli Skota, Selope Thema, Chief [Albert] Luthuli, Professor Z.K. Matthews, Moses Kotane, J.B. Marks and the amount of knowledge they had on African history was impressive.[1] Their chief strength lay in the fact that their feet were deeply planted in African soil and they used scientific knowledge to enrich our heritage and culture. They could trace the movements of each section of our people from the North, discuss competently the various theories on the subject, the reasons for the many clashes between our people throughout our history, contact with the whites and even attempt to predict the future course of events. The old generation that inherited the oral traditions of our ancestors has disappeared or is disappearing and science has developed modern techniques of acquiring knowledge in all fields, but even the younger generation of today still values the experience of elders. Young men who are grappling every day with fresh practical human problems like to test the knowledge acquired from the classroom and books against the experience of their mature seniors who have been in the field.

....

1. For notes on these individuals, see People, Places and Events.

Yes, the boarding master is the man who is in *charge* of the students in a college, yes. Now this was a remarkable man . . . He once gave a sermon [about] a man whose house was haunted by evil spirits. He did everything to drive them out, but he failed. Then he decided to leave his *kraal* [a rural settlement of huts and houses], packed all his things on a wagon and started driving away to settle elsewhere. Along the way, he met a friend and the friend asked, '*Where* are you going?' Before he answered, a voice came out of the wagon, 'We are trekking, we are leaving our *kraal.*' It was one of the evil spirits. He thought he was leaving them behind; he actually came along with them. And he says, the moral was '*Don't* run away from your problems; *face* them! Because *if you don't deal* with them, they will *always* be with you. *Deal* with a problem which arises; face it courageously.' That was the moral . . . I never forgot that, you see, and I accepted that if you have a problem, you must face it and not gloss over it. For example, you know, in politics, there are *very* sensitive issues and people normally don't want an unpopular approach. If people say 'We must go on action', very few people will say 'Have we got the resources? Have we made sufficient preparations? Are we in a position to undertake this action?' Some people like to give an impression of being militant and therefore *not* to face the problems, especially if they are the type of problems which are going to make you unpopular. Success in politics demands that you must take your people into confidence about your views and state them very clearly, very politely, very calmly, but nevertheless state them openly.

3. FROM A LETTER TO THE UNIVERSITY OF SOUTH AFRICA,
   DATED 22 DECEMBER 1987[2]

I hereby apply for exemption from Latin 1 on the following grounds: Although I obtained a pass in this subject in the 1938 matriculation examinations, and in spite of the fact that I passed a special course in the same subject at the University of the Witwatersrand in 1944, I have forgotten practically everything about it. If I am compelled to attempt the course, I will have to start right from the beginning. At the age of 69 years this will be a very difficult undertaking indeed. I am a qualified attorney, having practiced as such for nine years prior to my arrest and conviction. If I decided to resume practice as an attorney, I would not be required first to obtain a degree course in Latin. In actual fact, I have no intention of ever practicing law again either as an attorney or as an advocate. Even if I had intended practicing law some time in the future, I am not likely ever to do so, since I am serving a sentence of life imprisonment. If you grant this application I propose to register for African Politics in place of Latin 1.

4. FROM HIS UNPUBLISHED AUTOBIOGRAPHICAL MANUSCRIPT
   WRITTEN IN PRISON

My association with the African National Congress has taught me that a broad national movement has numerous and divergent contradictions, fundamental and otherwise. The presence in one organisation of various classes and social groups with conflicting long term interests that may collide at crucial moments brings its own train of conflicts. Contradictions of a different kind may split from top to bottom an otherwise homogeneous class or group, and the prejudices arising from

....

2.   Mandela continued his studies for a law degree while in prison and completed his degree in 1989.

different practices in regard to circumcision are amongst these. I still remember well my first reaction, and even revulsion, at Fort Hare when I discovered that a friend had not observed the custom. I was twenty-one then and my subsequent association with the African National Congress and progressive ideas helped me to crawl out of the prejudice of my youth and to accept all people as equals. I came to accept that I have no right whatsoever to judge others in terms of my own customs, however much I may be proud of such customs;[3] that to despise others because they have not observed particular customs is a dangerous form of chauvinism. I consider myself obliged to pay proper respect to my customs and traditions, provided that such customs and traditions tend to keep us together and do not in any way conflict with the aims and objects of the struggle against racial oppression. But I shall neither impose my own customs on others nor follow any practice which will offend my comrades, especially now that freedom has become so costly.

5.   FROM A CONVERSATION WITH RICHARD STENGEL

Oh, yes, yes. I was proud of that because we were told by our teachers, 'Now you are at Fort Hare, you are going to be a *leader* of your people.'[4] This was what was being drummed upon us, and of course in those days to have a degree as a black man was something very important. And so I had this feeling, and of course the King was very proud that he had a son, a member of the clan, who was at Fort Hare.

---

3. Circumcision is a traditional Xhosa ritual initiating a boy into manhood. Mandela was circumcised when he was sixteen years old.
4. Established in 1916, the University of Fort Hare was South Africa's first college for the higher education of black South Africans.

But the process of illusion and disillusionment is part of life and goes on endlessly. In the early [19]40s what struck me forcefully was the conflict between my expectations and actual experience. At College I had come to believe that as a graduate I would automatically be at the head, leading my people in all their efforts. In a sense that was true of the majority of the Fort Hare students. Many of them left the lecture room straight to some cosy job, with a steady income and carrying a measure of influence. It is also true that graduates do enjoy the respect of the community especially in the field of education.

But my experience was quite different. I moved in circles where common sense and practical experience were important, and where high academic qualifications were not necessarily decisive. Hardly anything I had been taught at College seemed directly relevant in my new environment. The average teacher had fought shy of topics like racial oppression, lack of opportunity for the black man and the numerous indignities to which he is subjected in his daily life. None had ever briefed me on how we would finally remove the evils of colour prejudice, the books I should read in this connection and the political organisations I should join if I wanted to be part of a disciplined freedom movement. I had to learn all these things by mere chance and through trial and error.

PART TWO

Drama

Nelson Mandela once played the part of John Wilkes Booth, the assassin of Abraham Lincoln, in a play performed at Fort Hare. He played the tyrant Creon when the prisoners put on Antigone on Robben Island. Ahmed Kathrada had ordered a whole lot of Greek plays ostensibly for his studies – these did not evoke any curiosity among the warders, so were allowed to come in without any problems. Playing the villain no doubt appealed to Mandela's wicked sense of humour. He sometimes quotes from Shakespeare and has a taste for Greek tragedy, which he first read on the Island. He joked at one time about being an actor and, during the years of his political apprenticeship, he learned the power of the dramatic gesture.

Indeed, his life from 1941 until his incarceration in 1962 was one of great public drama. From the late 1940s he began to assume leadership positions in the African National Congress (ANC), and through the 1950s and into the 1960s he participated prominently in every national campaign and event in the struggle against apartheid. By the time of his capture in August 1962, he was the leader of Umkhonto we Sizwe (MK) – the armed wing of the ANC – and arguably the most popular and well-known figure in the anti-apartheid struggle. He had become 'The Black Pimpernel', South Africa's most wanted man.

Not surprisingly, in the 1963–64 Rivonia Trial, the most dramatic and significant political trial in South Africa's history, Mandela stole the show.

His personal drama heightened when, after a couple of passing affairs, he married a young relative of Walter Sisulu, Evelyn Mase, in 1944. They had four children: a daughter, Makaziwe (Maki); two sons, Madiba Thembekile (Thembi) and Makgatho (Kgatho); and another daughter – their first, also named Makaziwe – who died aged just nine months. After a dozen years of marriage they separated with bitterness and acrimony, which caused considerable unhappiness in the family down the years.

In 1958, he married the radiantly beautiful Winnie Madikizela. Mandela always admired strong women, like Ruth Mompati, Lilian Ngoyi, Helen Joseph and Ruth First, but he did not, perhaps, appreciate how strong Winnie would turn out to be. They had two daughters: Zenani (Zeni) and Zindziswa (Zindzi). Mandela often called Winnie 'Zami', an abbreviation of her Xhosa name 'Nomzamo'. This second family was to feel as acutely as the first the impact of Mandela's public life. His drama was their pain.

CHAPTER THREE

Wings to the Spirit

'Only armchair politicians are immune from committing mistakes. Errors are inherent in political action. Those who are in the centre of political struggle, who have to deal with practical and pressing problems, are afforded little time for reflection and no precedents to guide them and are bound to slip up many times. But in due course, and provided they are flexible and prepared to examine their work self critically, they will acquire the necessary experience and foresight that will enable them to avoid the ordinary pitfalls and pick out their way ahead amidst the throb of events.'

....

From his unpublished autobiographical manuscript written in prison, see page 35.

1. FROM HIS UNPUBLISHED AUTOBIOGRAPHICAL MANUSCRIPT WRITTEN IN PRISON

Only armchair politicians are immune from committing mistakes. Errors are inherent in political action. Those who are in the centre of political struggle, who have to deal with practical and pressing problems, are afforded little time for reflection and no precedents to guide them and are bound to slip up many times. But in due course, and provided they are flexible and prepared to examine their work self critically, they will acquire the necessary experience and foresight that will enable them to avoid the ordinary pitfalls and pick out their way ahead amidst the throb of events.

2. FROM HIS UNPUBLISHED AUTOBIOGRAPHICAL MANUSCRIPT WRITTEN IN PRISON

In Alexandra, life was exciting and, although the racial policies of the present government have destroyed its social fabric and reduced it to a ghost town, thinking of it always evokes in me fond memories.[1] Here I learnt to adjust myself to urban life and came into physical contact with all the evils of white supremacy. Although the township had some beautiful buildings, it was a typical slum area – overcrowded and dirty, with undernourished children running about naked or in filthy rags. It teemed with all kinds of religious sects, gangsters and shebeens. Life was cheap and the gun and the knife ruled at night. Very often the police would raid for passes, poll tax and liquor and arrest large numbers. In spite of this, Alexandra was more than a home for its fifty thousand residents. As one of the few areas of the country where Africans could acquire freehold property, and run their own affairs free from the tyranny of municipal regulations, it

---

1. Mandela found accommodation in Alexandra, a crowded slum known as 'Dark City' due to the fact it had no electricity.

was both a symbol and a challenge. Its establishment was an acknowledgement that a section of our people had broken their ties with the rural areas and become permanent town dwellers. Drawn from all the African language groups, its population was politically conscious, more articulate and with a sense of solidarity which was causing increasing concern among the whites. It became clear to me that the leadership of my people would come from the urban areas where militant workers and an emergent class of prosperous and ambitious traders were suffering all the frustrations of racial prejudice. These are the straps that bind one tightly to Alex. Up to the actual moment of my arrest fourteen years ago, I regarded the township as a home in which I had no specific house, and Orlando, where my wife and children still live, as a place where I had a house but no home.

3. FROM HIS UNPUBLISHED AUTOBIOGRAPHICAL MANUSCRIPT
   WRITTEN IN PRISON

A warm friendship developed between me and Lazar Sidelsky and the numerous acts of kindness and assistance he gave me on all sorts of problems would fill a whole chapter.[2] A very special friend was John Mngoma, an orator and well versed in Zulu history. I would listen to him for hours relating interesting episodes from our past . . . As a result of these and other contacts I made during my early days in Johannesburg, I developed some inner strength and soon forgot about my difficulties and my poverty and suffering, my loneliness and frustrations. These connections gave me the confidence that I could stand on my own feet, enjoy the goodwill and support of worthy men and women I had not previously known and

---

2. Lazar Sidelsky, see People, Places and Events.

to whom I could turn in case of need. And now I had a home of my own choice far away from my birthplace and had made progress, however little, mainly through my own initiative and resources. I have a special attachment to the people who befriended me during times of distress. A feature of many of these friendships is that they were built around families rather than individuals, and they have scarcely been affected by the death of those members through whom they were founded.

4. CONVERSATION WITH RICHARD STENGEL

MANDELA: But there is a fellow I became friendly with at Healdtown, and that friendship bore fruit when I reached Johannesburg. A chap called Zachariah Molete. He was in charge of sour milk in Healdtown, and if you are friendly to him, he would give you very thick sour milk . . . When I arrived in Johannesburg in the early forties, I stayed in . . . Alexandra township, and I became a close friend of his, because his father had . . . a grocery shop, and he was the chief steward of the Wesleyan Church and he looked after me, because I was struggling, made sure I got some groceries. [On] one particular occasion he came to me and said, 'Look, you must be very careful at night because there is a gang which they call the Thutha Ranch.' Now '*thutha*' means collecting and taking away. They were such gangsters, such thieves, that when they raided your house they would remove everything – they got the name from there. And he says, 'They are operating in your area here.' Now I was staying . . . in a single room, and one night I woke up because there [was] noise of people walking outside, and I listened to this and I remembered what Zachariah had told me. And *then* there was an argument and the argument was clear. One chap says, 'No, let's get in, let's go in' and another one says, 'No, man, this chap has no money, he has nothing, he's a student.' Then they argued . . . but the other chap was tough. He said, 'Leave the student alone, man, leave him alone' . . . But apparently the chap who was insisting got so frustrated, so annoyed, that he *kicked* the door – it was a poor door you see and the bolt, you know, just snapped. But they didn't enter; they passed.

STENGEL: That was your door that he kicked?

MANDELA: My door, yes. And I got such a *shock*, such a *shock*, but they passed; they didn't enter . . . I changed my bed and I put it across the door there, you know, because it was the only way of closing the door and keeping it in place. That's how I slept. And I was very grateful because . . . whoever it was . . . who saved me from being robbed, one of them was kind enough, you know, to say, 'No, don't do that.'

5. FROM A LETTER TO ZINDZI MANDELA, DATED 9 DECEMBER 1979, WHICH WAS CONFISCATED BY PRISON CENSORS BECAUSE HE DIDN'T 'HAVE PERMISSION' TO INCLUDE IT IN HER CHRISTMAS CARD THAT YEAR

I sometimes wonder what happened to our boxing gym at what used to be called St Joseph's in Orlando East. The walls of that school and of the DOCC [Donaldson Orlando Community Centre] are drenched with sweet memories that will delight me for yrs [years]. When we trained at the DOCC in the early [19]50s the club included amateur and professional boxers as well as wrestlers. The club was managed by Johannes (Skip Adonis) Molosi, a former champ and a capable trainer who knew the history, theory and practical side of the game.[3]

Unfortunately, in the mid-50s he began neglecting his duties and would stay away from the gym for long periods.

----

3. His name was actually 'Johannes (Skipper Adonis) Molotsi'.

Nelson Mandela 466/64 _[signature]_   9 12·79

My darling Zindzi,

I sometimes wonder what happened to our boxing gymn at what used to be called St Joseph's in Orlando East. The walls of that school & of the D.O.C.C. are drenched with sweet memories that will delight me for yrs. When we trained at the D.O.C.C. in the early 50s the club included amateur & professional boxers as well as wrestlers. The club was managed by johannes [Skip Adonis] Molosi, a former champ & a capable trainer who knew the history, theory & practical side of the game.

Unfortunately in the mid-50s he began neglecting his duties & would stay away from the gymn for long periods. Because of this, the boxers revolted. Twice I settled the matter, but when Skip failed to pay heed to repeated protests from the boxers things reached breaking point. This time I was totally unable to reconcile the parties. The boxers left the D.O.C.C. & opened their own gymn at St. Joseph's. Thembi & I went along with them. Simon Tshabalala, who is now abroad, became the manager & the star boxer was, of course, still Jerry [Uyinjia] Moloi who later became the Joe lightweight champ & leading contender for the national

From a letter to Zindzi Mandela, dated 9 December 1979, see page 38. The letter was discovered in 2010 in the South African National Archives with a handwritten note in Afrikaans by a prison censor which read: 'The attached piece that prisoner Mandela included with his Christmas card will not be sent. The card will be sent. The prisoner has not been informed that this piece has been rejected. He does not have permission to include it with the card. I discussed this on 20 December 1979 with Brigadier du Plesssis and he agrees with the decision. Keep it in his file.'

Because of this, the boxers revolted. Twice I settled the matter, but when Skip failed to pay heed to repeated protests from the boxers, things reached breaking point. This time I was totally unable to reconcile the parties. The boxers left the DOCC and opened their own gym at St Joseph's. Thembi and I went along with them. Simon Tshabalala, who is now abroad, became the manager, and the star boxer was, of course, still Jerry (Uyinja) Moloi who later became the Tvl [Transvaal] lightweight champ and leading contender for the national title. Apart from Jerry we produced 3 other champs: Eric (Black Material) Ntsele who won the national bantamweight from Leslie Tangee, Freddie (Tomahawk) Ngidi who became Tvl flyweight champ, a title which was later held by one of our gym mates, Johannes Mokotedi. There were other good prospects like Peter, the flyweight, who built our garage at home. He hailed from Bloemfontein and was a student at the Vacation School in Dube. Thembi himself was a good boxer and on occasions I sat until very late at night waiting for him to return from a tournament in Randfontein, Vereeniging or other centres. I and my gym mates were a closely knit family and when Mum [Winnie] came into the picture that family became even more intimate. Jerry and Eric even drove Mum around when I could not do so and the entire gym turned up at our engagement party.

By the way, Freddie worked for our firm as a clerk. He was quiet and reliable and the entire staff was fond of him. But on one Xmas eve I returned to the office and who did I find lying flat and helpless in the passage just outside the general office? Freddie. His appearance so shocked me that I rushed him to a doctor. The quack gave him one quick look and assured me that the champ was OK but that he needed more sleep. He had succumbed to the usual Xmas sprees and over-indulged himself. I drove him to his home at OE [Orlando East] quite relieved. Incidentally, I should have told you that during the dispute at the DOCC Skip accused Jerry of stabbing him in the back just as Mark Antony betrayed his friend Caesar. Thembi asked who Antony and Caesar were. At the time Thembi was only 9. Skip explained, 'Don't tell us about people who are dead.' If I had not been there Skip would have pulled out the child's bowels, so furious he was. He bitterly complained to me about what he considered to be discourtesy on the part of the boy. I reminded him that in my house I was the patriarch and ruled over the household. But that I had no such powers in the gym; that Thembi had paid membership fees, we were perfect equals and I could give him no instructions.

We would spend about 1½ hrs in the gym and I was at home about 9 pm. Tired with hardly a drop of water in my body. Mum would give me a glass of fresh and cold orange juice, supper served with well-prepared sour milk. Mum was glow[ing] with good health and happiness those dys [days]. The house was like a beehive with the family, old school friends, fellow workers from Bara [Baragwanath Hospital],[4] members of the gym and even clients calling at the house to chat with her. For more than 2 yrs she and I literally lived on honeymoon. I quietly resisted any activity that kept me away from home after office hrs [hours]. Yet she and I kept warning each other that we were living on borrowed time, that hard times would soon knock at the door. But we were having a great time with good friends and we did not have much time for self-pity. It is more than 2 decades since then, yet I recall those dys so clearly as if everything happened yesterday.

----

4. Winnie was a social worker at Baragwanath Hospital.

STENGEL: During this time there was quite a lot of socializing, wasn't there? You mentioned before, when you first came to Johannesburg, you were taken to parties, Communist Party parties, and you met Michael Harmel,[5] and there's been a lot written about the mixing, in a social way, that was going on with Joe Slovo and Ruth First . . .[6]

MANDELA: No actually, it was not something extraordinary; just like anything that was happening in this country both amongst whites and blacks. The only difference is that here you had blacks and whites together.

STENGEL: But that was extraordinary, wasn't it?

MANDELA: . . . That mixing was extraordinary, but the parties themselves were something that were very frequent in the country. Yes, it was not something novel. And it didn't happen with such regularity. The point was that these groups were also used, certainly by the [Communist] Party, for the purpose of recruiting new members.

STENGEL: I see . . . at least among whites, didn't they feel that they were doing something that was very daring and exciting by having mixed parties like that?

MANDELA: No, no, no, I don't think so. Here were whites who were bred in the democratic tradition, in the proper sense of the word, who had committed themselves to the struggle by the oppressed people and therefore they wanted moments of relaxation and invited Africans, blacks.

STENGEL: And you would go to these parties?

MANDELA: Oh yes, yes. I was not a frequent [party goer]. In fact, at one time Joe complained to Walter [Sisulu] that 'Man, Nelson doesn't like parties.'

---

5. Michael Harmel, see People, Places and Events.
6. Joe Slovo, see People, Places and Events. Ruth First, see People, Places and Events.

MANDELA: I was being introduced to various strands of thought in Johannesburg.

STENGEL: And when you went to the meetings you would just sit and listen?

MANDELA: . . . I never spoke. The only thing I took part in was debates – not in political meetings but just academic debates. For example, there would be a team from Bloemfontein to Johannesburg; I would be invited to lead a discussion from Johannesburg. *That* I participated in, but in meetings I never did, until I joined the [ANC] Youth League. Even then I was very nervous. I was really very nervous.

STENGEL: Nervous why? Because it was a big step, or it was dangerous?

MANDELA: . . . I didn't know politics, you see? I was backward politically and I was dealing with chaps, you see, who knew politics, who could discuss what was happening in South Africa and outside South Africa. Chaps, some of whom had only Standard Four, academically very humble educational qualifications, but they knew *far* more than I did . . . At Fort Hare [University] I did two [BA] courses in History where I went into South African history very deeply and European history. But what Gaur Radebe knew was far more than I did because he learned not only just the facts;[7] he was able to get *behind* the facts and explain to you the causes for a particular viewpoint. And I learned history afresh and I met a number of them. Of course people like Michael Harmel with MAs, you know, and Rusty Bernstein was [a] BA from Wits [University of the Witwatersrand],[8] these chaps . . . were also very good in history and although I was not a [Communist] Party man, but

---

7. Gaur Radebe, see People, Places and Events.
8. Lionel (Rusty) Bernstein, see People, Places and Events. .

. . . I listened to them *very* carefully. It was very interesting to listen to them.

STENGEL: When you first went to the Communist Party meetings . . . you were very anti-communist then?

MANDELA: Yes quite, oh yes, oh yes.

STENGEL: So when you were going to the meetings it didn't make you sympathetic to the Communist Party? . . .

MANDELA: No, no, no, no, no, no. I was just going there because I was invited and I was keen to see. It was a new society where you found Europeans, Indians and Coloureds and Africans together. Something new to me. Which I had never known. And I was interested in that.

STENGEL: You were interested in being a social observer more than you were interested in the politics.

MANDELA: Oh, no, no, no. I was not interested really in the politics. I was interested, you see, yes, in the social aspect of it . . . I was impressed by the members of the Communist Party. To see whites who were *totally* divested of colour consciousness was something, you know, which . . . was a new experience to me.

STENGEL: So did that feel liberating in a way? Was that intoxicating?

MANDELA: No, it was interesting. I wouldn't say it was liberating. And that is why I attacked the communists, you see, when I [became] involved politically. And I didn't think it was liberating. I thought Marxism was something that actually was subjecting us to a foreign ideology.

8. FROM A LETTER TO WINNIE MANDELA, DATED 20 JUNE 1970[9]

Indeed, 'the chains of the body are often wings to the spirit'. It has been so all along, and so it will always be. Shakespeare in <u>As You Like It</u> puts the same idea somewhat differently:

> Sweet are the uses of adversity,
> Which like a toad, ugly and venomous,
> Wears yet a precious jewel in the head.[10]

Still others have proclaimed that 'only great aims can arouse great energies'.

Yet my understanding of the real idea behind these simple words throughout the 26 years of my career of storms has been superficial, imperfect and perhaps a bit scholastic. There is a stage in the life of every social reformer when he will thunder on platforms primarily to relieve himself of the scraps of undigested information that has accumulated in his head; an attempt to impress the crowds rather than to start a calm and simple exposition of principles and ideas whose universal truth is made evident by personal experience and deeper study. In this regard I am no exception and I have been victim of the weakness of my own generation not once but a hundred times. I must be frank and tell you that when I look back at some of my early writings and speeches I am appalled by their pedantry, artificiality and lack of originality. The urge to impress and advertise is clearly noticeable.

---

9. Winifred Nomzamo Madikizela-Mandela, see People, Places and Events.
10. 'Sweet are the uses of adversity/Which, like the toad, ugly and venomous/Wears yet a precious jewel in his head.' From *As You Like It*, William Shakespeare, act 2, scene 1.

9. FROM A CONVERSATION WITH RICHARD STENGEL ABOUT THE 1952 DEFIANCE CAMPAIGN AGAINST APARTHEID LAWS

Well, I had been in prison before that, but for minor violations and where I was detained for about a day, not even a full day. I was detained in the morning and released in the afternoon . . . I was arrested there, not because I had defied, but because I had gone and urinated in a, what-you-call, whites' toilet room, for whites only. Well we can say I went to wash my hands in a white lavatory and then they arrested me . . . [*chuckles*]. It was a mistake on my part; I didn't read the sign. So then they arrested me, took me to a police station. But at the end of the day they released me. Now, but *here* were people who were going to jail because of a principle, because they were protesting against a law which they regarded as unjust. Students who were my colleagues left classes and went to defy for the *love* of their people and their country. That had a tremendous impact on me.

10. FROM A CONVERSATION WITH RICHARD STENGEL

[I don't] . . . interfere in the affairs of others, unless I'm asked. Even when I'm asked, my own concern is always to bring people together. Even as a lawyer, when . . . a man or his wife comes to me to institute divorce action, I always say, 'Have you done everything in your power to resolve this problem?' . . . Some people welcome that, and in fact I have saved marriages in that way. And then some people of course resent it. She comes to you because they have quarrelled . . . and she feels bitter, and when you say, 'Can I call your husband?' You see? Oh, she gets terribly agitated. And from that moment even when you go to court she does not even want you to look at her husband . . . You see she wants you to adopt exactly the same position which she adopts. It becomes very difficult. But the point is that

NELSON MANDELA   27. 12. 84

Mum,

...s of the letter to Dalwonga, which I handed in this morning for dispatch
to Matata were summarised in the front page of today's Die Burger with the
following headline: Matanzima doen aanbod (Matanzima makes an offer)
Mandela verwerp vrylating (Mandela rejects release). This is the letter
cc Ngubengcuka,

Nobandla has informed me that you have pardoned my nephews, and I am
grateful for the gesture. I am more particularly touched when I think of my sisters
feeling about the matter and I thank you once more for your kind consideration.

          Nobandla also informs me that you have now been able to persuade the
Government to release political prisoners, and that you have also consulted with
the other "homeland" leaders who have given you their full support in the
matter. It appears from what she tells me that you and the Government intend
that I and some of my colleagues should be released to Umtata.

I perhaps need to remind you that when you first wanted to visit us in 1977
my colleagues and I decided that, because of your position in the implementation
of the Bantustan scheme, we could not accede to your request.

Again in February this year when you wanted to come and discuss the question
of our release, we reiterated our stand and your request was not acceded to.
In particular, we pointed out that the idea of our release being linked to a
Bantustan was totally and utterly unacceptable to us.

While we appreciate your concern over the incarceration of political prisoners, we
must point out that your persistence in linking our release with the
Bantustans, despite our strong and clearly-expressed opposition to the
scheme, is highly disturbing, if not provocative, and we urge you not to
continue pursuing a course which will inevitably result in an unpleasant
confrontation between you and ourselves.

We will, under no circumstances, accept being released to the Transkei
or any other Bantustan. You know very well fully well that we have spent the
better part of our lives in prison exactly because we are opposed to the
...ea of separate development, which makes us foreigners in our

---

From a letter to Winnie Mandela, dated 27 December 1984, see pages 48–49.

I have always tried to bring people together, you know? . . . But I don't always succeed.

11. FROM A LETTER TO WINNIE MANDELA, DATED 27 DECEMBER 1984, QUOTING FROM A LETTER TO K D MATANZIMA[11]

It appears . . . that you and the Government intend that I and some of my colleagues should be released to Umtata.[12] I perhaps need to remind you that when you first wanted to visit us in 1977 my colleagues and I decided that, because of your position in the implementation of the Bantustan Scheme, we could not concede to your request.[13] Again in February this year when you wanted to come and discuss the question of our release, we reiterated our stand and your plan was not acceded to. In particular we pointed out that the idea of our release being linked to a Bantustan was totally and utterly unacceptable to us. While we appreciate your concern over the incarceration of political prisoners, we must point out that your persistence in linking our release with Bantustans, despite our clearly expressed opposition to the scheme, is highly disturbing, if not provocative, and we urge you not to continue pursuing a course which will inevitably result in an unpleasant confrontation between you and ourselves. We will, under no circumstances, accept being released to the Transkei or any other Bantustan. You know fully well that we have spent the latter part of our lives in prison exactly because we are opposed to the very idea of separate development, which makes us foreigners in our own country, and which enables the Government to perpetuate our oppression to this very day. We accordingly request you to

---

11. Kaiser Daliwonga (K D) Matanzima, see People, Places and Events.
12. Mandela used both 'Umtata' (colonial spelling) and 'Mthatha' (post-apartheid spelling).
13. Under the Bantu Authorities Act, 1951, the apartheid government established 'homelands' or Bantustans for black South Africans.

desist from this explosive plan and we sincerely hope that this is the last time we will ever be pestered with it.

12. CONVERSATION WITH RICHARD STENGEL

STENGEL: We left off last time talking about your trip in September 1955 when your bans expired,[14] and you write quite a lot about it in your memoirs, in the manuscript, in great detail. Was the trip important to you because you felt like it was your last moment of freedom?

MANDELA: No, I had been banned from September, from December 1952. That was my first ban in terms of the Riotous Assemblies Act and that was for one year, and then on another occasion it was for two years. But in terms of the Suppression of Communism Act, I came to be banned and confined to Johannesburg for five years, and when the ban expired because it had not been possible for me to travel around, it was like a new chapter in my life and therefore I made it a point to see the country because I knew that the question of a ban and confinement to a particular area was something that was going to haunt me for the rest of my life as long as I was active politically. That really was the reason for the importance I attached to the trip.

13. CONVERSATION WITH RICHARD STENGEL

STENGEL: What was the International Club?

MANDELA: . . . The Johannesburg International Club was a club which made it possible for people of various national groups to meet . . . it was a place in town where people could meet and exchange views and receive visitors . . . and it served meals, there were games . . . debates, and so on. It was a place for social

---

14. Individuals and organisations could be banned by the government and subject to a variety of restrictions.

occasions. At one time there came an American, two American actors: Canada Lee . . . and this chap now, who is quite a top actor, Sidney Poitier. We entertained them there and it was a very interesting club; those days it was one of the few instances where you could have members of all national groups together.

STENGEL: And was it here in town? Where was it?

MANDELA: Yes, it was further down towards the west . . .

STENGEL: And you became secretary?

MANDELA: Yes, I became secretary.

STENGEL: There was also a fellow who – I believe he succeeded you as secretary, with whom you were friends – Gordon Bruce.

MANDELA: Gordon Bruce, yes, that's right.

STENGEL: So you socialised with people.

MANDELA: Yes, an Englishman, who came from England, and a very religious man, married to a Jewish lady, Ursula.[15] A blind lady, but very capable, very capable lady. She is now teaching; at least when I came out of jail I went to see them . . . One day Gordon was not going to be available at five o'clock to go and fetch his wife, so he asked me to [do it]. She was . . . working . . . a few blocks away from here in Commissioner Street. And I went there, I got hold of her. Now, because she was blind, she put her hand here [*gestures*], on the arm. And then I went out with her. The whites nearly killed me. Now she . . . was a beautiful woman . . . to see a black man holding a white lady like that? Oh, they almost killed me. But I can pretend . . . that I am brave, you know, and [that] I can beat the whole world, you see, so I just ignored them. And got into the car. [Later] when I was underground, I spent a lot of time with them. They were not very far from my hiding place and I used to visit them in the evening.

---

15. Gordon Bruce was not in fact religious, and was an agnostic. His wife was an observant Jew.

CONVERSATIONS WITH MYSELF

14. CONVERSATION WITH AHMED 'KATHY' KATHRADA ABOUT DR JAMES MOROKA,[16] WHO WANTED TO DISTANCE HIMSELF FROM THE NINETEEN OTHER ACCUSED, INCLUDING MANDELA AND KATHRADA, IN THE 1952 DEFIANCE CAMPAIGN TRIAL AND APPOINTED HIS OWN LAWYER[17]

KATHRADA: Ah, then page 61–62 [of *Long Walk to Freedom* draft]: 'I went to see Dr Moroka at his house in Thaba Nchu in the Orange Free State. At the outset of our meeting [I] suggested both of these courses of action to him. But he was not interested; he had a number of grievances that he wanted to air. Moroka could be quite haughty,' etcetera.

MANDELA: Could be 'quite haughty'?

KATHRADA: Haughty.

MANDELA: No, man . . . I don't like the description of Moroka like that.

KATHRADA: Aha.

MANDELA: . . . In the first place, Moroka was never haughty. And I don't like, in, a biography like this, you see, to make uncomplimentary remarks.

KATHRADA: Aha.

MANDELA: . . . I think we should have, we *can* say, 'It was a disappointment to see that the leader of the African National Congress should want to disassociate himself from actions and policies which were adopted under his leadership.' . . . But I don't want us to be going into the questions of him being haughty and betraying people.

KATHRADA: Aha.

MANDELA: I think we should avoid that . . . and . . . you know, his children, I wrote to them when I was in prison and they wrote back, you know, to say that for the first time a good

16. Dr James Sebe Moroka, see People, Places and Events.
17. Ahmed Mohamed (Kathy) Kathrada, see People, Places and Events.

word has been said about . . .

KATHRADA: About their father.

MANDELA: Their grandfather.

KATHRADA: Aha.

MANDELA: You see what we *say* about leaders, even though we may criticise them, it would be *good*, you see, to say that to compare him with [Yusuf] Dadoo[18] . . . [Walter] Sisulu[19], you know, these are people produced by the movement . . . who were committed, you know, to the *whole* culture of collective leadership . . . Dr Moroka came from another school and he had these limitations, but put it in a dignified way.

KATHRADA: Aha.

MANDELA: . . . You see criticism must be dignified. We must be factual, we must be realistic, we must be honest, but at the same time, you know, within a certain frame because we are *builders* . . .

KATHRADA: Ja, ja.

MANDELA: When you said that a writer from the movement is not just recording, also is a builder, must contribute, you see, to the building of the organisation and the trust, you know, that should be invested in that organisation. I think you've said that . . .

15. FROM A CONVERSATION WITH RICHARD STENGEL ABOUT
NON-VIOLENCE

The Chief [Albert Luthuli] was a passionate disciple of Mahatma Gandhi and he believed in non-violence as a Christian and as a principle . . .[20] Many of us did not . . . because when you regard it as a principle you mean throughout, whatever the position is, you'll stick to non-violence . . . We took up the attitude that we would stick to non-violence only insofar as the conditions

18. Dr Yusuf Dadoo, see People, Places and Events.
19. Walter Ulyate Max Sisulu, see People, Places and Events.
20. Chief Albert John Mvumbi Luthuli, see People, Places and Events.

permitted that. Once the conditions were against that we would automatically abandon non-violence and use the methods which were dictated by the conditions. That was our approach. Our approach was to empower the organisation to be *effective* in its leadership. And if the adoption of non-violence gave it that effectiveness, that efficiency, we would pursue non-violence. But if the condition shows that non-violence was not effective, we would use other means.

16. CONVERSATION WITH AHMED KATHRADA

KATHRADA: Did you read Gandhi too?

MANDELA: Oh yes. No, that's true. No, that's true.

KATHRADA: So, that's true?

MANDELA: But, Nehru was *really* my hero.

KATHRADA: . . . This is the way it's worded, page 62 [of *Long Walk to Freedom* draft]: 'He felt some pangs at abandoning his Christian beliefs which had fortified his childhood, like St Peter three times denying Christ.' Now, is it correct wording to say you 'abandoned your Christian beliefs'?

MANDELA: No, never.

KATHRADA: It would be wrong, isn't it?

MANDELA: . . . I say it's absolutely untrue. I never abandoned my Christian beliefs.

KATHRADA: OK.

MANDELA: And I think it's proper, you know, it could do a lot of harm.

KATHRADA: Exactly, ja.

MANDELA: Ja, could do a lot of harm.

17. CONVERSATION WITH RICHARD STENGEL

STENGEL: What was Ruth First like?

MANDELA: Ruth? Ruth – her death was a tragedy for South

Africa because she was amongst the brightest stars in the country, in the proper sense of the word.[21] I . . . [had] known Ruth from our university days. We were in the same university and she was progressive, and she was not the type of white who was progressive when she was with you in a room, or away from the public. If she met you in one of the corridors of the university or in the street, Ruth will stand and talk to you, *very* comfortable, in a very relaxed manner and she was *brilliant*. In any meeting where you sat with Ruth, there was just nothing but brilliance. And . . . she did not suffer fools, had no patience towards fools and she was energetic, systematic, hard-working and she would tax you on any type of job that you undertook and she would . . . make the *maximum* effort and to produce the best result. She was fearless, she could criticise *anybody* and she rubbed people, you know . . . in the wrong way at times. She was direct and outspoken. But at the same time she was very broad, just like her husband, Joe [Slovo], very broad. In those days when [they] were young communists, and very radical, they had friends amongst the Liberals and amongst prominent businessmen, and her house was a crossroad of people of different political persuasions. That was a wonderful girl, I loved very much. I loved and respected [her] very much and I was very sorry when I heard from prison that she had passed away.
STENGEL: And their house was, as you say, a kind of centre.
MANDELA: Oh yes.
STENGEL: And would you go there for dinner . . . ?
MANDELA: Oh very often, very often. I had a clash with her . . . in 1958, I appeared in a trial and . . . I lost the case, and some women were sent to jail, and she then criticised me in the way I handled the case. It was actually the criticism of somebody who

----

21. Ruth First was killed in Mozambique on 17 August 1982 after a parcel addressed to her exploded as she opened it.

was not conversant with the law. But it was over the telephone and I was hard-pressed because I was dealing, you see, with more than 2,000 women, trying to arrange defence [for] them. The whole day, you know, I'd be busy either actually defending them or arranging people to defend them. And . . . then I handled one case and I lost it and three women were sent to jail, although, of course we bailed them out. Then she, on the telephone, criticised the manner in which I had handled the case and I told her to go to hell. And then [*laughs*] immediately thereafter I realised, man, you see, this is a lady, and this is a *very* good comrade. However wrong she was, she believed in what she said. Then, at the end of the day, instead of going home, I went along with Winnie to her place and I found her with one of the lecturers . . . at university . . . I just came in, didn't say anything, just grabbed her, embraced her and kissed her and walked out. Walked away. [*laughs*] Ja, they tried to say sit down and so on – I just walked away. Yes. But I'd made peace. And Joe was saying, 'I told you Nelson would never have any grudges against you.' I walked away. So we made up. I didn't want any tension between us. Although I lost my temper I immediately realised that, no, I was unfair to her. She's a *very* sincere comrade, she should be entitled to criticise the way I behaved in anything where I made a mistake. But we made it up. I *really* respected Ruth and when subsequently I went underground she was one of my contacts.

18. FROM A CONVERSATION WITH AHMED KATHRADA

Gee whiz. I think we should describe, you see, what banning means . . . you are just prevented from attending gatherings and confined to a magisterial district. That was the first time, you know, I was banned, under the Riotous Assemblies Act in December 1952 . . . I was prohibited from attending public gatherings, and then I was confined to the magisterial district of Johannesburg. Now, it was a *new* experience in so far as I was concerned and the fact that I couldn't go beyond Johannesburg was, of course, something that affected me a great deal. But there was no *shunning* by people because not everybody in the first place knew when he met you that you are a banned person. The only case in which I came across this was, there used to be a chap called Benjamin Joseph, an attorney, where Harry Mokoena worked. One day . . . I was coming down Fox Street and he was coming towards me and as I approached he says, [*whispering*] 'Nelson, don't talk to me. Please just pass. Don't talk to me.' That was the *only* case I know.

19. FROM HIS UNPUBLISHED AUTOBIOGRAPHICAL MANUSCRIPT WRITTEN IN PRISON

Confined to Johannesburg for a whole two years and with the pressure of both my legal and political work weighing heavily on me, I was suffocated from claustrophobia and anxious for a bit of fresh air. Fourteen years of cramped life in South Africa's largest city had not killed the peasant in me and once again I was keen to see that ever beckoning open veld and the blue mountains, the green grass and bushes, the rolling hills, rich valleys, the rapid streams as they sped across the escarpment into the insatiable sea.

20. FROM HIS UNPUBLISHED AUTOBIOGRAPHICAL MANUSCRIPT WRITTEN IN PRISON

Duma Nokwe and others gathered at home one night to see me off.[22] The young and promising barrister was in his usual jovial mood and as the evening lengthened he became more lucid and

22. Mandela was about to embark on a working holiday to Durban, the Transkei and Cape Town, 1955. Philemon (Duma) Nokwe, see People, Places and Events.

loquacious and kept us roaring with laughter. Occasionally he would burst into song – Russian and Chinese – at the same time gesticulating zealously as if conducting an imaginary choir. We sat up until about midnight and as they were leaving the house my daughter Makaziwe, then two years old, awoke and asked me if she could come along with me. Although I had been confined to Johannesburg, pressure of work had allowed me little time to spend with the family and I was well aware of the longing that would eat away their insides as I drifted further and further from them on my way to the Transkei. For some seconds a sense of guilt persecuted me and the excitement about the journey evaporated. I kissed her and put her to bed and, as she dozed away, I was off.

CHAPTER FOUR

No Reason to Kill

'. . . Home is home even for those who aspire to serve wider interests and who have established their home of choice in distant regions. The happy lift that seized me as I drove into York Road, the main street, is beyond measure.'

Excerpt from his unpublished autobiographical manuscript written in prison, see page 61.

1. FROM HIS UNPUBLISHED AUTOBIOGRAPHICAL MANUSCRIPT
   WRITTEN IN PRISON

In the evening of the third I reached Mthatha, my home town.[1] Home is home even for those who aspire to serve wider interests and who have established their home of choice in distant regions. The happy lift that seized me as I drove into York Road, the main street, is beyond measure. I had been away for the long stretch of 13 years and although there were no fatted calves and festooned trees to welcome me I felt . . . like the Returned Wanderer of Biblical fame and looked forward to seeing my mother and humble home, the numerous friends with whom I grew up, that enchanting veld and all the paraphernalia that make up unforgettable days of childhood . . . I thought I had left the Security Police behind on the Rand and had not suspected that they had spread their tentacles as far afield as my home town. I was still drinking coffee with two chiefs in my room when early next morning my hostess brought in a white gentleman. Without any courtesies he arrogantly asked, 'Are you Nelson Mandela?' 'And who are you?' I countered. He gave his rank as a detective sergeant and his name. I then asked, 'May I see your warrant, please?' He resented my impertinence much more than I detested his own arrogance but after some hesitation he produced his authority. I then told him that I was Nelson Mandela. He requested me to accompany him to the police station and I asked whether I was under arrest to which he replied that I was not. I refused to go. Whereupon he fired a succession of questions while at the same time noting my remarks in his notebook: when did I leave Johannesburg, what places had I visited, how long did I intend remaining in the Transkei, exactly where would I go on leaving the area, did I have a permit to enter the Transkei? I told him where

1.   In this and the following two entries, Mandela is referring to a trip he took after his banning expired in 1955.

I would stay, that the Transkei was my home and that I did not need a permit to enter it, but refused to answer the other questions. When he left the chiefs criticized me for my abruptness, stressing that I could have answered some of the questions without any risk to myself. I explained that I had done so because of the man's discourtesy and haughtiness and that I had justly rewarded him for his arrogance. I don't think I convinced them . . . Being together with my mother in her home filled me with boyish excitement. At the same time I could not avoid a sense of guilt as my mother was living all alone and 22 miles from the nearest doctor. My sisters and I were each living on their own. Despite the fact that her children tried in their own way to render her financially comfortable, she chose to live an austere life and saving what one child gave her to distribute to any of her other children who happened to be in need. On previous occasions I endeavoured to persuade her to come and live with me in Johannesburg, but she could never face the wrench of leaving the countryside where she had lived all her life . . . I have often wondered whether a person is justified in neglecting his own family to fight for opportunities for others. Can there be anything more important than looking after your mother approaching the age of 60, building her a dream house, giving her good food, nice clothing and all one's love? Is politics in such cases not a mere excuse to shirk one's responsibilities? It is not easy to live with a conscience that raises such questions from time to time. Often I am able to persuade myself that I have done my best at all times to bring a measure of ease and comfort into my mother's life. Even when at times I am plagued with an uneasy conscience I have to acknowledge that my whole-hearted commitment to the liberation of our people gives meaning to life and yields for me a sense of national pride and real joy. This feeling has been multiplied a hundred times by the knowledge that right up to her last letter she wrote me

CONVERSATIONS WITH MYSELF

shortly before her death, my mother encouraged me in my beliefs and in fighting for them.

2. CONVERSATION WITH RICHARD STENGEL

MANDELA: By the way, when I was driving . . . driving out from Port Elizabeth, it was early in the morning, about ten. It was a hot day and as I was driving – it was quite a bushy area, a little wild area soon after leaving Port Elizabeth – I suddenly come across a snake crossing the road . . . It was already twisting, you see, because of the heat underneath – he couldn't bear the heat. And it was twisting but it was too close for me to do anything else, so I, what-you-call, [ran] over it. My heart was sore, you know? Because it jumped up, you know, as it was dying, you see. And I couldn't do anything; I just didn't see it, man. Yes, poor chap. And there was no reason *why* I should kill it you know? It was no threat to me, and left me with a very sad feeling.

STENGEL: The snake incident which you mention in the memoirs, were you also superstitious about running over a snake?

MANDELA: No, no, no.

STENGEL: That it was bad luck or a bad omen?

MANDELA: Oh no, no, no. I was not superstitious at all. But just to kill an animal, an innocent reptile, that was what worried me. And especially seeing it through the rear-view mirror, struggling, you know, to be alive. You know, it was a deplorable act on my part. But that was a beautiful area at the time . . . from Port Elizabeth to Humansdorp. You went through forest, you know, thick forest and where it was *absolutely* quite still, except . . . the noise of the birds and so on, but very still. *Beautiful* area! And . . . then wild, you see. Before I got to Knysna, I came across a baboon which crossed the road and stood behind a tree and kept on peeping at me, you know? And I liked . . .

such incidents . . . Ja, Knysna . . . I sincerely thought that if God came back to earth he would settle there, you know?

3. FROM A CONVERSATION WITH RICHARD STENGEL

I addressed that meeting of the Ministers' Interdenominational Society of the Western Cape . . . It's difficult now to remember the exact thing, but what I was saying was to stress the *role* of the church in the struggle and to say, that just as the Afrikaners use the pulpit in order to propagate their views, our priests should do exactly the same. And then there was a chap who prayed, Reverend Japhta, who made a very rather remarkable prayer and [he] said, 'God, we have been praying [to] you, pleading with you, asking you to liberate us. *Now* we are instructing you to liberate us.' Something along those lines, and I thought that was very significant.

4. FROM HIS UNPUBLISHED AUTOBIOGRAPHICAL MANUSCRIPT
    WRITTEN IN PRISON

Although I was now fully committed and had gained some idea of the hazards that accompanied the life of a freedom fighter, I had not seen any major political campaign by blacks and had not even begun giving serious attention to the question of methods. The sacrifices I was called on to make so far went no further than being absent from the family during weekends mainly, returning home late, travelling to address meetings and condemning government policy.

5. FROM HIS UNPUBLISHED AUTOBIOGRAPHICAL MANUSCRIPT
    WRITTEN IN PRISON

At that time my eldest son, Madiba [Thembi], was five. One day he asked his mother where I lived. I used to return home late at night and leave early in the morning before he was awake. I missed him a great deal during those busy days. I love playing and chatting with children, giving them a bath, feeding and putting them to bed with a little story, and being away from the family has troubled me throughout my political life. I like relaxing at the house, reading quietly, taking in the sweet smell that comes from the pots, sitting around the table with the family and taking out my wife and children. When you can no longer enjoy these simple pleasures something valuable is taken away from your life and you feel it in your daily work.

6. CONVERSATION WITH RICHARD STENGEL

STENGEL: So let's get to 1944, when you met Evelyn.[2]

MANDELA: Oh, I see, yes.

STENGEL: . . . You met her obviously through Walter [Sisulu] because she was Walter's cousin.

MANDELA: Yes, quite.

STENGEL: . . . Can you tell me about the circumstances that you met her?

MANDELA: Well, I wouldn't like to go into that matter. You know our people resent us talking about divorce, you know, and so on . . . I didn't mind myself . . . I didn't want to be presented in a way that omits the dark spots in my life, but I couldn't convince them, including people like Walter Sisulu. I just couldn't convince him on that question . . . because their view is that you are not only telling your life; we want you to be a model around which we are going to build our organisation. Now if I deal with Evelyn here, I will have to tell you why our marriage collapsed, because our marriage *really* collapsed because of differences in politics and I don't want to [say] that now against a poor woman, you know? Who can't

2. Evelyn Ntoko Mase, see People, Places and Events.

write her own story and put her own point of view. Although she has been interviewed by people, you see, and she has really distorted what actually happened . . . And once I start dealing with her, I must give the proper story, the full story. I would like to leave that out.

7. CONVERSATION WITH AHMED KATHRADA

KATHRADA: Now this is about Evelyn.

MANDELA: Uhuh?

KATHRADA: Now *that* you have corrected already. 'According to Evelyn, when Mandela complained that she was spoiling their son by giving him too much money he took her throat and the boy went to neighbours who came round and found scratches on her neck.'

MANDELA: Mmm!

KATHRADA: Not true?

MANDELA: That's not true. But what I wonder is *how* I could have not noticed these things.

KATHRADA: You see you have corrected this other thing where 'Evelyn became a dedicated Jehovah's Witness and spent much time reading the Bible. Mandela objected that the Bible tamed people's minds, that the whites had taken the Africans' land and left them with the Bible.' You have said, 'Not true.'

MANDELA: Yes, quite.

KATHRADA: But further on, this thing about 'taking her by the throat'.

MANDELA: No, definitely say 'Not true' for the whole thing.

KATHRADA: Oh, I see.

MANDELA: For the whole thing because there is no question of that, there's no question of that. I am sure she would have taken me to the police if I had done a thing like that. You know what happened?

KATHRADA: Ah.

MANDELA: We were arguing.

KATHRADA: Ah.

MANDELA: Now she had prepared for this, unknown to me. You remember those stoves, old stoves?

KATHRADA: Aha.

MANDELA: Coal stoves? We had an iron.

KATHRADA: Ja, a poker?

MANDELA: That's right, a poker.

KATHRADA: Ja.

MANDELA: So she had put this thing in the coal and it was *red* hot and as we were arguing she then *pulled* this thing out, you know, in order to, what-you-call, to *burn* my face. So I caught hold of her and twisted her arm, enough for me to take this thing out.

KATHRADA: The poker away.

MANDELA: That's all.

8. CONVERSATION WITH AHMED KATHRADA ABOUT THE POTATO BOYCOTT[3]

KATHRADA: All right, page 30 [of *Long Walk to Freedom* draft], still the questions from the publisher. Ah, what you are saying here: 'One of the most successful campaigns also occurred in 1959 and that was the Potato Boycott.'

MANDELA: Yes.

KATHRADA: '. . . It was well known that labour conditions on white farms in the Transvaal were grim but no one knew quite how grim they were until Henry Nxumalo, an intrepid reporter for the magazine posed as a worker himself and then

---

3. The 1959 Potato Boycott drew attention to the slave-like conditions suffered by black South African workers on potato farms.

wrote about it . . .'[4] Now you *are* going on with a paragraph or two about the the the Potato Boycott. He is saying, 'Were you involved in this in any personal way? If you were not, I'd be inclined to *delete* this material.'

MANDELA: Oh.

KATHRADA: That's what *he's* saying, although I would disagree with him because I think the Potato Boycott was such an important . . .

MANDELA: Oh yes, quite.

KATHRADA: . . . event for us.

MANDELA: Yes. I was . . . that was in 1959, hey?

KATHRADA: Somewhere there.

MANDELA: Yes, quite. Was it not [19]57?

KATHRADA: No, no . . .

MANDELA: I remember Lilian [Ngoyi] addressing a meeting with a potato and [s]he says, 'Look, I will never eat a potato in my life.[5] Look at this potato; it looks like a human being . . .'

KATHRADA: Aha.

MANDELA: And, 'Because it was fertilised, you see, out of human flesh.' Something like that. I think that was [19]57, but you may be right – it may have been [19]59 . . . I remember OR [Oliver Tambo],[6] [*chuckles*] when the boycott was [on], he bought fish and chips and started eating them. I think it was [Patrick] Mthembu who said, 'Look at the leading official of the ANC [African National Congress], breaking the boycott.'

KATHRADA: [*laughs*]

MANDELA: . . . OR was not aware of it and he says, 'Take this thing away! *Take* it away!' But he had already eaten it! [*laughs*]

---

4. Henry Nxumalo (1917–57). Journalist and assistant editor of *Drum* magazine who wrote an exposé on the potato farms.
5. Lilian Masediba Ngoyi, see People, Places and Events.
6. Oliver Reginald Tambo, see People, Places and Events.

9. CONVERSATION WITH AHMED KATHRADA ABOUT ANDERSON KHUMANI GANYILE'S USE OF TRADITIONAL MEDICINE

MANDELA: Gee whiz, [that] fellow believes in witch doctors. You know, when we took him to Lesotho, I went to fetch him in White City, in Mofolo, and I warned him beforehand that 'Look, I'll come at this particular time to pick you up' because I was in the Treason Trial. So I came very early in the morning, I think about seven o'clock, and he came out of a side room and said, 'Oh yes' and he went back. Man, I think he spent about thirty minutes and I got annoyed, you see, and I said, 'No, just pull him out.' He was busy having his medicine, washing himself. *Gee* whiz! And by the time he came out he was smelling, you know, like a what-you-call, a meer, a polecat. Smelling [of] all sorts of things, herbs and so on. I was annoyed with that boy.

KATHRADA: Ah.

MANDELA: He kept me for thirty minutes!

KATHRADA: While he was inyanga-ing himself.[7]

MANDELA: Ja.

10. CONVERSATION WITH AHMED KATHRADA ABOUT THE 1960 STATE OF EMERGENCY[8]

KATHRADA: Then, page 81 [of *Long Walk to Freedom* draft], you are saying, 'After one has been in prison it is the small things that one appreciates – the feeling of being able to take a walk whenever one wants, to cross a road, to go into a shop and buy a newspaper, to speak or choose to remain silent – the simple act of being able to control one's person. Free men do not always appreciate these things and one takes *joy* in them only

---

7. Ganyile was taking herbal medicine probably prescribed by a traditional healer or *inyanga*.
8. The 1960 State of Emergency was characterised by mass arrests, the imprisonment of most African leaders, including Mandela, and the banning of the ANC and PAC.

after one has been in chains.' Then, they [the publishers] are saying here, 'Any way to turn this abstraction into a description of what you did that day that seemed so sweet? More on your reunion with your family.' . . .

MANDELA: No, except that day I went to town with the car and I got two traffic tickets for . . .

KATHRADA: Speeding?

MANDELA: Hmm?

KATHRADA: For speeding?

MANDELA: No, no, no, for wrong parking.

KATHRADA: Oh.

MANDELA: And so on. Then Winnie then told me, look, this is the last time I'm driving.

KATHRADA: Aha.

MANDELA: That's all.

11. CONVERSATION WITH AHMED KATHRADA ABOUT WHETHER EVIDENCE INCRIMINATING HIM WAS REMOVED FROM LILIESLEAF FARM IN RIVONIA[9]

KATHRADA: Ja, well I remember I came to see you at a consultation in Pretoria, with Joe [Slovo].

MANDELA: Oh, I see.

KATHRADA: They at first said said no, but then Joe said, 'No, this is my defence witness so we have to consult' and we discussed it, and then you raised the question of your stuff at Rivonia and Joe said, 'Don't worry, *everything* is gone from there.'

MANDELA: [*laughs*] Ja, I know! I know!

KATHRADA: [*laughs*] *Everything* is gone.

MANDELA: Yes, I know.

[*both laugh*]

....

9. Mandela was captured on 5 August 1962. When police raided Liliesleaf Farm on 11 July 1963, they arrested MK operatives and seized incriminating documents.

KATHRADA: And then nothing was gone. They found *everything*.

MANDELA: Yes.

12. CONVERSATION WITH AHMED KATHRADA ABOUT BEING UNDERGROUND

MANDELA: We can also say that very big people, very important people who were not known . . . to have identified themselves with the movement used to be generous and to support us. And we won't deal with names, with specific names, but people *were* very generous, as long as they were sure that we would observe the element of confidentiality. Planning our visits meant that I would see the people, you know, in the infrastructure, to say, 'Today I am going to attend a meeting in Fordsburg', which is a real, a what-you-call, something that actually took [place].

KATHRADA: Ja.

MANDELA: Two cases, very striking cases, by the way, when I attended meetings in Fordsburg, and I saw [Ben] Turok and others on one occasion during the day and Maulvi [Cachalia] went to a family in Fordsburg.[10]

KATHRADA: In Vrededorp.

MANDELA: Vrededorp. That's right.

KATHRADA: Ja.

MANDELA: And said, 'Look, somebody is going to come and stay here tonight. Could you accommodate him?' *They* agreed very enthusiastically because they respected Maulvi. Now, I was wearing an overall, and very often, you see, I didn't comb my hair,[11] and I went to this house, you know, just to be aware of the house (Maulvi gave me the address) and to tell them that I'd come back in the evening. I knocked and a lady came forward, opened the door, says, 'Yes, what do you want?'

....

10. Ben Turok, see People, Places and Events. Ismail Ahmad (Maulvi) Cachalia, see People, Places and Events.
11. During his period underground Mandela adopted various disguises.

I said, 'Well, Maulvi Cachalia has arranged that I should stay here' and she says, 'I have no room for you.' Banged the door [*laughs*] because she saw this *wild* fellow you know?

13. FROM A CONVERSATION WITH RICHARD STENGEL ABOUT HIS ARREST ON 5 AUGUST 1962

At Howick, that's right, a car – a Ford V8 – passed and immediately ordered us to stop. And they selected the spot *very* well because on the left-hand side there was a steep bank like this, [*gestures*] and I was sitting, you see, to the left, on the left side . . . I was *very* fit those days, and I could virtually climb any wall. And then I looked at the back, just at the rear-view mirror, [and] I saw there were two cars behind. Then I felt that, no, it would be ridiculous for me to try and escape; they'll shoot me. And we stopped. So a fellow came – tall, slender fellow in private [plain clothes] – he came right to my side and he says, 'I am Sergeant Vorster' and took out his warrant . . . He was *very* correct in everything – very, very, very correct and courteous. And he says, 'May I know who your name is?' I said, 'I am David Motsamayi.' He says, 'No, but aren't you Nelson Mandela?' I said, 'I am David Motsamayi.' He says, 'Ag, you are Nelson Mandela. This is Cecil Williams.[12] I am arresting you. And we'll have to turn back and go to Pietermaritzburg.' I said, 'Very well.' And he says, '. . . the Major will get into your car, at the back of your car. You can just drive back.' So we turned back.

Now, I had a revolver which was unlicensed and I just took it out and put it in between the seats. There were seats – the driver's seat and my seat – but they were separate seats, but linked, and there was a *small* space here, which you can hardly

----

12. Cecil Williams (d. 1979) was a white theatre director and anti-apartheid activist.

see, and I just pushed it in. And also I had a notebook, and I took it out and I pushed it in, whilst I was talking to this major [in] the back. And at one time I thought I could open the door *fast* and roll down, but I didn't know how long, you know, this bank was and what was there. I was not familiar with the landscape. No, I thought that would be a gamble, and let me just go and think of a chance later. So we went to the police station and they locked me up.

14. CONVERSATION WITH AHMED KATHRADA ABOUT BEING
    ALLOWED TO VISIT HIS OFFICE DURING HIS 1960 STATE OF
    EMERGENCY DETENTION

KATHRADA: 'And I would stay there all day and evening. I walked downstairs to the ground floor, to the café to buy incidentals and he [the policeman] turned his head aside on one or two occasions when Winnie came to see me. We had a kind of a gentleman's code between us. I would not escape and thereby get him into trouble, while he would allow me a degree of freedom that I would not otherwise have [been] permitted.' The question they [the publishers] are asking, ah: '*Later* you say you were quite willing to try to escape.' 'Was that a philosophical change or simply a matter of personal loyalty versus a principle?'
MANDELA: That's a technical question, you know?
KATHRADA: Ah . . .
MANDELA: I mean, as a prisoner I would take any opportunity to escape, but when dealing with a particular individual whom you respected, you would not like to put into trouble. That was the position.
KATHRADA: Aha.

15. CONVERSATION WITH RICHARD STENGEL ABOUT THE RESORT TO ARMED STRUGGLE

MANDELA: There are stages when one in a position of authority has to go . . . public to commit the organisation. Because otherwise people are eloquent and you have an idea, and you have the *gut* feeling that this is a correct idea, but you deal with people, you know, who are *very* powerful, who can assemble facts and who can be systematic and so on. And they will sway everybody. Therefore, if you want to take an action and you are convinced that this is a correct action, you do so and confront that situation. It's not a question of being [un] disciplined. You have to *carefully* choose the opportunity and make sure that history would be on your side.

STENGEL: I'd like you to explain the whole process of how the decision to form MK [Umkhonto we Sizwe] was made.[13] At the Rivonia Trial you explain it in a general way. You said at the end, the second half of 1960, you and some colleagues reached the conclusion that violence was going to be inevitable. How did this whole process happen? Did you talk first privately with people and then there was the decision of the Working Committee? Was there a build-up to the decision?

MANDELA: No, what actually happened was I discussed the matter with Comrade Walter [Sisulu]. We discussed it because when Comrade Walter was going overseas, in 1953, I then said to him, 'When you reach the People's Republic of China, you must tell them, ask them, that we want to start an armed struggle and get arms,' and then I made that speech in Sophiatown. I was pulled up for this but I remained convinced that this was the correct strategy for us.[14] And then when I was underground I then discussed the matter with Comrade

---

13. Umkhonto we Sizwe (MK), see People, Places and Events.
14. In his address Mandela had said that the time for passive resistance had ended.

Walter and we decided to *raise* it at a meeting of the Working Committee. We raised the matter but, as I told you, I was dismissed very cheaply, because [Moses] Kotane – the secretary of the Party and of course a member of the Working Committee and the National Executive – *his* argument was the time had not come for that: 'Because of the severe measures taken by the government you are unable to continue in the old way.[15] The difficulties have paralysed you and you now want to talk a revolutionary language and talk about armed struggle, when in fact there is still room for the old method that we are using *if* we are imaginative and determined enough. You just want to expose people, you see, to massacres by the enemy. You have not even thought very carefully about this.' So he dismissed me like that and he was *quick* to speak and everybody supported him. I discussed the matter with Walter afterwards . . . The opposition was so heavy that Walter did not even dare to say a word. [*laughs*] But he has always been a very diplomatic chap, you know, but *reliable*, you know, when you take a decision with him. Very reliable. And so we reviewed the matter, and he has always been resourceful, and he says, 'No, call him alone; discuss it with him. I'll arrange for him to come and see you' because I was already underground. So Kotane came and we spent the whole day together. This time I was *very frank* and I said, 'You are doing precisely what the Communist Party in Cuba did – they said the conditions for a revolution had not yet arrived. Following the old methods, you see, which were advocated by Stalin – how a revolutionary situation can be identified, that is, by Lenin and Stalin. Here we have to decide from our own situation. The situation in this country is that it is time for us to consider a revolution, an armed struggle, because people are already forming military units in order to

15. Moses Kotane, see People, Places and Events.

start acts of violence. And if we don't do so, they are going to continue. They haven't got the resources, they haven't got the experience, they haven't got the political machinery to carry out that decision. The only organisation that can do so is the African National Congress which commands the masses of the people. And you must be creative and *change* your attitude because your attitude really is the attitude of a man who is leading a movement in the old way when we were legal, who is not considering leading now in terms of the illegal conditions under which we are operating.' So I was able to be blunt in order to challenge him, you know . . . I was able to challenge him. So he says, 'Well, I'm not going to promise anything, but raise it again.' So I went and raised it and he said, 'Well I'm still not convinced, but let's give him a chance. Let him go and put these ideas to the Executive, with our support.' So we then went down and everybody agreed. We went down to Durban at a meeting of the National Executive of the ANC. Then Chief [Albert Luthuli], Yengwa and others opposed this very strongly.[16] So we knew of course that we were going to get opposition from the Chief, because he *believed* in non-violence as a *principle*, whereas we believed in it as a *tactic*, although we couldn't say so to court . . . To the court, that is [during] the Treason Trial, we said we believe in non-violence as a principle, because if we had said [we believed in it] as a tactic it would give a loophole to the crown, to the state, to say that at any time, when it suited us, we would use violence, and that in fact, that is what we had been doing. So we avoided that, but *only* for that reason. We have always believed in non-violence as a tactic. *Where* the conditions demanded that we should use non-violence we would do so; where the conditions demanded that we should depart from non-violence we would do so. So, but we knew

16. Masabalala Bonnie (M B) Yengwa (1923–87). Anti-apartheid activist and minister of religion. Member of the ANC.

I

I was one of those who formed MK, and my
instructions from the NEC of the ANC was to
attend the Pafmecsa Conference in Addis
Ababa in February 1962, to visit the independent
African States, and to ask them to give military
training to our people, and to raise funds for the
struggle.
I had lived underground for almost 10 mnths,
and it was exciting indeed to look forward to
free and unfettered movement in day time,
without fear of arrest
I looked forward to visiting new countries
and meeting famous freedom fighters, who
were dominating the liberation movement in
various parts of the Continent.
Above all, I looked forward to meeting Comrade
Tambo and his capable Team which was
mobilising international support for our
struggle. They had done impressive spade work and
helped to put our struggle on the map. Emergence of
MK had boosted their efforts. but socio-economic problems
were frightening.

....

From a notebook, about Mandela's involvement in the formation of Umkhonto we Sizwe (MK),
the armed wing of the ANC, and going underground.

that Chief was . . . would oppose this, *and* he opposed it *very* well, but we persuaded him . . .

16. FROM A CONVERSATION WITH RICHARD STENGEL ABOUT THE FORMATION OF UMKHONTO WE SIZWE (MK)

Then they said, 'Very well, you have made a case. We now authorise you. We give you permission. You can go and *start* this organisation. That is, you, Mandela, you can go and start this organisation . . . and you can join with others and so on: collaborate with others, cooperate with others. But *we*, as the ANC [African National Congress], we are formed to prosecute a non-violent policy; this decision can only be changed by a national conference. We are going to *stick* to the old policy of the ANC.' That turned out to have been a good decision because when we came to court . . . [and] when the state looked at these minutes . . . they found that [they] . . . did not support their case at all, because *here* is the ANC deciding. People like . . . Chief Luthuli, like Moses Kotane, like Dr Monty Naicker, who was the chairperson of the South African Indian Congress, all of them were saying, 'Let us not embark on violence; let us continue with non-violence.'[17] And when they couldn't resist the argument I was putting forward, they said, 'You go and start that organisation. We will not discipline you because we understand the conditions under which you have taken this line. But don't involve us; we are going to continue with non-violence.' The state found that, those minutes, they [proved our] whole case and they did not hand it in. We, the defence, handed that document in to say, '*Support* for our point of view is this.' So, that is what happened, you see, with Umkhonto we Sizwe.

....

17. Dr Gangathura Mohambry (Monty) Naicker, see People, Places and Events.

MANDELA: All that we have to say is that the number depended, you see, on the conditions in each particular area. There was no set number and most of the people were trained abroad, but a little later we felt it would be valuable to train people in the area where they were going to operate. But it must be understood that it was extremely difficult to do so, because we were dealing with a strong government, [a] strong enemy . . . who had the facilities to move around and to be able to detect what was being done on the ground. Under those circumstances we could only train just a few.

KATHRADA: Aha. All right, then, page 135 [of *Long Walk to Freedom* draft] you are saying, 'On the orders of MK [Umkhonto we Sizwe] High Command, in [the] early morning hours of December the 16th, home-made bombs were exploded at electric power stations and government offices in Jo'burg, PE [Port Elizabeth], Durban. One of our men was inadvertently killed, the first MK soldier to die in the line of duty.'

MANDELA: That's [Petrus] Molefe hey?[18]

KATHRADA: Ja, now he says, 'Was this the first death associated with MK? Did you have a feeling of responsibility?'

MANDELA: Well, we say so, that he was the very first.

KATHRADA: Ja.

MANDELA: And naturally we had a sense of responsibility because he was our soldier, our cadre, and the death, you know, indicated . . . that we had not sufficiently trained people, and it was something very disturbing. But we took that, you see, in [our] stride; and casualties – you can't avoid casualties when you are starting a new method of political activity.

....

18. Petrus Molefe was killed when a bomb he placed on 16 December 1961 exploded prematurely.

STENGEL: But the story where the Chief [Albert Luthuli] asked you why you hadn't consulted with him about, about the formation of MK, was that on this trip or was that when you came back from Africa?

MANDELA: No, no, no. It was before we took the trip . . . But the Chief had actually forgotten because, as I told you, we had a meeting of the ANC National Executive in which we discussed the question of taking up arms. We eventually agreed after he had advised against it, and when we went to the joint meetings now of the ANC, the South African Indian Congress, the South African Congress of Trade Unions, the Federation of [South] African Women, *then* the Chief asked us, 'Well, my comrades, we have taken this decision.' In fact he asked at the meeting, 'We have taken this decision that we must start violence and establish an army, but I would like to appeal to you: let's take our original positions' and as if the ANC has taken no decision. We agreed and we spent the *whole* night – we never slept – spent the *whole* night discussing the question of the formation – the start of the acts of violence. So for him to say that we didn't consult him was just the fact that he was ill and he forgot very easily . . . But the matter was *thoroughly* debated.

19. CONVERSATION WITH AHMED KATHRADA ABOUT WILDLIFE

KATHRADA: Did you ever go to the zoo? In Johannesburg?

MANDELA: Oh, I see, yes, yes. Yes, I had seen most of the animals in the zoo.

KATHRADA: But you've never been to the Kruger National Park, at that time?

MANDELA: No, no. I only went to the Kruger National Park . . .

KATHRADA: After you came back.

MANDELA: . . . after I came back from jail.

KATHRADA: Aha.

MANDELA: Have you ever been there?

KATHRADA: Ja. I went there, last December, also. Not this December, the December before.

MANDELA: And you saw?

KATHRADA: . . . The first time, ay man, we saw *nothing*.

MANDELA: Yes.

KATHRADA: What had happened is that it had rained.

MANDELA: Oh, I see.

KATHRADA: And the radio said it's useless going because once it has rained the animals won't come to their normal watering places.

MANDELA: Yes, quite. Yes, that's true.

KATHRADA: So we saw just about nothing.

MANDELA: Mmm. But there, you know, to shoot an impala, you see, is just like committing suicide, you know; it's murder.

KATHRADA: Ja.

MANDELA: Because they are so *trustworthy*. They are so *used* to visitors that they come and just watch you, and they don't run away.

KATHRADA: Ja.

MANDELA: You *can't*. I could never have the courage to shoot at those.

20. CONVERSATION WITH RICHARD STENGEL

STENGEL: Have you ever used that comparison before or since? The one with Christ and the money changers?

MANDELA: Yes. Yes. I think I must have done so, or might have done, because I know it very well . . .

STENGEL: Explain it to me now, how you would use that analogy . . .

MANDELA: . . . Whether you have to use peaceful methods or

violent methods . . . is determined purely by the conditions . . . Christ used force because in *that* situation it is the *only* language that he could use. And . . . therefore there is no principle that force may not be used. It depends on the conditions. That is how I would approach the matter.

STENGEL: So under the circumstances then, it's even Christian to use force because Christ had to resort to force?

MANDELA: Well, *everybody* – when the only way of making a forward movement, of solving problems, is the use of force: when peaceful methods become inadequate. That is a lesson of history, right down the centuries and . . . in every part of the world.

CHAPTER FIVE

Bursting World

Pages from the diary Mandela kept during his trip through Africa and to London, UK, in 1962.

1. EXTRACTS FROM THE DIARY HE KEPT DURING HIS TRIP
   THROUGH AFRICA AND TO LONDON IN 1962

17 JANUARY 1962

The immigration officer sees me again and appeals to me that on no account must I move around as I might be kidnapped by the SAP [South African Police].

I gain the impression that whilst there may [be] genuine concern for my safety, he also wishes to make sure that I should meet people in the BP [Bechuanaland Protectorate].

29 JANUARY 1962

I call for a visa at the Ethiopian Embassy. On the way we pass the Conference Hall and I am told to take cover and look the other way as Colin Legum might recognise me.[1]

15 APRIL 1962

I spend the day quietly reading in my hotel.

19 APRIL 1962

I fly from Freetown to Monrovia. The aerodrome, Robertsfield is 48 miles away from the city.

I lodge at the Monrovia City Hotel.

20 APRIL 1962

I spend the day reading.

23 APRIL 1962

I spend the day quietly in the hotel reading.

25 APRIL 1962

2 pm

....

1. Colin Legum (1919–2003). Author, journalist, anti-apartheid activist.

I meet the President.[2] He informs me that the people of Liberia would do everything in their power to help our people in their struggle for self-determination. Sends his regards to Chief [Albert Luthuli].

26 APRIL 1962

I miss my plane to Accra and I book for the following day at 9 am.

5 MAY 1962

OR [Oliver Tambo] phones to say he will arrive on 7/5. He telephones from Stockholm.

7 MAY 1962

OR arrives at lunch time. We meet head of African mission at 7/30 pm and have a friendly chat with him.

27 MAY 1962

We leave Lagos by Pan Am for Monrovia on our way to Conakry. After stopping for 45 minutes at Accra, plane reaches Monrovia at 12 noon. We drive to Monrovia City Hotel.

1 JUNE 1962

We fly to Dakar and put up at Hotel de La Paix.

7 JUNE 1962

We fly by BOAC to L[ondon].

15 JUNE 1962

I meet David Astor, Editor of the 'Observer'.[3] Michael Scott

---

2. President William Vacanarat Shadrach Tubman (1895–1971). President of Liberia, 1944–71.
3. David Astor (1912–2001). English newspaper publisher and editor.

and Colin Legum are present.[4] I explain the situation in SA. Discussions are most cordial and each expresses flattering and inspiring comments.

16 JUNE 1962
I see film of Zami, Zeni, Zindzi, Gompo and other scenes in South Africa.[5]

18 JUNE 1962
OR and I fly by BOAC to Khartoum. We cross the Alps at about 6 pm and reach Rome at about 7 pm.

26 JUNE 1962
7/20 am we fly to Addis Ababa and are taken to Ras Hotel.

29 JUNE 1962
First lesson on demolitions start. Instructor Lt. Befekadu.

30 JUNE 1962
I have practice in demolitions.

1 JULY 1962
I spend the day writing up notes.

7 JULY 1962
Lt. Befekadu takes me out to a restaurant serving national dishes.

8 JULY 1962
Col Tadesse, Lt. Befekadu and I dine in small restaurant in town and thereafter go to the cinemas.

4. Michael Scott (1907–83). Cleric, film-maker, anti-apartheid activist.
5. Winnie and their two daughters. Gompo was the family dog.

2. CONVERSATION WITH AHMED KATHRADA ABOUT HIS TRIP
   THROUGH AFRICA IN 1962

KATHRADA: Then 'a plane was arranged for, and our first destination was a town in northern Botswana, Bechuanaland, called Kasane . . .'

MANDELA: Yes.

KATHRADA: '. . . that was strategically situated at the point where almost the whole of southern Africa met: Angola, Northern and Southern Rhodesia and South West Africa, as all these states were then known.' Now, he is asking, this was your first plane trip, wasn't it?

MANDELA: Yes.

KATHRADA: Your very first?

MANDELA: No, no, no, no, no. It was not. During the Defiance Campaign in 1952, I travelled a couple of times on a plane.

KATHRADA: Aha.

MANDELA: To Port Elizabeth.

KATHRADA: 'If it was your first trip, were you apprehensive or eager? What kind of a plane was it? It may seem trivial but this is just the sort of telling human moment that readers will care about. The paradoxical combination of your important mission with your first trip abroad.'

MANDELA: . . . No, it was not the first time, but nevertheless, there were some scary moments . . . we came across a storm and the turmoil, you know, was very disturbing, and then we reached the hotel at Kasane and the one landing strip was waterlogged, and by the time we came there, elephants and other animals – zebras – were grazing there and so we couldn't land . . . because you can easily frighten animals, you see, by flying low . . . So we went to land elsewhere and we flew over the hotel . . . And we flew over the lodge to indicate to the hotel owner that we had arrived and pointed out, you know, where we were going to land, which was further away from the hotel. . . . He [the hotel owner] came late and . . . said that along the way they came across elephants . . . [that] refused to move away . . . for some time, so they had to stop there to wait for them to move . . .

KATHRADA: Ah.

MANDELA: It was already dusk and as we were going back we saw a lioness sleeping across the road . . . just more or less a track.

KATHRADA: Ja.

MANDELA: . . . That was my first experience of the bush, really. And during the night the lions, you see, were roaring, man, and it appeared as if they were just outside the rondavel. Because when [they] roared, you know . . . the window – the glass – vibrated, and I was frightened to go out.

3. CONVERSATION WITH RICHARD STENGEL ABOUT MEETING EMPEROR HAILE SELASSIE OF ETHIOPIA

STENGEL: So tell me about the Emperor, Haile Selassie. You met him.

MANDELA: *That* was an impressive fellow, man, very impressive. It was my first time to watch . . . a head of state going through the formalities . . . the motions of formality. This chap came wearing a uniform and he then came and bowed. But it was a bow which was not a bow – he stood erect, you see, but just brought down his head . . . then . . . took his seat and addressed us, but he spoke in [Amharic] . . . Then, at the end of the conference he saw every, each delegation . . . and Comrade Oliver Tambo asked me to speak for our delegation, to speak to him. And I explained to him very briefly what was happening in South Africa . . . He was seated on his chair, listening like a log . . . not nodding, just immovable, you know, like a statue

. . . The next time I saw him was when we attended a military parade, and *that* was very impressive [*whistles*], absolutely impressive. And he was then giving awards . . . to the soldiers; everyone who had graduated got a certificate . . . A very fine ceremony – a very dignified chap – and he also gave medals. There [were] American military advisors . . . [and] groups of military advisors from various countries . . . And so he gave medals to these chaps too. But to see whites going to a black monarch emperor and bowing was also very interesting.

4. CONVERSATION WITH AHMED KATHRADA ABOUT HIS
   MILITARY TRAINING

KATHRADA: Then, they want to know on the same page 166 [of *Long Walk to Freedom* draft], 'Did you ever become proficient with a pistol? Did you receive more military instruction than this at Oujda?'
MANDELA: Oh yes, at Oujda, yes, I did. But the perfection was in Ethiopia because I spent two months there and I was taught now how to fire various guns [at] different targets, you know? . . . And different distances, stationary targets and then a moving target, you see. They would, what-you-call, they would bring it up and then it would disappear, come up [and] . . . disappear. It would run, you see, and you had to hit it, you see, running. So all that perfection, you see, took place in . . . Ethiopia. And then the fatigue marches . . . where you have a very *heavy* bag, you know – round[s] of bullets around the waist. Then you carry on you [a] knapsack, a lot of provisions and so on, and a water bottle, and your gun, you know . . . and you travel over mountains and so on. A bit . . . strenuous.

KATHRADA: Then . . . this is about the training you were having: 'I had never fired a gun before, but it felt comfortable in my hands. I aimed, pulled the trigger and the next thing I know the bullet had raised some powder on the rock. My instructors began to exclaim something in Arabic and complimented me on my shot. But as it turned out, it was a lucky one for I did not hit the rock again in several more attempts.'

MANDELA: Actually, no, even the *first* one, I didn't hit the rock.

KATHRADA: Oh.

MANDELA: But it was *next* to the rock.

KATHRADA: Aha.

MANDELA: And having regard to the distance because we had the river in between us. We had a valley, a long valley, and the river and then this target was right across, and I just hit next to the stone.

KATHRADA: Aha.

MANDELA: And that was sufficiently . . . close to them for a man who was handling the gun for the first time. I think I told you how this chap taught me – he couldn't speak the language.

KATHRADA: Ja.

MANDELA: Arabic.

KATHRADA: Carry on.

MANDELA: Yes, you know? I think I demonstrated – I don't know whether I did to you, but he couldn't speak English and *all* that he did was to take the gun, you see, and it was a heavy Mauser. He took the gun and said [*sound of quick tapping*], you see?

KATHRADA: Ah.

MANDELA: I should hold it *tight*, and then he said I should, what you call, I should stand *firmly* on the ground, he says [*sound of foot stomping once*].

KATHRADA: Ah.

MANDELA: [*another foot stomp*] You see?

KATHRADA: Ah.

MANDELA: And he was very good, you see; I mean without being able to talk [English] . . .

KATHRADA: Aha.

MANDELA: But he really was a very good chap. But I didn't *hit* the stone.

KATHRADA: Aha.

MANDELA: I hit next to it.

KATHRADA: Next to it.

MANDELA: Yes.

6. FROM HIS UNPUBLISHED AUTOBIOGRAPHICAL MANUSCRIPT
    WRITTEN IN PRISON

In spite of plunder by the colonialists Egypt still is a country of fabulous wealth in ancient art and culture. I have always been anxious to see the pyramids, the sphinx and the embalmed body of Ramses II, perhaps one of the strongest pharaohs that ever ruled that country. I spent the whole morning at the museum making detailed notes and later Oliver [Tambo] took me to Gizeh where we saw the colossal stone structure with its square base firmly planted on the ground where the sloping sides met at the apex, all done with mortar and giant blocks of stone with which a monumental edifice was built, held in position by their own weight.

Oliver took me for a boat ride around the island on the Nile and as a boy of about 9 skillfully manoeuvred the boat we were going to use, my otherwise fearless and calm comrade-in-arms widened his eyes, watched the whole operation suspiciously and explained: 'Are we going to be driven by this small boy? Oh no.' At the same time he stepped back and stood at a safe distance. But when an elderly man took the controls we relaxed and I thoroughly enjoyed the one hour ride on Africa's longest river.

My chief interest was to find out the type of men who founded the high civilisation of olden times that thrived in the Nile Valley as far back as 5000 B.C. This was not merely a question of archaeological interest but one of cardinal importance to African thinkers who are primarily concerned with the collection of scientific evidence to explode the fictitious claim of white propagandists that civilisation began in Europe and that Africans have no rich past that can compare with theirs. I discussed the matter with one of the curators at the museum but he was extremely cautious and although he drew my attention to several theories on the matter, for which I was extremely grateful, I was no wiser on the subject than I was before I entered the museum.

7. CONVERSATION WITH RICHARD STENGEL ABOUT ALGERIAN
   FREEDOM FIGHTERS

MANDELA: Mostefai? Yes, yes, he was the head of the Algerian delegation in Morocco.
STENGEL: Right. Now he talked to you quite extensively, didn't he?
MANDELA: Oh, yes, for several days.
STENGEL: Right.
MANDELA: Reviewing the Algerian Revolution. Oh, that was a masterpiece, man, I can tell you. Very few things inspired me as the briefing from Dr Mostefai.
STENGEL: Really, how come? Why?
MANDELA: . . . He was reviewing to us, you know, the *history* of the Algerian Revolution. The problems that they had. How they started. They started thinking that they would be able to

defeat the French in the battlefield, inspired by what happened in . . . Vietnam. Dien Bien Phu. They were inspired by that, and they thought they could defeat the French . . . He says even their uniforms, their outfits, were so designed for an army that was going to defeat the French. Then they realised that they could not do so. They have to fight guerrilla warfare, and he says even their own, their uniform, changed because it was now an army that would be on the run, either attacking [or] moving away fast. They had what-you-call trousers, you see, which were narrow down there, you know, and lighter shoes. It was *most* fascinating, and then they kept the French army moving.

They would attack from the Tunisian side, launch an offensive that side, and then the French – because of this – they would *move* their army from the western side, from the Moroccan border, because the Algerians were fighting from Tunisia and from Morocco. Although they had also units operating inside, but the main army was fighting from these two areas, two countries . . . Then they would then start an offensive from Tunisia, *deep* into Algeria, and the French would *move* their army from the west, from the borders of Morocco in order to stop this offensive. And when they *moved* that army, the offensive would start on the Moroccan side, you see? And the French would again move, you know, their forces to the Moroccan side, and they kept them moving like that. Now *all* those, man, were very interesting, absolutely interesting.

STENGEL: And were you thinking this might be a model for how MK [Umkhonto we Sizwe] would be in South Africa?

MANDELA: Well, it was information on which we could work out our own tactics.

8. FROM HIS 1962 NOTEBOOK ON HIS TRAINING IN MOROCCO
WITH THE NATIONAL LIBERATION FRONT IN ALGERIA (ALN)

Maroc

18/3

R [Robert Resha][6] and I leave [Rabat] for the border village of Oujda, the HQ of the ALN in Maroc. We leave by train and reach at 8 am on 19/3.

19/3

An officer meets us at the station and drives us to [HQ]. We are received by Abdelhamid [Brahimi],[7] head of the political section of the ALN.

Present are Si Jamal, Aberrahman, Larbi, Noureddine Djoudi. A general discussion on the situation in SA [South Africa] ensues and pertinent and searching questions are put to us. The discussion is thereafter adjourned to enable us to see things in training camps and in the front lines.

At 4 pm, accompanied by Djoudi and another officer we drive to training base of Zegangan situate[d] in what was known as Spanish Morocco. We arrive there at 6 pm and are met by the Commander of the camp Si Jamal. He shows us the army museum containing an interesting collection of armaments of the ALN, starting with those used during the uprising of November 1, 1954, to the latest equipment.

After dinner we visit the soldiers' theatre and listen to music and sketches. The two sketches presented contain terrific propaganda against French rule in Alg[eria]. After the show we return to our quarters and sleep.

---

6. Robert Resha, see People, Places and Events.
7. Dr Abdelhamid Brahimi (1936–). Later became the prime minister of Algeria, 1984–88.

21/3

After visiting the ALN printing works and transmission HQ we proceed, in the company of two officers to Bouleker. We first visit the HQ of the battalion on the northern division. It is situated suitably in the most strategic area and heavily guarded. We have lunch there consisting of rabbit meat and fresh bread.

Thereafter we proceed to the HQ of one of the battalions situated right on the Alg border. We see and enter the dugouts. There are a lot of refugees around the camp and their appearance was most touching. Later we return to Oujda for a discussion.

The discussion starts at 6.30 pm and we were to leave at 9.45 back to Rabat. At 9.30 it was decided that we should leave by car for Rabat the next day as we had hardly disposed of ¼ of our business.

9.   FROM HIS 1962 NOTEBOOK

Another point . . . that Capt Larbi made was that the country's elite must be made to realise that the masses of the people, however poor and illiterate they might be, are the country's most important investment. In all activities and operations there must be a thorough diffusion of the intelligentsia and the masses of the people – peasants and labourers, workers in the cities, etc.

Thirdly, the masses of the people must be made to realise that political action, of the nature of strikes, boycotts and similar demonstrations, has become ineffective standing just by themselves. Action must be accepted as the primary and most essential form of political activity.

10. FROM HIS 1962 NOTEBOOK

Whilst political consciousness is vital in the formation of an army and in mobilising mass support, practical matters must not be lost sight of. For example, a woman who is not politically developed may do a great deal for the revolution simply because her boyfriend, husband or son is in the army. Also villages may show individual initiative which must be encouraged.

There is a case where one village attacked a French post without instructions from the ALN [National Liberation Front in Algeria]. In another village, the people dug an underground tunnel on their own.

It is also known that at a certain stage the ALN prevented its soldiers from getting married. Later on this was modified and general permission to marry was granted. Those women who were now married to the soldiers of the ALN, including their families, immediately became supporters of the ALN and the revolution.

11. FROM HIS 1962 NOTEBOOK

There are certain vital matters which have to be borne in mind in building up a revolutionary army:

Whilst it is important to have your people trained by friendly countries . . . this should only be part of the plan. The essential point to grasp is to produce your own schools [which] will establish training centres either inside or on the borders of the country.

You must also plan and provide for replacements simply because in combat you will [lose] many men. You will break the revolution if you do not take the necessary preparations. You will also give confidence to the enemy. On the contrary, and right from the beginning you must show him that your strength is increasing.

You must be flexible and original otherwise the enemy will smash your forces.

Account must also be taken for the fact that the longe[r] the war lasts, the more the massacres increase, and the people get tired.

12. FROM HIS 1962 NOTEBOOK

Spectacular and successful attacks by the revolutionaries enabled the Alg[erian] people to recover their dignity. In Alg[eria] they established zonal commando[s] who had a specialised function. Their activities have no economic advantage but [are] extremely useful in building up the people's morale. But such action must not fail. Examples of commando operations consist in surface attacks on French soldiers in cities, explosions in cinemas.

You must also not rely merely on a declaration by a prospective recruit that he is ready to fight. You must test him. In one village 200 people declared that they were ready to join the ALN [National Liberation Front in Algeria]. They were then told that the following day there would be an attack on the enemy. Volunteers were called for and only 3 came forward. In yet another case new recruits were told to march to a certain point at night where they were promised weapons. They reached the place at midnight and they were told that the man who had promised to deliver the weapons had not arrived, and were advised to return the next night. Those who complained revealed that they would not be reliable under more difficult conditions.

13. FROM HIS 1962 NOTEBOOK

There must be proper coordination of guerrilla activities in the towns and country areas.

Considerations to be born in mind when starting Rev[olution].

There must be an absolute guarantee that all precautions have been taken to ensure success – organisation is extremely important. There must be a network throughout the country first and foremost . . . We must make a thorough study of all revolutions including those that failed. Good organisation is absolutely essential. In the wilaya [province] a year was taken to build a proper organisation.

An uprising that is local must be avoided. Many uprising[s] failed because the revolutionary idea was not shared by all.

An uprising must be organised in such a way as to ensure its continuity.

15. FROM HIS 1962 NOTEBOOK

Organisers of rev[olution] must not be unduly worried by lack of military training on the part of the masses of the people. The best commanders and strategists in the ALN [National Liberation Front in Algeria] have mainly been those people who have no previous military experience. There is also a difference between being military and militant. In Alg[eria] women not only could shoot but they could dismantle a rifle and assemble it again.

16. FROM HIS 1962 NOTEBOOK

Date of commencement must be chosen when it is absolutely certain that rev[olution] will succeed and it must be related to other factors. For example, the French Minist[er] of Defence, after touring Tunisia and Morocco made a statement that Alg[eria] was peaceful. The uprising occurred the next day.

Thereafter, he made a statement that the uprising was confined to certain areas and not countrywide. Soon thereafter it was extended throughout the country. Choosing of date[s] should be influenced by psychological opportunity.

17. FROM HIS 1962 NOTEBOOK

We must have the courage to accept that there will be reprisals against the population. But we must try and avoid this by a careful selection of targets. It is better to attack targets which are far away from the population than those that are near. Targets must be near as possible to the enemy. To the people and the world the uprising must assume the character of a popular revolutionary movement. To the enemy it must appear as an uprising of a few only.

We must seek the support of the entire population with a perfect balance of social classes. The base of your support will be amongst the common people, poor and illiterate but the intellectuals must be brought in.

Finally, there must be perfect harmony between the external delegation of the revolutionary movement and the high command. Both must consist of similar and equally developed personnel.

18. FROM HIS 1962 NOTEBOOK

14/3/62 Dr Mostefai
The original objective of the Alg[erian] Revolution was the defeat of the French by military action as in Indo-China. Settlement by negotiation was not visualised.

Conception of the struggle when you begin will determine failure or success of the revolution.

You must have a general plan which governs all our daily operations. In addition to the general plan which deals with the total situation, you must have a plan, say for the next 3 months. There must be no action for the sake of action. Every individual action must be done to implement the strategic aim. You must have

a) Military objective
b) Political objective
c) Psychological objective

This is the strategic aim for a limited time. The strategic aim may create a new situation which may make it necessary to alter the general plan. Your tactical plans are governed by strategy. Your tactics will not only be confined to military operations but they will also cover such things as the political consciousness of the masses of the people, the mobilisation of allies in the international field. Your aim should be to destroy the legality of the Government and to institute that of the people. There must be parallel authority in the administration of justice, in administration and in supplies.

The political organisation must be in complete control of the people and their activity. Your soldiers must live amongst the people like fish in water.

The aim should be that our forces should develop and grow and those of the enemy should disintegrate.

To start a revolution is easy but to continue and maintain it is most difficult. Duty of a commander is to make a thorough analysis of the situation before a start is made.

19. CONVERSATION WITH AHMED KATHRADA ABOUT HIS TRIP TO
    LONDON IN 1962

MANDELA: Yes, well actually, the British gave me a hard time at the airport. Not rude; you see they are very subtle.
KATHRADA: Ja.
MANDELA: . . . I had to produce my passport, but in the first

place, you see, Oliver [Tambo] says, 'You go to that table; I'll go to that other one.' And we parted, and so I gave this chap my passport, and he looked at it and greeted me very politely, and he says, 'What are you coming to England for?' So I say, 'I came to the library, to the museum, because I am writing a book.' And he says, 'What book is this?' So I say, 'Well, the subject is the evolution of political thought in Africa' and he says, 'Oh, sir, wonderful – it's a wonderful title, and how long do you want?' I say, 'I just want two weeks.' He says, 'No, don't ask for two weeks; ask for a month.' And I thought . . . I'm going to have a wonderful time, and I say, 'No, I'll get a month,' and he said, 'Have you got a return ticket . . .'

KATHRADA: Ah.

MANDELA: '. . . with you?' . . . I was *shaken* by this. I say, 'No, but I've got some money.' In fact I think I've got about 20 rands or something. [*laughs*] And I said, 'I've got some money' and I found my hand going to the pocket, but he says, 'No, no, no, no. Don't worry.' Because . . . he knew . . . the fact that I had the money and he didn't want to do that. They are very subtle.

KATHRADA: Ja.

MANDELA: 'No, no, no, no, don't do that.' And then, *as* he was talking to me, the chap in that counter signalled to him, says [*gestures*] . . . to Oliver, you see? In other words, he was saying that 'This is a chap in a . . .', what-you-call, 'in the black list.'

KATHRADA: Aha.

MANDELA: And he was *tipping* [off] this chap, and he was asking very subtle questions, but *coming* up, you know, with something devastating, you know?

KATHRADA: Ah.

MANDELA: And eventually [he] says, 'I'm going to give you Form so-and-so', you know, 'which will enable you to stay for a month,' and then wished me well. In the meantime they were plotting . . . They discovered that, no, we are freedom fighters.

But I had quite a lovely time because I saw British politicians, and they welcomed me *very* well. I saw this chap Denis Healey, of the Labour Party,[8] and I saw . . . the chap Hugh Gaitskell[9] . . . Now they wanted me to meet [Prime Minister] Macmillan but . . . we were foolish; you see, our programme was too tight, seeing people like David Astor, Anthony . . . [10]

KATHRADA: Sampson.[11]

MANDELA: Sampson and others . . .

KATHRADA: You didn't stay with Astor did you?

MANDELA: No, no, no, no. I stayed with Oliver, yes.

KATHRADA: Aha.

MANDELA: . . . It was, of course, exciting to be in England and the capital of [the] once . . . powerful British Empire. I enjoyed that, and then in going, you know, to their bookshops and so on and getting literature on guerrilla warfare.

20. CONVERSATION WITH RICHARD STENGEL ABOUT GUERRILLA WARFARE

MANDELA: The revolution in China was a masterpiece, a *real* masterpiece. If you read how they fought that revolution, you believe in the impossible. It's just miraculous. Who is the American man who wrote the book *Red Star Over China*?

STENGEL: Yes.

MANDELA: What was his name? Famous name, man.

STENGEL: Snow.

MANDELA: Edgar Snow.

STENGEL: Right.

MANDELA: That was the first book I read about China.

STENGEL: Oh is it really?

---

8.   Denis Healey (1917–). British Labour Party politician.
9.   Hugh Gaitskell (1906–63). British Labour Party politician. Leader of the Labour Party, 1955–63.
10. Harold Macmillan (1894–1986). British prime minister, 1957–63.
11. Anthony Sampson, see People, Places and Events.

MANDELA: Yes. *Red Star Over China* – Edgar Snow . . . *Red Star Over China* – Edgar Snow. Well written, simple and sympathetic, but not a communist. You know? Not a communist, that was the . . . advantage because he could also criticise. *But* it was a constructive work, and when he described its origin in the south-eastern part of China where they started, and then how Chiang Kai-shek and others tried, you know, to circle, encircle this area and to *squeeze* it and to *crush* this revolution, and how they fought against it. And when it became clear that if they *remain* there they would be crushed, they decided to *break* through this steel wall and went down [to] China and then went *right* up to the borders of the Soviet Union and that is where they started the offensive fight.

STENGEL: Right, the long march.

MANDELA: Yes, that long march, you see? That was just a miracle. Some of the incidents just showed, you know, it was just like magic, how they escaped.

STENGEL: So what, from your reading, what were the lessons that you learned that you wanted to apply to MK [Umkhonto we Sizwe] in the sense that you had read about movements that failed? So what did you want to avoid to prevent MK from failing that you learned as a result of the reading?

MANDELA: Well it was really to find out firstly, what are the fundamental principles of starting a revolution? An armed revolution, armed warfare. That's why I read Clausewitz because it did not deal with guerrilla warfare; it deals with the rules of war, you know, principles of war . . . Oh, by the way, I read also *The Revolt* by Menachem Begin.

STENGEL: Oh.

MANDELA: Yes, *The Revolt* by Menachem Begin. Now, that was now something which was very encouraging to us, because here was a movement in a country which had no mountains and . . . their base was inside Israel . . . which was occupied by the British Army from top to bottom, you see? From border to border. But they conducted that struggle in a *very* powerful way and that really was very interesting. I also read about the Partisans in France, Mitterrand, and in Eastern Europe. And so this is the type of literature I read.

21. CONVERSATION WITH RICHARD STENGEL

MANDELA: That period underground . . . I read Clausewitz, I . . . read *Commando* by Deneys Reitz. And I . . . read two books . . . on Malaysia, and I . . . read this book on the Philippines, on the Hukbalahap, and *Born of the People* by Luis Taruk. And I had read the works of Mao Zedong. But here I was just . . . learning how to use a gun [in Ethiopia].

STENGEL: Right. It was practical.

MANDELA: It was practical, yes.

STENGEL: Oh, so you went there to two shooting ranges, is that right, that you went to?

MANDELA: Yes, that's right. There was a shooting range for all the soldiers, which was quite some distance away from the camp. Then there was one for . . . the Emperor's guard – guard of honour – and which was nearer. I went to those two.

STENGEL: What kind of a shot were you?

MANDELA: No, for a . . . I mean, reasonable, I was reasonable, because in [Morocco] that was where I used – I handled a gun for the first time. And they just taught you, you know, how you handle a gun and its mechanism, you see. They stripped it, and you knew the various parts. They put it together and they asked you to do that several times until you are quite perfect.

22. FROM A CONVERSATION WITH AHMED KATHRADA ABOUT THE ARMED STRUGGLE

Well . . . one of the controversial issues when we established MK was . . . control. We wanted to avoid militarism; we wanted to create . . . a military force which was under a central political organisation where they took instructions from the political organisation, and that is the principle on which it was established . . . We stressed that that training must go hand in hand with political training. They must know why they are going to take up arms and fight. They must be taught that the revolution was not just a question of pulling a trigger and firing – it was an organisation that was intended to take over political power. That is what we stressed.

CHAPTER SIX

The Chains of the Body

'. . . In my current circumstances, thinking about the past can be far more exacting than contemplating the present and predicting the course of future events. Until I was jailed I never fully appreciated the capacity of memory, the endless string of information the head can carry.'

Excerpt from a letter to Hilda Bernstein, dated 8 July 1985, see pages 115–116.

1. FROM A CONVERSATION WITH RICHARD STENGEL

Plays like *Antigone* . . . Those Greek plays, you know, are really worth reading. It's like the classics, you know the works of Tolstoy and so on, because after reading . . . that literature, you always come out . . . feeling very elevated and your sensitivities to . . . fellow human beings having been deepened. It is one of the greatest experiences . . . you can have, you know, to read a Greek tragedy and Greek literature in general . . .

2. CONVERSATION WITH AHMED KATHRADA ON WHETHER
   HE WAS BETRAYED

KATHRADA: You know, of course, that they phoned Walter [Sisulu] to say that *I* had given you up?[1]
MANDELA: The . . . press?
KATHRADA: No, it was an anonymous phone call . . . he tells Walter . . . 'I'm just tipping you off that the person who gave up Mandela is Kathrada.'
MANDELA: Yoh!
KATHRADA: [*laughs*]
MANDELA: Yoh! . . . Good God. Because those things are smashed by events.
KATHRADA: Ja, well remember they blamed Albertina [Sisulu] also.[2]
MANDELA: Yes, yes quite. Yes. I know they blamed Albertina and Walter.
KATHRADA: Ja.
MANDELA: *That* touched me. I didn't know about yours.
KATHRADA: Ja.

....

1. Kathrada is referring to how Mandela came to be arrested on 5 August 1962.
2. Nontsikelelo (Ntsiki) Albertina Sisulu, see People, Places and Events.

MANDELA: But the one of Walter, man. You know, in fact, when he came to see me in jail, you know he didn't look like Walter; he seemed to have been shaken by that accusation.

KATHRADA: I think the press even came out with something that Albertina and Winnie [Mandela] had a fight about this, about this accusation that . . . Walter and Albertina had given you up . . .

MANDELA: No, I know, what happened, you see, because I was reading the papers and this question about Walter was mentioned there.

KATHRADA: Ah.

MANDELA: And I had to discuss with him that 'Look, I've got *complete* confidence in you . . . don't even *worry* about that,' and he *was* worried about that because people, you know will take advantage.

3. CONVERSATION WITH AHMED KATHRADA ABOUT HIS ARREST

KATHRADA: The publisher is asking, '*More* on your emotions . . . at realising that the game was up. Were you frightened that you might be shot?'[3]

MANDELA: No, I had no such fright, you see, because I considered my options immediately this car passed and signalled us; because I looked at the rear-view mirror and I could see that there were cars behind and then they selected a very strategic place with a high bank on my left where I couldn't run, run away, and I decided that the game was up. I could see the mountains, the Lesotho mountains . . . but I decided, you see, that it would be a risky thing and I decided just to remain. I had no fears of being shot, you know, once I decided I was not going to run away.

....

3. See note 1, this chapter.

4. FROM A LETTER TO HILDA BERNSTEIN, DATED 8 JULY 1985,
    ABOUT THE RIVONIA TRIAL[4]

How is your memory? It may well be that you no longer need it, with all the modern facilities which surround you – newspapers, good literature, archives, libraries, radio, television, videos, computers, and what have you. In my current circumstances, thinking about the past can be far more exacting than contemplating the present and predicting the course of future events. Until I was jailed I never fully appreciated the capacity of memory, the endless string of information the head can carry.

I still remember the day you sat behind me in Pretoria as Rusty [fellow accused Bernstein] was busy parrying off some of [prosecutor Percy] Yutar's onslaughts. Quite early during the exchanges, I got the impression that it was not Yutar, but the man from Observatory, who was calling the shots. It also seemed to me that even [the judge, Quartus] de Wet was being disarmed, if not enchanted, by the gentle and self-assured manner with which the witness was brushing aside all that Yutar could throw in.

As we adjourned, I could not resist telling you that the witness was good. Can you recall how Mrs Bernstein retorted? 'What do you mean good? He was brilliant!' she shot back. Indeed, he was. If he had been as flat-footed as we were, he would also have been languishing in the cooler, never attended Tony's wedding and, who knows, manpower problems in the family might have been compounded. For Keith, Francis, Patrick, Tony [Bernstein's children] and you his return was certainly an unforgettable day.[5]

....

4. Hilda Bernstein, see People, Places and Events.
5. Rusty Bernstein was acquitted in the Rivonia Trial.

I also remember that on the first day of the Pretoria exercise you had expressed some concern about how I and a colleague looked in our khaki outfits. But now, after praising your husband, you had some good things to say about our appearance. I can no longer recall whether I was able to chat to you the day Rusty was discharged. All I can remember now is reading a newspaper in a rubbish dump on Robben Island to the effect that he was in Zambia.[6]

5. CONVERSATION WITH AHMED KATHRADA ABOUT PAC (PAN AFRICANIST CONGRESS) LEADER ROBERT SOBUKWE[7]

KATHRADA: And Sobukwe was kept with the criminals in the cell next door.

MANDELA: Oh yes.

KATHRADA: And we managed to talk to him.

MANDELA: Aha.

KATHRADA: Of course, they treated him very badly.

MANDELA: Yes.

KATHRADA: Short trousers, no shoes.

MANDELA: Yes, that's right.

KATHRADA: And we managed to speak to him and asked him . . . whether we could do anything for him. His request was tobacco and a spoon. So then, you know, there was this little hole.

MANDELA: *Ah* yes.

KATHRADA: We then smuggled in tobacco for him and, and a spoon and possibly some food, but I can't remember that. But his *main* request was tobacco.

MANDELA: Yes, I know. I think that's one of the things that killed him.

6. Following the trial the Bernsteins fled South Africa.
7. Robert Mangaliso Sobukwe, see People, Places and Events.

KATHRADA: Oh ja, lung cancer.

MANDELA: Mmm. Yes. Because he had TB [tuberculosis], you see.

KATHRADA: Aha.

6. CONVERSATION WITH AHMED KATHRADA

KATHRADA: Then you, page 15 [of *Long Walk to Freedom* draft], you are talking of the visit . . . the first visit that you got from Winnie [Mandela] at the Fort now. Ah, you are saying, 'I thanked her for it' – the clothes and a parcel she brought. Ah, 'I thanked her for it and although we did not have much time, we quickly discussed family matters and I assured her of the strength of our cause, the loyalty of our friends and how it would be her love and devotion that would see me through whatever transpired'.

MANDELA: By the way, she brought me some silk pyjamas and nightgown, you see?

KATHRADA: Ja.

MANDELA: And I said, 'No . . .'

KATHRADA: [*laughs*]

MANDELA: '. . . this outfit is not for this place.' [*chuckles*]

7. CONVERSATION WITH RICHARD STENGEL

STENGEL: Tell me about when you had a blackout and you fainted.

MANDELA: Oh, I see. Ha! No I went with [Robert] Sobukwe to the hospital, to hospital, the what-you-call, prison hospital. I just fell. I wasn't aware that there was anything wrong, and I even bruised . . . the side of my face and I had an opening somewhere. That's all. I just fell and then got up – ooh, the reports that circulated outside – yussis! That this man is sick. He's very sick. And I hadn't felt anything. I don't know why

I fell. But I certainly was dizzy, and but after that, you see, nothing happened. I don't know what had happened.

8. CONVERSATION WITH AHMED KATHRADA ABOUT
   ROBERT SOBUKWE

MANDELA: No, I was never confrontational towards Sobukwe. You must remember that Sobukwe was my client. I was his lawyer, and we respected each other very much, Sobukwe, because he was a very pleasant chap.
KATHRADA: Ja.
MANDELA: And a gentleman and there was never any confrontation and I got on *very well* with him in prison.

9. FROM A CONVERSATION WITH RICHARD STENGEL
   ABOUT NONRACIALISM

We have never accepted really multiracialism. Our demand is for a *nonracial* society, because when you talk of multiracialism, you are multiplying races; you are saying that you have in this country so many races. That is in a way to perpetuate the concept 'race', and we preferred to say we want a nonracial society.

. . . We discussed and said exactly what we are saying, that we are not multiracialist, we are nonracialist. We are fighting for a society where people will cease thinking in terms of colour . . . It's not a question of race; it's a question of ideas.

10. CONVERSATION WITH AHMED KATHRADA ABOUT CONSTABLE JOHANNES GREEFF, A POLICEMAN WHO HELPED FOUR COMRADES ARRESTED IN CONNECTION WITH THEIR CASE ESCAPE FROM CUSTODY[8]

KATHRADA: You see, our chaps had promised him to pay him two thousand pounds and the money was delivered to Laloo [Chiba].[9]

MANDELA: I see.

KATHRADA: And he was now . . . continuing the arrangement they had already started. The main bribery as far as I can remember, or persuading the chappie, was Mosie [Moolla].[10]

MANDELA: I see.

KATHRADA: And to some extent, I suppose it was more of a collective thing, really.

MANDELA: Yes, quite, yes.

KATHRADA: And then . . . the arrangement was that Laloo will pay him and the money was then brought to Laloo's place and this chap was supposed to pick it up, but when they wanted to pay him, he was there with the cops, you see, so they didn't pay him.

MANDELA: *Oh!*

KATHRADA: Ah.

MANDELA: Gee whiz!

KATHRADA: And then the fellow got arrested and he got six years . . .

MANDELA: *Oh!*

KATHRADA: . . . this Greeff, and they released him after three years or something. He did serve a sentence, you see.

MANDELA: Is that so?

....

8. The four comrades were Abdulhay Jassat, Moosa (Mosie) Moolla, Harold Wolpe and Arthur Goldreich. On 11 August 1963 they escaped the Marshall Square police station in Johannesburg by bribing Johannes Greeff.
9. Isu (Laloo) Chiba, see People, Places and Events.
10. Moosa Mohamed (Mosie) Moolla, see People, Places and Events.

KATHRADA: And, I'm still going to get you this cutting that Harold [Wolpe] says in which you are quoted as saying that we must honour that debt.[11]

MANDELA: No, we must actually. If *that* was the, the background, if the young fellow was sent to jail.

KATHRADA: Oh *yes*! He served three years, at least, out of a six-year sentence. Now I was just mentioning to Joel the other day when we were talking about this. You know 2,000 pounds in those years, today what is its value, its worth?

MANDELA: Yes.

KATHRADA: A hang of a lot more.

MANDELA: Yes, mmm.

KATHRADA: And I was just thinking that perhaps what we should do is to give him one of these ANC [African National Congress] cars, which won't cost us anything. And they *are* going to go to waste, a lot of these cars, I'm sure.

MANDELA: Just make a note of that man, just make a note.

KATHRADA: Mmm. I've got a note already, about Greeff, but I was going to take it further with you when we get this cutting from Harold, wherein, you are, you know, you are reported as having said that we must honour this . . .

MANDELA: Yes, quite.

KATHRADA: . . . this debt, but that was . . .

MANDELA: . . . You see, I would strongly urge, man, that we should honour it.

KATHRADA: Ja. It'll also give us good publicity.

MANDELA: Yes, yes.

KATHRADA: This chap is now settled in the Cape . . .

MANDELA: Greeff?

KATHRADA: Greeff and . . .

MANDELA: And what is he doing?

---

11. Harold Wolpe (1926–96). Economist, writer and anti-apartheid activist. Member of the SACP.

KATHRADA: He's farming, I think.

MANDELA: Shame, he might be in difficulty, I'm telling you. Farming is not an easy thing.

KATHRADA: So I think that we should . . .

MANDELA: No, no, no, let's discuss that. Let's discuss that.

11. CONVERSATION WITH AHMED KATHRADA ABOUT PLEADING NOT GUILTY IN THE RIVONIA TRIAL

MANDELA: We never pleaded guilty in the Rivonia Trial. We pleaded *not* guilty, remember?

KATHRADA: Ja.

MANDELA: We said that it is the government . . .

KATHRADA: Exactly.

MANDELA: . . . that is the criminal and that should be . . .

KATHRADA: Exactly. What he is mistaking it with is that . . .

MANDELA: Yes.

KATHRADA: . . . in your statement . . .

MANDELA: That's right.

KATHRADA: . . . from the dock, you had admitted to . . .

MANDELA: Yes.

KATHRADA: . . . a lot of things.

MANDELA: That's right.

KATHRADA: But that wasn't a plea of guilty.

MANDELA: Yes, yes, quite.

KATHRADA: Of guilt.

MANDELA: Mmm.

12. FROM THE END OF HIS 20 APRIL 1964 SPEECH FROM THE DOCK IN THE RIVONIA TRIAL

During my lifetime I have dedicated myself to this struggle of the African people. I have fought against White domination, and I have fought against Black domination. I have cherished the ideal of a democratic and free society in which all persons live together in harmony and with equal opportunities. It is an ideal which I hope to live for and to achieve. But if needs be, it is an ideal for which I am prepared to die.

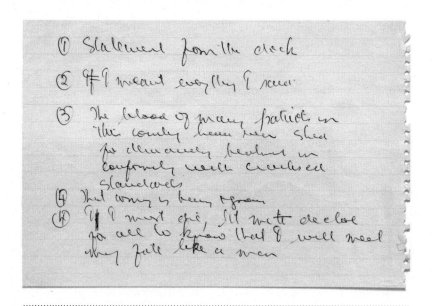

Five points jotted down by Mandela in preparation for sentencing on 12 June 1964 in the Rivonia Trial, in which he and his fellow trialists were facing the death penalty. It reads:

1. *Statement from the dock*
2. *I meant everything I said*
3. *The blood of many patriots in this country have [has] been shed for demanding treatment in conformity with civilised standards*
4. *That army is beginning to grow*
5. *If I must die, let me to declare for all to know that I will meet my fate like a man*

13. FROM A CONVERSATION WITH AHMED KATHRADA ON THE
    PROSPECT OF THE DEATH SENTENCE

We discussed it, as I say, and we said that it was necessary for us to think, not only just in terms of ourselves, who were in this situation, but of the struggle as a whole. We should disappear under a cloud of glory, we should fight back. This is the service we can render to our organisation and to our people. And of course, when you are alone in your cell you also thought in terms of yourself and the fact that you are likely not to live and that is . . . only but human. But, *collectively*, we took this decision and it also made us happy, you know, that this was the *last* service we can give to your people and your organisation.

14. CONVERSATION WITH AHMED KATHRADA ABOUT THE DAY OF SENTENCING IN THE RIVONIA TRIAL

KATHRADA: 'I was disturbed to discover that first day that Winnie [Mandela] was unable to attend. Because of her banning and her restrictions to Johannesburg, she needed police permission to come to court. She applied and was refused. Around the same time, I also learned that our house had recently been raided and the police detained a young relative of Winnie's who had been staying there. Winnie was not the only wife to be harassed. Albertina Sisulu, Caroline [Motsoaledi],' etc.[12] Now they wanted to know, the publishers, on page 93 [of *Long Walk to Freedom* draft]: 'Were you concerned for the safety of your children?'
MANDELA: Yes, of course, naturally. Why should they even ask that question?

15. FROM A LETTER TO SEFTON VUTELA, DATED 28 JULY 1969[13]

As disciplined and dedicated comrades fighting for a worthy cause, we should be ready to undertake any tasks which history might assign to us however high the price to be paid may be. This was the guiding principle throughout our political careers,

....

12. Caroline Motsoaledi. Wife of Elias (Mokoni) Motsoaledi. For Elias (Mokoni) Motsoaledi, see People, Places and Events.
13. Sefton Siphiwo Vutela. Married to Winnie's sister, Nancy Madikizela.

and even as we went through the various stages of the trial. I must, however, confess that for my own part the threat of death evoked no desire in me to play the role of martyr. I was ready to do so if I had to. But the anxiety to live always lingered. But familiarity does breed contempt even for the hideous hand of death. The critical phase lasted a few hours only, and I was a worried and exhausted man as I went to bed the day I heard of the Rivonia swoop. But when I got up in the morning the worst was over and I had somehow mustered enough strength and courage even to rationalize that if there was nothing else I could do to further the cause we all so passionately cherished, even the dreadful outcome that threatened us might serve a useful purpose on wider issues. This belief served to feed and replenish my slender resources of fortitude until the last day of the proceedings. It was reinforced by the conviction that our cause was just and by the wide support we received from influential bodies and individuals on both sides of the Colour line. But all the flourish of trumpets and the hosannas sung by us and our well-wishers in the course of the trial would have been valueless if courage had deserted us when the decisive moment struck.

16. CONVERSATION WITH AHMED KATHRADA ABOUT THEIR
   THOUGHTS BEFORE SENTENCING AT THE RIVONIA TRIAL

MANDELA: Well, it's easy, of course, *now* to say I didn't care, but *we* did expect a death sentence, and in fact in the morning before the judge delivered his judgement, the *sentence*, because he had already found us guilty, but before he delivered the sentence, you remember he . . . seemed . . . to have been *nervous*, and we said, 'Well, it's very clear, he's going to pass the death sentence.' . . .
KATHRADA: Aha.
MANDELA: We *were* expecting a death sentence and we had

resigned ourselves to it. But of course, it's a very *serious* experience where you feel that somebody is going to turn to you and tell you now, that 'This is the end of your life' and *that* was a matter of concern, but nevertheless we had tried, you know, to steel ourselves for this eventuality, tragic as it was.

KATHRADA: Aha.

MANDELA: And I was with brave colleagues; they appeared to be braver than myself. I would like to put that on record.

KATHRADA: Aha. Well, I think that ends this chapter, at least.

MANDELA: Good.

PART THREE

Epic

Viewed from the vantage point of the present, the whole of Nelson Mandela's life seems to have carried the energy of legend and the weight of epic narrative. His story was woven into the story of South Africa's journey from colonialism, through apartheid, to democracy. That long walk to freedom of a nation was unimaginable without Mandela's personal long walk. But it was during the more than twenty-seven years of his incarceration that his life assumed its epic proportions. Mandela became an international symbol of the struggles for justice. He was without doubt the most famous prisoner in the world. A prisoner ready by 1990, on his release, to stride across a global stage.

Conditions on Robben Island were, for the first years, very harsh. The food was poor, the work was hard, the summers hot, the winters very cold and the warders brutal. Initially only one short letter and one short visit were allowed every six months. Physical suffering was significant; psychological pain was worse. The petty-mindedness of the authorities was unrelenting. The glass partition in the visitors' room was an obscenity. Surveillance was invasive. Every letter to a loved one about deeply personal things was written with the knowledge that a third person, the censor, was also reading it.

Over the years Mandela accommodated himself to circumstances, as the prison authorities (under pressure from the political prisoners, who fought the prison system relentlessly on issues of principle) made their own accommodations. Mandela's privileges, and his capacity to secure leverage with the authorities, grew after his move to Pollsmoor Prison in 1982, especially after he inaugurated talks about talks with the apartheid regime in 1985. By the time he was moved to Victor Verster Prison in December 1988, where he occupied a spacious bungalow house of his own, he could see or communicate with whomever he liked. Frequently he was taken on trips out of prison, sometimes for high-level meetings, sometimes simply to see the sights. He was already a president-in-waiting.

CHAPTER SEVEN

Unaccommodated Man

'Zami and I met you at the party the same night but you were soon gone. A few days thereafter I bade farewell to Zami and kids and now I'm a citizen across the waves.'

....

Excerpt from a letter to Amina Cachalia, dated 8 April 1969, see page 133.

1. FROM A LETTER TO ARCHIE GUMEDE, DATED 8 JULY 1985[1]

In conclusion, I would like to draw your attention to a letter in a JHB [Johannesburg] daily which dealt with the case of 9 men who were condemned to death by Queen Victoria for treason. As a result of protests from all over the world the men were banished. Many years thereafter, the Queen learned that one of these men had been elected PM [prime minister] of Australia, the second was appointed Brigadier-General in the USA Army, the third became Attorney-General for Australia, the fourth succeeded the third as A.G [attorney general], the fifth became Minister of Agriculture for Canada, the sixth also became Brigadier-General in the USA, the seventh was appointed Governor-General of Montana, the eighth became a prominent New York politician, and the last was appointed Governor-General of Newfoundland.

2. FROM A LETTER TO AMINA CACHALIA, DATED 8 APRIL 1969, ABOUT THE DAY THE TREASON TRIAL ENDED[2]

Zami and I met you at the party the same night but you were soon gone. A few days thereafter I bade farewell to Zami and kids and now I'm a citizen across the waves.

It was not an easy decision to make. I knew the hardship, misery and humiliation to which my absence would expose them. I have spent anxious moments thinking of them and have never once doubted Zami's courage and determination. But there are times when I even fear receiving letters from her, because on every occasion she comes down I see with my own eyes the heavy toll on her health caused by the turbulent events of the last 8 yrs.

1. Archibald Gumede (1914–88). Lawyer and anti-apartheid activist. Member of the ANC. Co-founder and president of the United Democratic Front (UDF).
2. Amina Cachalia, see People, Places and Events.

3. FROM HIS UNPUBLISHED AUTOBIOGRAPHICAL MANUSCRIPT
   WRITTEN IN PRISON, ABOUT THE FIRST TIME HE WAS SENT TO
   ROBBEN ISLAND[3]

One night towards the end of May 1963 I was ordered to pack my personal belongings. At the reception office I found three other political prisoners . . . I learnt from Col. Aucamp who was then officer commanding, Pretoria Local, that we were being transferred to Robben Island. I hate being moved from one prison to another. It involves much inconvenience and degrading treatment. One is handcuffed and sometimes even manacled, and often it involves being exposed to prison officials and members of the public at each stop at different prisons en route while one is dressed in the humiliating prison outfit. But I was excited at the prospect of seeing Robben Island, a place that I had heard of since the days of my childhood, a place that our people talked of as esiqithini (at the Island). The Island became famous among the Xhosa people after Makana also known as Nxele, the commander of the Xhosa army in the so called Fourth Xhosa War was banished and was subsequently drowned when he tried to escape from the Island by swimming to the mainland.[4] His death was a sad blow to the hopes of the Xhosas and the memory of that blow has been woven into the idioms of the people who speak of a 'forlorn hope' by the phrase 'Ukuza kuka Nxele'. Makana was not the first black hero to be banished and confined to Robben Island. That honour goes to Autshumayo, known to white historians as Harry the Strandloper. Autshumayo was banished by [Jan] Van Riebeeck to Robben Island at the end of the 1658 War between the Khoi Khoi and the Dutch. The honour is even more fitting in that Autshumayo was also the

3. Mandela was imprisoned on Robben Island twice. The first time was for two weeks in 1963 while he was serving a five-year prison sentence for incitement to strike and leaving the country without a passport.
4. Mandela is actually referring to the fifth Xhosa war, 1818–19.

first and so far the only person to successfully escape from the Island. After several attempts he finally succeeded in making his break in an old boat that was ridden with holes and considered completely unseaworthy. At different times many other patriots and freedom fighters found themselves held prisoner on Robben Island. Heroes like [Chief] Maqoma, who was commander in the so called Fifth Xhosa War of 1834,[5] Langalibalele, the Hlubi Chief who was sentenced for High Treason by a special court in Natal in 1873, Sheikh Abdul Rahman Mantura, a political exile from Java, are part of the history of the Island.[6] Just as the Portuguese colonialists gave a unique place in history to the Island of Fernando Po by imprisoning their numerous African patriots, the British held Indian patriots on the Andaman Islands, and in the same way as the French held Ben Bella on [Aix] Island,[7] so too have the rulers of South Africa determined that Robben Island should live in the memory of our people. Robben Island – one-time leper colony, Second World War naval fortress guarding the entrance to Cape Town harbour – a tiny outcrop of limestone, bleak, windswept and caught in the wash of the cold Benguela current, whose history counts the years of our people's bondage. My new home.

4. FROM HIS UNPUBLISHED AUTOBIOGRAPHICAL MANUSCRIPT
   WRITTEN IN PRISON, ABOUT BEING SENT BACK TO PRETORIA

I have never been able to ascertain why after just 2 weeks on Robben Island I was transferred back to Pretoria. But I do know that the Department of Prisons released a press statement claiming that I had been removed for my own safety because PAC [Pan Africanist Congress] prisoners on the Island

----

5. Mandela is actually referring to the sixth Xhosa war, 1834–36.
6. Sheikh Abdul Rahman Mantura. Muslim cleric who was imprisoned on Robben Island in the eighteenth century.
7. Ahmed Ben Bella (1918–). President of Algeria, 1963–65.

intended to assault me. This was a blatant falsehood because the only group of PAC prisoners with whom I had contact on the Island were my nephew and his friends with whom I was on the best terms. And subsequent meetings with various members of the PAC convinced me that the authorities fabricated this story – perhaps to cover their own reasons, perhaps as part of a deliberate design to foment and fan animosities between members of the PAC and ANC [African National Congress] both inside and outside prison. The transfer certainly had no connection with the fact that I was subsequently charged in the Rivonia Trial because the arrest which eventually led to that case took place on the 11th July 1963, almost a month after I was removed from the Island.

5. CONVERSATION WITH AHMED KATHRADA ABOUT
   PRISON WARDERS

KATHRADA: Ah, then you are saying, 'The warders were, without exception, white and Afrikaans-speaking.' That's not quite accurate.
MANDELA: Yes.
KATHRADA: Because there was Southerby there.
MANDELA: Aha.
KATHRADA: There was Mann there, there were some English-speaking.
MANDELA: Yes, mostly.
KATHRADA: Mostly Afrikaners, ja. And though this thing about 'baas'.[8]
MANDELA: [*laughs*] You could remember that Southerby?
KATHRADA: Ja.
MANDELA: Big stomach hey?

....

8. Under the apartheid system, black South Africans were expected to call white men 'baas', which is Afrikaans for 'boss'.

KATHRADA: Ja, Southerby.

MANDELA: What did he say?

KATHRADA: When [Andrew] Mlangeni, Mlangeni hit him on the stomach, he said . . .[9]

MANDELA: [*laughs*]

KATHRADA: . . . 'Captain, where do you get this big stomach from?'

MANDELA: Gee whiz!

KATHRADA: Don't you remember? Ja, Mlangeni.

MANDELA: Yes, I think I remember that.

KATHRADA: [*laughs*] Ja.

MANDELA: But he said something to me, man, you know? And he was quite *good*, you know, in his repartee. I can't remember now, but he thought that I had exaggerated the importance of myself, you know? But it was very witty, you know, and very *sharp*.

KATHRADA: Ja. No, no, something is registering.

MANDELA: I can't remember, I can't remember.

KATHRADA: I can't remember also. Ah, 'Though we were ordered to say "baas", we never did.'

MANDELA: Yes.

6. CONVERSATION WITH AHMED KATHRADA ABOUT NEEDING SUNGLASSES ON ROBBEN ISLAND

KATHRADA: *Then*, when you talk about sunglasses, ah, at the quarry, even when they granted us [permission], we had to *buy* the sunglasses.[10]

MANDELA: Yes.

KATHRADA: They didn't provide them for us.

---

9. Andrew Mokete Mlangeni, see People, Places and Events.
10. Prisoners were put to work in a lime quarry on Robben Island. Many prisoners' eyes, including Mandela's, were damaged by the harsh glare of the sun striking off the white stones.

MANDELA: Yes, yes. Well they *did* provide *cheap* ones, you remember, which were . . .

KATHRADA: Which were useless.

7. CONVERSATION WITH AHMED KATHRADA ABOUT WORKING AT THE QUARRY

KATHRADA: Then you are talking of lunch-time in the quarry where you are saying we sat on the ground. We didn't really. What we did is, remember there were bricks and then we put wood, pieces of wood there.

MANDELA: Oh, I see.

KATHRADA: To sit on.

MANDELA: That's right, that's right.

KATHRADA: So we didn't sit on the ground.

MANDELA: Yes, yes, yes.

KATHRADA: Then page 49 [of *Long Walk to Freedom* draft], is it true that the present trouble you are having with your eyes also had something to do with the . . . lime?

MANDELA: Ah. No, that's what this specialist said . . .

KATHRADA: Ah.

MANDELA: Amoils is . . . a top specialist who actually attended to the eyes of Mrs [Margaret] Thatcher.

KATHRADA: Ah.

MANDELA: And he was given an award by Harvard University. No, he examined me very carefully; he says that there are perforations in my eyes arising out of the quarry, the lime quarry. He also treats Steve [Tshwete].[11] He says he has exactly the same condition as mine.

KATHRADA: Is that so?

---

11. Steve Vukhile Tshwete, see People, Places and Events.

MANDELA: Yes. He says it's a situation that is caused, you see, by . . . looking at bright sand and so on.

KATHRADA: Oh . . . we must add that.

MANDELA: Yes, quite.

KATHRADA: It's an important thing.

MANDELA: Ja, it's what he said.

KATHRADA: Because we tried to make an issue of it.

MANDELA: Yes.

KATHRADA: And those doctors just dismissed it.

MANDELA: Yes, quite . . .

8. CONVERSATION WITH AHMED KATHRADA ABOUT COMMON-LAW CRIMINALS ON ROBBEN ISLAND

KATHRADA: When you talk of criminals being brought to Robben Island, they were also brought there to *teach* us how to work.

MANDELA: We should also not refer to them as criminals.

KATHRADA: Ja, I know. We are saying 'non', I mean 'common-law'.

MANDELA: Common-law prisoners . . .

KATHRADA: Common-law prisoners were brought to the quarry also to teach us. If you remember, this fat one.

MANDELA: I see. *Oh* yes!

KATHRADA: And that other guy, Tigha who used to also give us haircuts now and then.

MANDELA: Oh I see, I see.

KATHRADA: They were really brought, some of them, to spy on us.

MANDELA: [*laughs*] Clearly.

KATHRADA: And also to *teach* us how to work.

MANDELA: Yes, that's right.

KATHRADA: Ah. They tried to demonstrate with pick and shovel so that we could work harder.

9. CONVERSATION WITH AHMED KATHRADA ABOUT THE
   BANK ROBBER

KATHRADA: Page 51 [of *Long Walk to Freedom* draft]: 'There was, for example, a bank robber among us whose name was Joe My Baby.'
MANDELA: Ah, I see, his surname is Sihlabane . . . You see, I don't know what his boxing name was. Even if he was a bank robber, man, I don't think we should say that.
KATHRADA: Ah.
MANDELA: Because he's doing a responsible job.
KATHRADA: Ja.
MANDELA: He was one of our best chaps.
KATHRADA: He's very good, ja.
MANDELA: *Very* good . . .
KATHRADA: It was Poppies and him, remember?
MANDELA: Huh? Yes, that's right.
KATHRADA: Poppies and him.
MANDELA: Yes, yes.
KATHRADA: They had decided among the two of them that one of them would be in charge of the political prisoners, smuggling things to us and Poppies would be looking after the common-law prisoners who came to do three meals or something.[12]
MANDELA: Oh, I see.
KATHRADA: And they used to smuggle food.
MANDELA: Yes, yes, yes.
KATHRADA: To the people who were punished.
MANDELA: Mmm.

....

12. 'Three meals' is a punishment where a prisoner is put in isolation without meals for a day.

KATHRADA: But both of them are very good.

MANDELA: Very good men.

KATHRADA: Poppies was, was really the expert in car, car theft.

MANDELA: I believe so, yes.

KATHRADA: Then, of course, he used to sell back-door goods to the Indians.

[*both laugh*]

He used to name them to me, who the Indians were, and I knew them all.

MANDELA: *Yes?*

KATHRADA: Poppies used to supply them with stuff.

MANDELA: *Hey*, that was an excellent chap, man. It's a pity that he died.

KATHRADA: He *died*?

MANDELA: Yes, he was shot.

KATHRADA: Poppies?

MANDELA: Yes.

KATHRADA: Oh.

MANDELA: Yes, shortly after he had come out, they shot him.

KATHRADA: Oh, I see.

MANDELA: In Meadowlands.

KATHRADA: Ay, he was a very intelligent chap.

MANDELA: Very intelligent.

KATHRADA: Articulate fellow.

MANDELA: Mmm.

10. CONVERSATION WITH RICHARD STENGEL ABOUT SINGING
    IN PRISON

STENGEL: Singing was banned?

MANDELA: Yes, yes, yes, at first that is. Singing anywhere in prison especially when you are working . . . They took us to the quarry to dig lime. Now that is a very difficult operation because you use a pick. The lime is in layers of rock. You find a rock layer . . . and to get to the lime you have to *break* that layer . . . They *sent* us there, because they wanted to show us that to come to jail is not an easy thing, it's not a *picnic* and you must never come to jail again. They wanted to *break* our spirits. So what we did was to sing freedom songs as we were working and *everybody* was inspired, you know; went through the work . . . with *high* morale, and then of course dancing to the music as we were working, you know? Then the authorities realized that . . . These chaps, you see, are too militant. They're in high spirits and they say, 'No singing as you are working.' So you *really* felt the *toughness* of the work . . . And of course, they had a regulation in the disciplinary code which banned singing, [and] they enforced it . . . Although we listened to them . . . when we went back to our cells, especially on the eve of Christmas and New Year, we organised singing concerts and we sang. So they eventually got used to that.

11. FROM A CONVERSATION WITH RICHARD STENGEL ABOUT THE ASSASSINATION ON 6 SEPTEMBER 1966 OF PRIME MINISTER H F VERWOERD[13]

Well, the death – the assassination – of any individual is never anything pleasant. We would prefer that the community should convey its disapproval of his policies without using methods like assassination. Because that can leave scars which we would find very difficult to remove for generations to come. Today, in this country, the Anglo-Boer War, which was fought in 1899 to 1902, you would think when you listen to Afrikaners *and* English speaking, that the . . . war is still raging today. Because of the scars of the past. Even . . . the present cabinet is drawn completely from Afrikaners. Englishmen are two or

13. Dr Hendrik Frensch Verwoerd, see People, Places and Events.

three, but the entire cabinet is of Afrikaners, and that is because they failed to . . . use peaceful methods of resolving their problems . . . Although Verwoerd was one of the most *insensitive* of prime ministers in this country . . . who regarded Africans as animals, worse than animals in many cases. Nevertheless, one didn't feel happy that he was assassinated. What is even more, is the way the prison authorities retaliated for his assassination, as if we were responsible for that. They brought Warder Van Rensburg from another prison . . . and he was most brutal. He was a very untidy chap in his habits. When – just by way of illustration – we would be working in the quarry . . . he would stand on a particular spot. And when he felt he should urinate, relieve himself, he would just urinate where he was standing, instead of going away, you know, to urinate a bit privately, secretly from us. He would urinate where he was standing. In fact, we lodged a *very* strong complaint against him because one day he was standing next to the table where we dish our food, and then when it came, when the time came for him to urinate, he just urinated where he was standing, and although he didn't urinate on the table itself . . . but it was just next to the leg of the table . . . we lodged a very strong protest . . . He was not a man of clean habits and he was also very insensitive. What happened was that they would decide in the morning before we [went] to work, that today so-and-so and so-and-so should be punished. And once they took that decision, it did not matter how hard you worked that morning; you would be punished at the end of the day.

12. CONVERSATION WITH RICHARD STENGEL ABOUT TRUMPED-UP CHARGES ON ROBBEN ISLAND[14]

STENGEL: Didn't you have to retain lawyers?

MANDELA: Yes, we did . . . We took up lawyers, you see, for all these charges . . . But we were convicted nonetheless . . . Isolation and being deprived [of] certain diet, certain meals . . . Rice water, that's all. Sometimes when the sentence is long, you fast. I'm not sure now whether it's for two days, and then you have a break, you eat, and the next day you continue fasting and then on the fifth day, they give you food again.

STENGEL: How do you deal with the hunger?

MANDELA: It's relatively easy. You *feel* it the first day, but the second day . . . you get used to it. Third day, you don't feel anything except that you are not as energetic as you used to be. But it's something . . . You get used to it. The human body has got enormous capacity for adjusting, especially if . . . you can coordinate your thinking, your whole spiritual approach to the physical one. And if you are convinced that you are doing something right, that you are demonstrating to the authorities that you can defend your rights and fight back, you don't feel it at all.

13. FROM A LETTER TO THE MINISTER OF JUSTICE, DATED 22 APRIL 1969

My colleagues have requested me to write and ask you to release us from prison and, pending your decision on the matter, to accord us the treatment due to political prisoners. At the outset we wish to point out that in making this application we are not pleading for mercy but are exercising the inherent rights of all people incarcerated for their political beliefs . . . Prior to our conviction and imprisonment we are members of well-known

---

14. Officials would regularly fabricate charges against prisoners as it gave them an excuse to punish them.

political organisations which fought against political and racial persecution, and which demanded full political rights for the African, Coloured and Indian people of this Country. We completely rejected as we still do, all forms of white domination, and more particularly the policy of separate development, and demanded a democratic South Africa free from the evils of Colour oppression, and where all South Africans, regardless of race or belief, would live together in peace and harmony on a basis of equality.

All of us, without exception, were convicted and sentenced for political activities which we embarked upon as part and parcel of our struggle to win for our people the right of self-determination, acknowledged throughout the civilized world as the inalienable birthright of all human beings. These activities were inspired by the desire to resist racial policies and unjust laws which violate the principle of human rights and fundamental freedoms that form the foundation of democratic government.

In the past the governments of South Africa have treated persons found guilty of offences of this nature as political offenders who were released from prison, in some cases, long before their sentences expired. In this connection we refer you to the cases of Generals Christiaan De Wet, JCG Kemp and others who were charged with high treason arising out of the 1914 Rebellion. Their case was in every respect more serious than ours. 12,000 rebels took to arms and there were no less than 322 casualties. Towns were occupied and considerable damage caused to government installations, while claims for damage to private property amounted to R500,000. These acts of violence were committed by white men who enjoyed full political rights, who belonged to political parties that were legal, who had newspapers that could publicise their views. They were able to move freely up and down the country espousing their cause and rallying support for their ideas. They had no justification whatsoever for resorting to violence. The leader of the Orange Free State rebels, De Wet, was sentenced to 6 years imprisonment plus a fine of R4,000. Kemp received a sentence of 7 years and a fine of R2,000. The rest were given comparatively light sentences.

In spite of the gravity of their offences, De Wet, was released within 6 months of his conviction and sentence, and the rest within a year. This event occurred a little more than half a century ago, yet the Government of the day showed much less intransigence, in its treatment of this category of prisoner than the present Government seems prepared to do 54 years later with black politicians who have even more justification to resort to violence than the 1914 rebels. This Government has persistently spurned our aspirations, suppressed our political organisations and imposed severe restrictions on known activists and field workers.

It has caused hardship and disruption of family life by throwing into prison hundreds of otherwise innocent people. Finally it has instituted a reign of terror unprecedented in the history of the Country and closed all channels of constitutional struggle. In such a situation resort to violence was the inevitable alternative of freedom fighters who had the courage of their convictions. No men of principle and integrity could have done otherwise. To have folded arms would have been an act of surrender to a Government of minority rule and a betrayal of our cause. World history in general, and that of South Africa in particular, teaches that resort to violence may in certain cases be perfectly legitimate.

In releasing the rebels soon after their convictions the Botha Smuts Government acknowledged this vital fact. We firmly believe that our case is no less different, and we accordingly ask you to make this privilege available to us. As indicated above, there were 322 casualties in the Rebellion.

By way of contrast, we draw attention to the fact that in committing acts of sabotage we took special precautions to avoid loss of life, a fact which was expressly acknowledged by both the trial Judge [and] the prosecution in the Rivonia case.

An examination of the attached schedule shows that if we use De Wet's case as the standard, then every one of us ought to have been released by now. Of the 23 persons whose names are listed therein, 8 are doing life imprisonment, 10 are serving sentences ranging from 10 to 20 years, and 5 between 2 and 10 years . . . The only way to avert disaster is not to keep innocent men in jail but to abandon your provocative actions and to pursue sane and enlightened policies. Whether or not evil strife and bloodshed are to occur in this country rests entirely on the Government. The continued suppression of our aspirations and reliance on rule through coercion drives our people more and more to violence. Neither you nor I can predict [what] the country will have to pay at the end of that strife. The obvious solution is to release us and to hold a round table conference to consider an amicable solution.

Our main request is that you release us and pending your decision, to treat us as political prisoners. This means that we should be provided with good diet, proper clothing outfits, bed and mattresses, newspapers, radios, bioscope [and] better and closer contact with our families and friends here and abroad. Treatment as political prisoners implies the freedom to obtain all reading material that is not banned and to write books for publication, we would expect to be given the option to work as one desires and to decide the trades one would like to learn . . . In this situation the Government regards the prison not as an institution of rehabilitation but as an instrument of retribution, not to prepare us to lead a respectable and industrious life when released, and to play our role as worthy members of society, but to punish and cripple us, so that we should never again have the strength and courage to pursue our ideals. This [is] our punishment for raising our voices against the tyranny of colour. This is the true explanation for the bad treatment we receive in prison – pick and shovel work continuously for the last 5 years, a wretched diet, denial of essential cultural material and isolation from the world outside jail. This is the reason why privileges normally available to other prisoners, including those convicted of murder, rape and crimes involving dishonesty are withheld from political offenders . . . In conclusion we place on record that the years we have spent on this Island have been difficult years. Almost every one of us has had [our] full share in one way or another of the hardships that face non-white prisoners. These hardships have at times been the result of official indifference to our problems, other times they were due to plain persecution. But things have somewhat eased and we hope even better days will come. All that we wish to add is that we trust that when you consider this application you will bear in mind that the ideas that inspire us, and the convictions that give form and direction to our activities constitute the only solution to the problems of our country and are in accordance with the enlightened conceptions of the human family.

14. FROM A CONVERSATION WITH RICHARD STENGEL ABOUT BEING PUT IN ISOLATION[15]

To be *alone* in prison is a difficulty. You must never try it. So what they did then was to *isolate* me without actually, you know, punishing me in the sense of depriving me of meals. But they made sure that I did not see a *face* of a prisoner. I saw a warder all the time; even my food was brought in by a warder.

....

15. Mandela was talking about being in solitary confinement at Pretoria Local Prison while awaiting trial in 1962.

[*chuckles*] And they would let me out for thirty minutes in the morning and thirty minutes in the afternoon, and when the *other* prisoners were locked up.

15. CONVERSATION WITH RICHARD STENGEL ABOUT THE BUCKET SYSTEM IN PRISON

MANDELA: Yes, you had a bucket, you see, for your room . . . We didn't have a water-borne sewerage in each cell. In the big cells, you had water-borne sewerage, but in the actual single rooms themselves, you didn't have that, yes. You just have these buckets which you used for the night.

STENGEL: I don't remember who it was, but someone who was new on the Island, who was very fastidious, said that you once helped him clean out his bucket because he didn't want to do it?

MANDELA: Well, no, I . . . There *was* a chap, one of our fellows, a trained member of Umkhonto we Sizwe; he was to go to . . . to Cape Town and . . . they used to leave very early, sometimes about five o'clock . . . before the cell was actually opened for us to go and empty our toilets [buckets]. So he then asked the chap opposite and he left for the city. Now he was next door to me. So the fellow opposite him, I reminded him, you see: 'Please, so-and-so has asked you to clean his bucket.' He says, 'No, I'm not prepared to do that. I will not do that. I will not clean a bucket for another man.' So I then cleaned it for him because it meant nothing for me; I cleaned my bucket every day [*chuckles*] and I had no problem, you see, in cleaning the bucket of another. That's what happened, you see. And it was just to help a friend, you know, who was let down by his own friend.

16. FROM A LETTER TO FRIEDA MATTHEWS,
DATED 25 FEBRUARY 1987[16]

A visit to a prisoner always has significance difficult to put into words. Routine is the supreme law of a prison in almost every country of the world, and every day is for all practical purposes like the day before: the same surroundings, same faces, same dialogue, same odour, walls rising to the skies, and the ever-present feeling that outside the prison gates there is an exciting world to which you have no access. A visit from your beloved ones, from friends and even from strangers is always an unforgettable occasion, when that frustrating monotony is broken and the entire world is literally ushered into the cell.

17. CONVERSATION WITH RICHARD STENGEL ABOUT VISITS
IN PRISON

STENGEL: How long were the visits?

MANDELA: At first, thirty minutes. So you have to wait for six months and only to speak for thirty minutes. Then they extended it to an hour, but they made thirty minutes your right, and the other thirty minutes a privilege. They could refuse if they wanted to. For example, whilst we were getting an hour, I was – they used to tell you beforehand, 'You are going to have so-and-so visiting you.' But one day they just said, 'You have a visit.' And I asked, 'Now who is it?' They said, 'No, we don't know.' Then I said, 'Well, ask the Commanding Officer; I want to see the Commanding Officer' and the Commanding Officer came and I said, 'Well, I've got a visit. I've asked the warders to tell me who the visitor is, and they say they don't know.' He says, 'Well, I'll investigate and see who your visitor is.' He never came back and I was taken to the visiting booth

16. Frieda Matthews (née Bokwe). Married to Professor Zachariah Keodirelang (Z K) Matthews. For Professor Zachariah Keodirelang (Z K) Matthews, see People, Places and Events.

without knowing who it was. *Suddenly*, Professor Fatima Meer came. So they didn't want to tell me because Fatima Meer was *marked* already and was [on] a black list, their black list. And they didn't want to tell me beforehand, but they were *forced* to allow her to come and see me. So, and then I thought it was [going to be for] an hour. After thirty minutes, they said, 'No, visit up!' and so I said, 'But you are supposed to give me an hour.' He said, 'No, you are entitled to thirty minutes. The other thirty minutes is discretionary; it's at our discretion. The visit is over.' And they were very, quite tough, quite abrupt. And so that was the position at the beginning, but . . . that hour, they continued, they never exceeded it. It was not until I went to Victor Verster, where I was kept . . . under conditions which were between a prisoner and a free man.[17] I was put in a cottage. I stayed in this cottage alone. It was not locked and I could stay outside until midnight. And I was provided with a warder who cooked my food; but we'll come to that a bit later.

18. FROM HIS UNPUBLISHED AUTOBIOGRAPHICAL MANUSCRIPT
    WRITTEN IN PRISON

A man who rises to the position of premier in any country must be a man of ability, forceful personality and uprightness in his public life. (d) Even making allowances for all that behind-the-scenes manoeuvres and pulling of strings, enough funds to run campaigns and to secure the support of influential individuals and propaganda agencies I believe that [Prime Minister] B.J. Vorster is on merit a man deserving the highest honours in so far as white conservative politics are concerned.[18] (e) His treasonable activities during the Second World War and his internment marked him as a man of strong beliefs prepared

----

17. Mandela was transferred to Victor Verster Prison in 1988, see People, Places and Events.
18. Balthazar Johannes (B J) Vorster, see People, Places and Events.

2.4.69

From a letter to Winnie Mandela, dated 2 April 1969. For other extracts from this letter, see pages 153–154.

to fight for them even when he is in a minority and to pay the penalty for them. (f) In a democratic South Africa where all its people enjoy franchise rights there would be many men who would stand head and shoulders above him both in regard to personality and their views. Nevertheless, among whites as presently constituted he seems to stand out prominently.

19. FROM A LETTER TO WINNIE MANDELA, DATED 2 APRIL 1969

A family photo at last! – 'what a masterpiece'! Kgatho and sisters are terrific and it gave me such joy to see ma's photo.[19] Your small picture almost created an upheaval. 'Ayingo Nobandla lo!' 'Is this not her younger sister!' 'Madiba has been long in jail,[20] he does not know his sister-in-law,' all these remarks were flung at me from all directions.

To me the portrait aroused mixed feelings. You look somewhat sad, absent-minded and unwell but lovely all the same. The big one is a magnificent study that depicts all I know in you, the devastating beauty and charm which 10 stormy years of married life have not chilled. I suspect that you intended the picture to convey a special message that no words could ever express. Rest assured I have caught it. All that I wish to say now is that the picture has aroused all the tender feelings in me and softened the grimness that is all around. It has sharpened my longing for you and our sweet and peaceful home.

These days my thoughts have wandered far and wide; to Hans St[reet] where a friend would jump into a blue van and unburden herself of all the solemn vows that are due from fiancée to her betrothed and immediately thereafter dash across to an Olds[mobile] on the opposite end of the block with

---

19. Makgatho (Kgatho) Mandela, see People, Places and Events.
20. Madiba is Mandela's clan name.

vows equally sweet and reassuring; the skill with which she manipulated her evening 'studies' in Chancellor House and made it possible to receive and entertain old friends as soon as new ones proceeded to a boxing gym. All these have come back over and over again as I examine the portrait.

CHAPTER EIGHT

Arras

'I last saw my mother on September 9 last year. After the interview I was able to look at her as she walked away toward the boat that would take her to the mainland and somehow the idea crossed my mind that I would never again set my eyes on her.'

....

From a letter to K D Matanzima, dated 14 October 1968, see page 159.

1. FROM A LETTER TO K D MATANZIMA, DATED 14 OCTOBER 1968, ABOUT THE DEATH OF MANDELA'S MOTHER[1]

I last saw my mother on September 9 last year. After the interview I was able to look at her as she walked away toward the boat that would take her to the mainland and somehow the idea crossed my mind that I would never again set my eyes on her. Her visits had always excited me and the news of her death hit me hard. I at once felt lonely and empty. But my friends here, whose sympathy and affection have always been a source of strength to me, helped to relieve my grief and to raise my spirits. The report on the funeral reinforced my courage. It was a pleasure for me to be informed that my relatives and friends had turned up in large numbers to honour the occasion with their presence and was happy to be able to count you amongst those who paid their last respects.

2. FROM A LETTER TO P K MADIKIZELA, DATED 4 MAY 1969[2]

I had never dreamt that I would never be able to bury ma. On the contrary, I had entertained the hope that I would have the privilege of looking after her in her old age, and be on her side when the fatal hour struck. Zami and I had tried hard to persuade her to come and live with us in Johannesburg, pointing out that she would be nearer Baragwanath Hospital which would ensure for her regular and proper medical attention, and that moving to the Reef would enable Zami to give her effective and all-round attention. I further discussed the matter with ma when she visited me on 6/3/66 and again on 9/9/67. But she spent all her life in the countryside and became attached to its plains and hills, to its fine people and simple ways. Although she had spent some years in Johannesburg,

1. Mandela's mother, Nosekeni Fanny Mandela, died of a heart attack on 26 September 1968.
2. Nophikela Madikizela. Winnie's stepmother.

The first page of one of Mandela's prison correspondence journals.

she found it very difficult to leave the home and the family graves. Though I fully appreciated her views and feelings I still hoped I might eventually succeed in persuading her to go up [to Johannesburg].

3. FROM A LETTER TO HIS DAUGHTERS ZENI AND ZINDZI
   MANDELA, THEN AGED NINE AND TEN, DATED 23 JUNE 1969

Once again our beloved Mummy has been arrested and now she and Daddy are away in jail. My heart bleeds as I think of her sitting in some police cell far away from home, perhaps alone and without anybody to talk to, and with nothing to read.[3] Twenty-four hours of the day longing for her little ones. It may be many months or even years before you see her again. For long you may live like orphans without your own home and parents, without the natural love, affection and protection Mummy used to give you. Now you will get no birthday or Christmas parties, no presents or new dresses, no shoes or toys. Gone are the days when, after having a warm bath in the evening, you would sit at table with Mummy and enjoy her good and simple food. Gone are the comfortable beds, the warm blankets and clean linen she used to provide. She will not be there to arrange for friends to take you to bioscopes, concerts and plays, or to tell you nice stories in the evening, help you read difficult books and to answer the many questions you would like to ask. She will be unable to give you the help and guidance you need as you grow older and as new problems arise. Perhaps never again will Mummy and Daddy join you in House no. 8115 Orlando West, the one place in the whole world that is so dear to our hearts.

This is not the first time Mummy goes to jail. In October 1958, only four months after our wedding, she was arrested

---

3. In 1969 Winnie was detained and placed in solitary confinement for seventeen months.

23. 6. 69

My darlings,

Once again our beloved Mummy has been arrested and now she and Daddy are away in jail. My heart bleeds as I think of her sitting in some police cell far away from home, perhaps alone and without anybody to talk to, and with nothing to read. Twenty-four hours of the day longing for her little ones. It may be many months or even years before you see her again. For long you may live like orphans without your own home and parents, without the natural love, affection and protection Mummy used to give you. Now you will get no birthday or Christmas parties, no presents or new dresses, no shoes or toys. Gone are the days when, after having a warm bath in the evening, you would sit at table with Mummy and enjoy her good and simple food. Gone are the comfortable beds, the warm blankets and clean linen she used to provide. She will not be there to arrange for friends to take you to bioscopes, concerts and plays, or to tell you nice stories in the evening, help you read difficult books and to answer the many questions you would like to ask. She will be unable to give you the help and guidance you need as you grow older and as new problems arise. Perhaps never again will Mummy and Daddy join you in House no. 8115 Orlando West, the one place in the whole world that is so dear to our hearts.

This is not the first time Mummy goes to jail. In October 1958 only four months after our wedding, she was arrested with 2000 other women when they protested against passes in Johannesburg and spent two weeks in jail. Last year she served few days, but now she has gone back again and I cannot tell you how long she will be away this time. All that I wish you to always bear in mind is that we have a brave and determined Mummy who loves her people with all her heart. She gave up pleasure and comfort in return for a full life of hardship and misery, because of the deep love she has for her people and country. When you become adults and think carefully of the unpleasant experiences Mummy has gone through, and the stubbornness with which she has held to her beliefs, you will begin to realise the importance of her contribution in the battle for truth and justice and the extent to which she has sacrificed her own personal interests and happiness.

Mummy comes from a rich and respected family. She is a qualified Social with 2000 other women when they protested against passes in Johannesburg and spent two weeks in jail. Last year she served four days, but now she has gone back again and I cannot tell you how long she will be away this time. All that I wish you always to bear in mind is that we have a brave and determined Mummy who loves her people with all her heart. She gave up pleasure and comfort in return for a life full of hardship and misery because of the deep love she has for her people and country. When you become adults and think carefully of the unpleasant experiences Mummy has gone through, and the stubbornness with which she has held to her beliefs, you will begin to realise the importance of her contribution in the battle for truth and justice and to the extent to which she has sacrificed her own personal interests and happiness . . . Since then Mummy has lived a painful life and had to try and run a home without a fixed income. Yet she somehow managed to buy you food and clothing, pay your school fees, rent for the house and to send me money regularly. I left home in April 1961 when Zeni was two years and Zindzi three months. Early in January 1962 I toured Africa and visited London for ten days, returned to South Africa towards the end of July the same year. I was terribly shaken when I met Mummy. I had left her in good health with a lot of flesh and colour. But she had suddenly lost weight and was now a shadow of her former self. I realised at once the strain my absence had caused her. I looked forward to some time when I would be able to tell her about my journey, the countries I visited and the people I met. But my arrest on August 5 put an end to that dream. When Mummy was arrested in 1958 I visited her daily and brought her food and fruits . . . She told me [during a visit to him in custody in 1962] that although she would most probably be arrested and sent to jail, as every politician fighting for freedom must expect, she would

Special letter to Zami   16 7 69

My darling,

This afternoon the Commanding Officer received the following
telegram from attorney Mendel Levin:

"Please advise Nelson Mandela his Thembekile passed
away 13th instant result motor accident in Cape Town."

I find it difficult to believe that I will never see Thembi again.
On February 23 this year he turned 24. I had ~~last~~ seen him towards
the end of July 1962 a few days after I had returned from the trip abroad.
Then he was a lusty lad of 17 that I could never associate with death.
He wore one of my trousers which was a shade too big & long for him.
The incident was significant & set me thinking. As you know he had
a lot of clothing, was particular about his dress & had no reason
whatsoever for using my clothes. I was deeply touched for the
emotional factors underlying his action were too obvious. For days
thereafter my mind & feelings were agitated to realise the psychological
strains & stresses my absence from home had imposed on the children.
I recalled an incident in December 1956 when I was an awaiting-
trial prisoner at the Johannesburg fort. At that time Kgatho was 6
& lived in Orlando East. Although he well knew that I was in
jail he went over to Orlando West & told Ma that he longed for me.
That night he slept in my bed.
But let me return to my meeting with Thembi. He had come to bid me
farewell on his way to a boarding school. On his arrival he greeted me very
warmly, holding my hand firmly & for some time. Thereafter we sat
down & conversed. Somehow the conversation drifted to his studies,
& he gave me what I considered, in the light of his age, at the time, to be an
interesting appreciation of Shakespeare's Julius Caesar which I very
much enjoyed. We had been corresponding regularly ever since he
went to school at Matatiele & when he later changed to Wodehouse.
In December 1960 I travelled some distance by car to meet him. Throughout this
period I regarded him as a child & I approached him mainly from this
angle. But our conversation in July 1962 reminded me I was no longer
speaking to a child but to one who was beginning to have a
settled attitude in life. He had suddenly raised himself from a son
to friend. I was indeed a bit sad when we ultimately parted. I

....

From a letter to Winnie Mandela, dated 16 July 1969, about his son Thembi's death,
see pages 165–167.

nevertheless remain in the country and suffer with her people. Do you see now what a brave Mummy we have?

4. FROM A 'SPECIAL LETTER' TO WINNIE MANDELA, DATED 16 JULY 1969, ON THE DEATH OF HIS SON THEMBI[4]

This afternoon the Commanding Officer received the following telegram from attorney, Mendel Levin:

'Please advise Nelson Mandela his [son] Thembekile passed away 13th instant result motor accident in Cape Town.'

I find it difficult to believe that I will never see Thembi again. On February 23 this year he turned 24. I had seen him towards the end of July 1962 a few days after I had returned from the trip abroad. Then he was a lusty lad of 17 that I could never associate with death. He wore one of my trousers which was a shade too big and long for him. The incident was significant and set me thinking. As you know he had a lot of clothing, was particular about his dress and had no reason whatsoever for using my clothes. I was deeply touched for the emotional factors underlying his action were too obvious. For days thereafter my mind and feelings were agitated to realise the psychological strains and stresses my absence from home had imposed on the children. I recalled an incident in December 1956 when I was an awaiting trial prisoner at the Johannesburg Fort. At that time Kgatho was 6 and lived in Orlando East. Although he well knew that I was in jail he went over to Orlando West and told Ma that he longed for me. That night he slept in my bed.

But let me return to my meeting with Thembi. He had come to bid me farewell on his way to boarding school. On his arrival he greeted me very warmly, holding my hand firmly

---

4. A special letter is when a prisoner's letter is not taken from their quota. Permission was usually given for special letters after a death or in connection with studies.

and for some time. Thereafter we sat down and conversed. Somehow the conversation drifted to his studies, and he gave me what I considered, in the light of his age at the time, to be an interesting appreciation of Shakespeare's Julius Caesar which I very much enjoyed.

We had been corresponding regularly ever since he went to school at Matatiele and when he later changed to Wodehouse.

In December 1960 I travelled some distance by car to meet him. Throughout this period I regarded him as a child and I approached him mainly from this angle. But our conversation in July 1962 reminded me I was no longer speaking to a child but to one who was beginning to have a settled attitude in life. He had suddenly raised himself from a son to [a] friend. I was indeed a bit sad when we ultimately parted. I could neither accompany him to a bus stop nor see him off at the station, for an outlaw, such as I was at the time, must be ready to give up even important parental duties. So it was that my son, no! my friend, stepped out alone to fend for himself in a world where I could only meet him secretly and once in a while. I knew you had bought him clothing and given him some cash, but nevertheless I emptied my pockets and transferred to him all the copper and silver that a wretched fugitive could afford.

During the Rivonia Case he sat behind me one day. I kept looking back, nodding to him and giving him a broad smile. At the time it was generally believed that we would certainly be given the extreme penalty and this was clearly written across his face. Though he nodded back as many times as I did to him, not once did he return the smile. I never dreamt that I would never see him again. That was 5 years ago . . . Never before have I longed for you than at the present moment. It is good to remember this in this day of bitter misfortune and reverses. The writer, P J Schoeman, tells the story of an African Commander-in-Chief who took his army of magnificent black warriors for a hunt. During the chase the son of the Commander was killed by a lioness and the Commander himself was badly mauled by the beast. The wound was then sterilised with a red-hot spear and the wounded dignitary wreathed [sic] with pain as the wound was being treated. Later Schoeman asked how he felt and he replied that the invisible wound was more painful than the visible one. I now know what the Commander meant.

5. FROM A LETTER TO EVELYN MANDELA, DATED 16 JULY 1969, ABOUT THEMBI'S DEATH

This afternoon the Commanding Officer informed me of a telegram received from attorney Mendel Levin of Johannesburg in which he reported the death of Thembi in a motor accident in Cape Town on July 13.

I write to give you, Kgatho and Maki[5] my deepest sympathy. I know more than anybody else living today just how devastating this cruel blow must have been to you, for Thembi was your first born and the second child that you have lost. I am also fully conscious of the passionate love that you had for him and the efforts you made to train and prepare him to play his part in a complex modern industrial society. I am also aware of how Kgatho and Maki adored and respected him, the holidays and [the] good time they spent with him in Cape Town.

In her letter written in October 1967 Maki told me that Thembi helped you in buying them all they needed. My late Ma gave me details of the warm hospitality she received from him when she visited me on the Island. Throughout the last five years up to March this year, Nobandla gave me interesting accounts of his attachment and devotion to the family and the

---

5. Makaziwe (Maki) Mandela, second-born daughter to his first wife, Evelyn, see People, Places and Events.

personal interest he took in all his relatives. I last saw him five years ago during the Rivonia Trial and I always looked forward to these accounts for they were the main channel through which I was able to hear something of him.

The blow has been equally grievous to me. In addition to the fact that I had not seen him for at least sixty months, I was neither privileged to give him a wedding ceremony nor to lay him to rest when the fatal hour had struck. In 1967 I wrote him a long letter drawing his attention to some matters which I thought were in his interest to attend to without delay. I looked forward to further correspondence and to meeting him and his family when I returned. All these expectations have now been completely shattered for he has been taken away at the early age of 24 and we will never again see him. We should all be consoled and comforted by the fact that he had many good friends who join with us in mourning his passing away. He fulfilled all his duties to us as parents and has left us with an inheritance for which every parent is proud – a charming Molokazana and two lovely babies.[6]

Once more I extend to you, Kgatho and Maki my sincere condolences and trust that you will muster enough strength and courage to survive this painful tragedy.

6. FROM A LETTER TO THE COMMANDING OFFICER OF ROBBEN ISLAND PRISON, DATED 22 JULY 1969

My eldest son, Madiba Thembekile, aged twenty-four, passed away in Cape Town on July 13, 1969, as a result of injuries he sustained in a motor-car accident.

I wish to attend, at my own cost, the funeral proceedings and to pay my last respects to his memory. I have no information as to where he will be buried, but I assume that this

---

6. Thembi's wife, Thoko, and two daughters, Ndileka and Nandi.

will take place either in Cape Town, Johannesburg or Umtata. In this connection I should be pleased if you would give me permission to proceed immediately, with or without escort, to the place where he will be laid to rest. If he will already have been buried by the time you receive this application, then I would ask that I be allowed to visit his grave for the purpose of 'laying the stone', the traditional ceremony reserved for those persons who miss the actual burial.

It is my earnest hope that you will on this occasion find it possible to approach this request more humanely than you treated a similar application I made barely ten months ago, in September 1968, for leave to attend my mother's funeral. Approval of that application would have been a generous act on your part, and one which would have made a deep impression on me. Such a humanitarian gesture would have gone a long way in softening the hard blow and painful misfortune of an imprisoned man losing a mother, and would have afforded me the opportunity to be present at the graveside. I might add that I saw my late son a little more than five years ago and you will readily appreciate just how anxious I am to attend the funeral.

Finally, I should like to point out that precedents exist when Governments have favourably considered applications of this nature.

7. FROM A LETTER TO NOLUSAPHO IRENE MKWAYI,
   DATED 29 SEPTEMBER 1969[7]

Ten months before this I had made a similar application when my mother passed away, although the authorities had then adopted a hard line in refusing what I considered in all the circumstances to be a reasonable request, I nonetheless

---

7. Nolusapho Irene Mkwayi. Wife of Wilton Zimasile Mkwayi. For Wilton Zimasile Mkwayi, see People, Places and Events.

vaguely hoped that this time the death of two members of the family occurring so soon after the other would probabl[y] induce the authorities to give me the one opportunity I had in life of paying my last respects to Thembi . . . my application was simply ignored and I was not even favoured with the courtesy of an acknowledgement. A further request for permission to obtain copies of press reports on the fatal accident were turned down, and up to now I have no authentic information whatsoever as to how Thembi died . . . Not only was I deprived of the opportunity of seeing for the last time my eldest son and friend, and the pride of my heart; I am kept in the dark on everything relating to him and his affairs.

8. FROM A LETTER TO IRENE BUTHELEZI, DATED 3 AUGUST 1969[8]

I was moved by the message of condolence contained in the telegram sent by my chief, Mangosuthu [Buthelezi], on behalf of the family and which I received on July 18 (my birthday), and I should like him to know that I deeply appreciate it.[9] 1968 and 1969 have been difficult and trying years for me. I lost my mother only 10 months ago. On May 12 my wife was detained indefinitely under the Terrorist Act [sic], leaving behind small chdn [children] as virtual orphans, and now my eldest son is gone never to return. Death is a frightful disaster no matter what the cause and the age of the person affected. Where it approaches gradually as in the case of normal illness, the next-of-kin are at least forewarned and the blow may not be so shattering when it ultimately lands. But when you learn that death had claimed a strapping and healthy person in the prime of his life, then one must actually live through the experience to realise how completely paralysing it can be. This

8. Irene Buthelezi. Wife of Mangosuthu Buthelezi. See note 9, below.
9. Mangosuthu Buthelezi, see People, Places and Events.

was my experience on July 16 when I was first advised of my son's death I was shaken from top to bottom and for some seconds I did not know exactly how to react. I ought to have been better prepared for Thembi was not the first child I lost. Way back in the Forties I lost a 9 months baby girl.[10] She had been hospitalised and had been making good progress when suddenly her condition took a grave turn and she died the same night. I managed to see her during the critical moments when she was struggling desperately to hold within her tender body the last sparks of life which were flickering away. I have never known whether or not I was fortunate to witness that grievous scene. It haunted me for many days thereafter and still provokes painful memories right up to the present day; but it should have hardened me for similar catastrophes. Then came Sept[ember] 26 (my wife's birthday) when I was advised of my mother's death. I had last seen her the previous Sept when she visited me on the Island at the ripe age of 76 having travelled alone from Umtata. Her appearance had much distressed me. She had lost weight and although cheerful and charming, she looked ill and tired. At the end of the visit I was able to watch her as she walked slowly towards the boat which would take her back to the mainland, and somehow the thought flashed across my mind that I had seen her for the last time. But as the months rolled by the picture I had formed of her last visit began to fade away and was altogether dispelled by the exciting letter she wrote thereafter testifying to her good health. The result was that when the fatal hour struck on Sept[ember] 26 I was again quite unprepared and for a few days I spent moments in my cell which I never want to remember. But nothing I experienced in the late Forties and in Sept[ember] last year can be likened to what I went through on July 16. The news was broken to

....

10. Makaziwe Mandela, see People, Places and Events.

me about 2.30 pm. Suddenly my heart seemed to have stopped beating and the warm blood that had freely flown in my veins for the last 51 years froze into ice. For sometime I could neither think nor talk and my strength appeared to be draining out. Eventually, I found my way back to my cell with a heavy load on my shoulders and the last place where a man stricken with sorrow should be. As usual my friends here were kind and helpful and they did what they could to keep me in good spirits.

9. FROM A LETTER TO NOLUSAPHO IRENE MKWAYI,
   DATED 19 NOVEMBER 1969

I had also been anxious to attend the funeral and to pay my last respects to Thembi just as I has been keen to do so in the case of the death of ma. Though I had never hoped to succeed, my heart bled when I finally realised that I could not be present at the graveside – the one moment in life a parent would never like to miss. Many people who ponder on the problems of the average prisoner tend to concentrate more on the lengthy sentences still to be served, the hard labour to which we are condemned, the coarse and tasteless menus, the grim and tedious boredom that stalks every prisoner and the frightful frustrations of a life in which human beings move in complete circles, landing today exactly at the point where you started the day before. But some of us have had experiences much more painful than these, because these experiences eat too deeply into one's being, into one's soul.

10. FROM A LETTER TO HIS SON MAKGATHO, DATED 28 JULY 1969

I hate giving lectures, Kgatho, even to my own children and I prefer discussing matters with everyone on a basis of perfect equality, where my views are offered as advice which the person affected is free to accept or reject as it pleases him. But I will be failing in my duty if I did not point out that the death of Thembi brings a heavy responsibility on your shoulders. Now you are the eldest child, and it will be your duty to keep the family together and to set a good example for your sisters, to be a pride to your parents and to all your relatives. This means that you will have to work harder on your studies, never allow yourself to be discouraged by difficulties or setbacks, and never give up the battle even in the darkest hour. Remember that we live in a new age of scientific achievement, the most staggering of which is the recent landing of man on the moon. That is a sensational event that will enrich man's knowledge of the universe and that may even result in a change or modification of many fundamental assumptions in many fields of knowledge. The younger generation must train and prepare themselves so that they can easily grasp the far-reaching repercussions of developments in the realm of space. This is an era of intense and vicious competition in which the richest rewards are reserved for those who have undergone the most thorough training and who have attained the highest academic qualifications in their respective fields. The issues that agitate humanity today call for trained minds and the man who is deficient in this respect is crippled because he is not in possession of the tools and equipment necessary to ensure success and victory in the service of country and people. To lead an orderly and disciplined life, and to give up the glittering pleasures that attract the average boy, to work hard and systematically in your studies throughout the year, will in the end bring you coveted prizes and much personal happiness. It will inspire your sisters to follow the example of their beloved brother, and they will benefit greatly through your scientific knowledge, vast experience, diligence and achievements. Besides, human beings like to be associated with a hardworking, disciplined and successful person and by carefully cultivating these qualities you will win yourself many friends.

STENGEL: The letters to your wife that I have read . . . they are very, very passionate, and it is an unusual combination, because the letters were very passionate and yet you were very much in control of yourself at all times. How do you explain that?

MANDELA: Well it was, it is [a] difficult thing to explain, but here I was with a woman with whom I have [been] married . . . for four years when I was sent to jail, and she was a very young person, inexperienced; she had two children and she couldn't bring them up properly because of the harassment, and persecution by the police.

STENGEL: And so how does that explain the passion in your letters?

MANDELA: Well, you know, I was thinking of her, of course, every day and also I wanted to give her encouragement, to know that there is somebody somewhere who cares for her.

STENGEL: Yes. Well that's obvious from the letters. How do you yourself deal with the idea that your wife . . . that you were sentenced to life in prison, you were gone for many, many years. She has a life outside, she meets other men . . . it must be very difficult to think about that; that perhaps she, you know, meets other men that she might like or might take your place temporarily. How did you deal with that?

MANDELA: Well that was a question, you know, which one had to wipe out of his mind. You must remember that I was underground for almost two years before I went to jail. I took a deliberate decision to go underground . . . In other words . . . those issues were not material issues to me, and then one had to accept the human issue, the human fact, the reality that a person will have times when he wants to relax and one must not be inquisitive. It is sufficient that this is a woman who is loyal to me, who supports me and who comes to visit me, who writes to me. That's sufficient.

STENGEL: And then everything else you . . . that's sufficient and you put the other things out of your mind?

MANDELA: Oh, yes.

STENGEL: Because they are not important.

MANDELA: Yes.

STENGEL: And it doesn't alter her relationship to you, and your relationship to her.

MANDELA: No.

STENGEL: What about, in the same vein, the fact again that you think you might be in prison for life, and the idea that you might never make love to a woman again; that your sexuality would just atrophy. How do you deal with that in prison?

MANDELA: . . . Oh, well, one gets used to that, and it's not that [hard] to control yourself; I mean I was brought up in high schools, boarding schools, where you were without women for almost six months, and you exercised discipline of yourself. And then when I went to prison, I resigned myself to the fact that I had no opportunity for sexual expression and I could deal with that.

12. FROM A LETTER TO WINNIE MANDELA, DATED 23 JUNE 1969

For one thing those who have no soul, no sense of national pride and no ideals to win can suffer neither humiliation nor defeat; they can evolve no national heritage, are inspired by no sacred mission and can produce no martyrs or national heroes. A new world will be won not by those who stand at a distance with their arms folded, but by those who are in the arena, whose garments are torn by storms and whose bodies are maimed in the course of contest. Honour belongs to those who never forsake the truth even when things seem dark and grim, who try over and over again, who are never discouraged by insults, humiliation and even defeat. Since the dawn of history, mankind has honoured and respected brave and honest people, men and women like you darling – an ordinary girl who hails from a country village hardly shown in most maps, wife of a kraal which is the humblest even by peasant standards.

My sense of devotion to you precludes me from saying more in public than I have already done in this note which must pass through many hands. One day we will have the privacy which will enable us to share the tender thoughts which we have kept buried in our hearts during the past eight years.

13. FROM A LETTER TO ADELAIDE TAMBO, DATED 31 JANUARY 1970[11]

Time was when I would have found it very difficult to manage without seeing Zami indefinitely and without receiving letters or hearing from her and the children. But the human soul and human body has an infinite capacity of adaptation and it is amazing just how hardened one can come to be; and how concepts which we once treated as relatively unimportant suddenly become meaningful and crucial.

I never dreamt that time and hope can mean so much to one as they do now. An important personage commented on the death of Thembi and Ma, and on the incarceration of Zami and said: for you it never rains but pours. That is how I also felt at the time. But the numerous messages of condolence and solidarity that we received gave us a lot of encouragement and spirits are as high as you have always known them to be.

....

11. Adelaide Frances Tambo, see People, Places and Events. A note was written on this letter by a prison censor indicating that this was a 'letter to Adelaide Tambo' – Mandela had used a pseudonym. It is unlikely to have been posted.

Hope is a powerful weapon even when nothing else may remain.

What has sustained me even in the most grim moments is the knowledge that I am a member of a tried and tested family which has triumphed over many difficulties. In such a large and broad family opinions can be diverse on almost everything, but we have always succeeded in sorting out things together and going forward all the same. This fact endows my spirits with powerful wings.

14. CONVERSATION WITH RICHARD STENGEL ABOUT HIS MOTHER

STENGEL: Did she [your mother] understand your struggle and your beliefs and sacrifices?

MANDELA: Yes, she did. But at first she didn't understand at all. Because one day, I came back home after work, from work, and she was waiting for me. 'My child, you must go back to the Transkei because there were two white men here, who came here and they spoke *very* good Xhosa and they said, "Look, your son is wasting his time. He is a lawyer. He is with people who are just wanting to create trouble, who have no profession, like Mr [Walter] Sisulu and you'd better save your child. Your child should go back to the Transkei."' And she was saying, 'No, no, no, let's go back. Let's go back to the Transkei.' So I realised that I hadn't done my work properly. Instead of starting preaching to my mother here, I was preaching, you know, to the public. I must start here. So I then started explaining to her why I'm in politics. And later, she would say, 'Look if you don't join other children in politics, I will disinherit you!' Yes. But it took *some* time before she could say so. Mmm.

March 1, 1971.

My Darling,

Friday the 5th February this year was your 12th birthday and in January I sent you a card containing my congratulations and good wishes. Did you get it? Again I say: many happy returns.

It is not easy for me to believe that our Zeni who was only a baby when I last saw her is now a big girl doing Standard V at a Boarding School, and studying subjects I never learnt at school, like French, Physical Science and Maths. I still remember clearly the night when you were born in 1959. On February 4th that year I returned home very late and found Mummy highly restless. I rushed for the late Aunt Phyllis Mzaidume, and the two of us drove Mummy to Baragwanath Hospital. It was a remarkable coincidence. Aunt Phyllis was herself born on the 5th February and on our way to Bara she hoped that you would be born on the same date, and that is exactly what happened. When she heard of the news of your arrival, she was as happy as if she had created you.

Your birth was a great relief to us. Only three months before this, Mummy had spent fifteen days in jail under circumstances that were dangerous for a person in her condition. We did not know what harm might have been done to you and to her health, and we are happy indeed to be blessed with a healthy and lovely daughter. Do you realise understand that you were nearly born in prison? Not many people have had your experience of having been in jail before they were born. You were only 25 months old when I left home and, though I met you frequently thereafter until January 1962 when I left the country for a short period, we never lived together again.

You will probably not remember an incident that moved me very much at the time and about which I never like to think. Towards the end of 1961 you were brought to the house of a friend and I was already waiting when you came. I was without wearing a jacket and hat. I took you into my arms and for about ten minutes we hugged and kissed and talked. Then suddenly you seemed to have remembered something. You pushed me aside and began searching the room. In a corner you found the rest of my clothing. After collecting it, you gave it to me and asked me to go home. You held my hand for quite some time, pulling desperately and begging me to return. It was a difficult moment for both of us. You felt I had deserted you and Mummy and your request was a reasonable one. It was similar to the note that you added to Mummy's letter of the 3rd December 1968 where you said: "Will you come home next year, my mother will fetch you with her car." Your age in 1961 made it difficult for me to explain my conduct to you, and the worried expression that I saw in your face

MANDELA: And of course, King Sabata . . . the father of the
present king. That is my nephew and he looked after my mother
very well and he is the person who buried her. Yes . . . I was
sorry when he died when I was in jail.

STENGEL: That was very difficult for you? The idea that you were
the breadwinner and now you were in prison and couldn't . . .

MANDELA: Yes, quite, oh yes. That was a difficult thing. And I
sometimes used to think – search my soul – whether I had done
the right thing, because not only my mother, but my sisters were
struggling; although two of them were married, but they were
struggling and . . . I wondered whether I had done the right
thing to try and help the public, and get your parents and your
family in such difficulties. But every time, I used to end up by
saying, 'Well, this was the correct decision on my part.'

STENGEL: But then there was a struggle between your personal
obligations to your family and your larger obligations to society?

MANDELA: Yes, yes, quite.

STENGEL: And that's the argument that you were . . . ?

MANDELA: Yes, quite. Yes, yes. Have I taken the right decision?
Can the decision be right, which means that your family should
suffer as they do? And my mother struggled, you know, to send
me to school, and although I was later taken by a member of
our clan . . . Chief Jongintaba Dalindyebo, who was acting
for Sabata, he was regent for Sabata.[12] He brought me up and
treated me *very* well, you know, like one of his children. I never
had complaints with him, you know, under him and his wife
. . . But . . . my duty was that as soon as I was able to be a
breadwinner, I should look after my mother and my sisters.
I couldn't, at a critical moment.

---

12. Chief Jongintaba Dalindyebo, see People, Places and Events.

STENGEL: Because, in moral philosophy, there are those who can say that your first obligation is to those around you?

MANDELA: The family, mmm.

STENGEL: And so that it's a hard – it's difficult?

MANDELA: Very difficult indeed. *Very*, very, very difficult. But one had to endure it, you see, because when I sat down to think about this, I said, 'Well nevertheless, I have taken a decision, a correct decision' because they are not the only people who are suffering. *Hundreds*, *millions*, in our country are suffering and so I felt I had taken a correct decision.

16. FROM A LETTER TO ZENI AND ZINDZI MANDELA,
    DATED 1 JUNE 1970

It is now more than 8 years since I last saw you, and just over 12 months since Mummy was suddenly taken away from you.

Last year I wrote you 2 letters – one on the 23rd June and the other on 3rd August. I now know that you never received them. As both of you are still under [16], and as you are not allowed to visit me until you reach that age, writing letters is the only means I have of keeping in touch with you and of hearing something about the state of your health, your school-work and your school progress generally. Although these precious letters do not reach, I shall nevertheless keep on trying by writing whenever that is possible. I am particularly worried by the fact that for more than a year I received no clear and first-hand information as to who looks after you during school holidays and where you spend such holidays, who feeds you and buys you clothing, who pays your school fees, board and lodging, and on the progress that you are making at school. To continue writing holds out the possibility that one day luck may be on our side in that you may receive these letters. In the meantime the mere fact of writing down my thoughts and expressing my feelings gives me a measure of pleasure and satisfaction. It is some means of passing on to you my warmest love and good wishes, and tends to calm down the shooting pains that hit me whenever I think of you.

17. FROM A LETTER TO SENATOR DOUGLAS LUKHELE IN SWAZILAND, DATED 1 AUGUST 1970[13]

Letters from me hardly ever reach [their] destination and those addressed to me [fare] no better. I am hoping that the remorseless fates, that consistently interfere with my correspondence and that have cut me off from my family at such a critical moment, will be induced by considerations of honour and honesty to allow this one through. I know that once it reaches your hands my troubles will be virtually over.

You know that I am essentially a rustic like many of my contemporaries, born and brought up in a country village with its open spaces, lovely scenery and plenty of fresh air. Although prior to my arrest and conviction 8 years ago I lived for 2 decades as a townsman, I never succeeded in shaking off my peasant background, and now and again I spent a few weeks in my home district as a means of recalling the happy moments of my childhood. Throughout my imprisonment my heart and soul have always been somewhere far beyond this place, in the veld and the bushes. I live across these waves with all the memories and experiences I have accumulated over the last half century – memories of the grounds in which I tended stock, hunted, played, and where I had the privilege of attending the traditional initiation school. I see myself moving into the Reef in the early forties, to be caught up in the ferment of the radical ideas that were stirring the more conscious of the African

....

13. Douglas Lukhele. Lawyer. Senator and attorney general in Swaziland. He did his articles at Mandela and Tambo. See note 14, this chapter.

youth . . . I remember the days when I served articles, licking stamps, daily running all sorts of errands, including buying hair shampoo and other cosmetics for white ladies. Chancellor House![14] It was there that OR [Oliver Tambo] and I became even more intimate than we were as College mates and as [Youth] Leaguers. Around us there developed new and fruitful friendships – Maindy, Zubeida Patel and Winnie Mandleni, our first typists; the late Mary Anne, whose sudden and untimely death greatly distressed us; Ruth, Mavis, Godfrey; boxing Freddy and Charlie the upright and popular caretaker and cleaner who never missed a day at Mai-Mai.[15] For some time you battled almost alone and against formidable difficulties to keep the firm afloat when OR and I were immobilised by the Treason Trial.[16] I even recall the strange incident that occurred when you visited Zami and I at our home in Orlando West in Dec. '60. As you approached the gate a bolt of lightning split out with such tremendous force that Zeni, then only 10 months, was flung to the ground where she remained motionless for some seconds. What a relief it was when she came round and started yelling; it was a close shave . . . Spiritual weapons can be dynamic and often have an impact difficult to appreciate except in the light of actual experience in given situations. In a way they make prisoners free men, turn commoners into monarchs, and dirt into pure gold. To put it quite bluntly, Duggie, it is only my flesh and blood that are shut up behind these tight walls.

Otherwise I remain cosmopolitan in my outlook; in my thoughts I am as free as a falcon.

The anchor of all my dreams is the collective wisdom of mankind as a whole. I am influenced more than ever before by

14. Chancellor House was the building in which Mandela and Oliver Tambo started their own law practice, Mandela and Tambo, in 1952.
15. The Mai Mai Market is Johannesburg's oldest and foremost market for traditional medicines.
16. Mandela and Oliver Tambo were two of the 156 members of the Congress Alliance arrested and charged with high treason in 1956, see People, Places and Events.

the conviction that social equality is the only basis of human happiness ... It is around these issues that my thoughts revolve. They are centred on humans, the ideas for which they strive; on the new world that is emerging; the new generation that declares total war against all forms of cruelty, against any social order that upholds economic privilege for a minority and that condemns the mass of the population to poverty and disease, illiteracy and the host of evils that accompany a stratified society.

18. FROM A LETTER TO WINNIE MANDELA, THEN IN PRETORIA CENTRAL PRISON, DATED 1 AUGUST 1970

The crop of miseries we have harvested from the heartbreaking frustrations of the last 15 months are not likely to fade away easily from the mind. I feel as if I have been soaked in gall, every part of me, my flesh, bloodstream, bone and soul, so bitter I am to be completely powerless to help you in the rough and fierce ordeals you are going through. What a world of difference to your failing health and to your spirit, darling, to my own anxiety and the strain that I cannot shake off, if only we could meet; if I could be on your side and squeeze you, or if I could but catch a glimpse of your outline through the thick wire netting that would inevitably separate us.

Physical suffering is nothing compared to the trampling down of those tender bonds of affection that form the basis of the institution of marriage and the family that unite man and wife. This is a frightful moment in our life. It is a moment of challenge to cherished beliefs, putting resolutions to a severe test. But as long as I still enjoy the privilege of communicating with you, even though it may only exist in form for me, and until it is expressly taken away, the records will bear witness to the fact that I tried hard and earnestly to reach you by writing every month. I owe you this duty and nothing will distract me from it. Maybe this line will one day pay handsome dividends. There will always be good men on earth, in all countries, and even here at home. One day we may have on our side the genuine and firm support of an upright and straightforward man, holding high office, who will consider it improper to shirk his duty of protecting the rights and privileges of even his bitter opponents in the battle of ideas that is being fought in our country today; an official who will have a sufficient sense of justice and fairness to make available to us not only the rights and privileges that the law allows us today, but who will also compensate us for those that were surreptitiously taken away.

In spite of all that has happened I have, throughout the ebb and flow of the tides of fortune in the last 15 months, lived in hope and expectation. Sometimes I even have the belief that this feeling is part and parcel of my self. It seems to be woven into my being. I feel my heart pumping hope steadily to every part of my body, warming my blood and pepping up my spirits. I am convinced that floods of personal disaster can never drown a determined revolutionary nor can the cumulus of misery that accompany tragedy suffocate him. To a freedom fighter hope is what a life belt is to a swimmer – a guarantee that one will keep afloat and free from danger. I know, darling, that if riches were to be counted in terms of the tons of hope and sheer courage that nestle in your breast (this idea I got from you) you would certainly be a millionaire. Remember this always.

19. FROM A LETTER TO WINNIE MANDELA, DATED 31 AUGUST 1970

If there was ever a letter which I desperately wished to keep, read quietly over and over again in the privacy of my cell, it was that one. It was compensation for the precious things your arrest deprived me of – the Xmas, wedding anniversary, birthday cards – the little things about which you never fail to think. But I was told to read it on the spot and [it] was grabbed away as soon as I had reached the last line.

Brig. [Brigadier] Aucamp attempted to justify this arbitrary procedure with the flimsy excuse that in the letter you gave his name for your address instead of your prison. He went on to explain that my letters to you were handled in exactly the same way, and that you were not allowed to keep them. When I pressed him for an explanation he was evasive. I realised there were important issues at stake which necessitate the making of serious inroads on your right as an awaiting-trial prisoner to write and receive letters and curtailment of my corresponding privilege. Our letters are subject to a special censorship. The real truth is that the authorities do not want you to share the contents of the letters I write you with your colleagues there, and vice versa. To prevent this they resort to all means, fair and foul. It is possible that communication between us may be whittled down still further, at least for the duration of the trial. As you know, the privilege as far as my normal monthly letters to and from friends and relations practically disappeared with your arrest. I have been trying to communicate with Matlala since January last and with Nolusapho since November.

On June 19 Brig. Aucamp explained that another department had instructed him not to forward these letters, adding at the same time that he was not in a position to give me reasons for these instructions, but that such instructions were not influenced by the contents of the letters. This revelation solved the riddle of the mysterious disappearance of most of the letters I wrote over the past 15 months. The matter entails even more serious implications. I should like to be in the position where I can always rely on what officials tell me, but I'm finding it increasingly difficult to square up wishes with experience. Twice during July and early this month, I was informed that your letter had not arrived. I have now established that the letter was actually here when I was being given assurances to the contrary.

20. FROM A LETTER TO NONYANISO MADIKIZELA, DATED 1 NOVEMBER 1970[17]

If there was ever a time for Zami to remain calm, cautious and calculating, *a time to think, and think, and think*, it is now. Let her be careful. There are those who do not want to see her free and who will use any pretext to pounce upon her.

When all Zami's shortcomings have been listed, she still emerges as a woman of great ability and ambition, endowed with qualities far more superior to anything I have ever possessed, and I have the highest regard for her. She deserves encouragement and support. One of my greatest regrets is to be unable to protect her – the one woman who has first claim to everything that I command in the form of knowledge, experience and advice. For courage and dedication she is second to none. But, however much she may be affected by the ideals that have moved other great women, she still lives here on mother earth. She must eat, bring children up, maintain me and have a decent home. One of my fervent hopes had once been that I would give her all these things, which would leave her free to strive to realise her aspirations with a measure of independence. That chance never came, and I never succeeded in providing for her and the children. With her numerous restrictions, no one is prepared to employ her and she finds it difficult to earn her living. What a catastrophe for a young woman of 36! Never shall I regret the decision I made in '61, but I wish one day my conscience would sit easy in my bosom.[18] Look after her, Nyanya. I have given you a glimpse of the woman I adore, the

---

17. Nonyaniso Madikizela. Winnie's sister.
18. Mandela is referring to his decision in 1961 to go underground and form MK.

human being behind the veil of fine garments she wears and attractive features for which she is widely known.

21. FROM A LETTER TO WINNIE MANDELA,
DATED 16 NOVEMBER 1970

You looked much better than I expected, but far from what you were when we last met in Dec. '68. The cumulative effect of a thousand and one strains was clearly visible. As I walked back to the jail after the interview, I was preoccupied with the fear that now that you have to live alone for 12 hours in the night, loneliness and anxiety might worsen your condition. This fear still haunts me.

Incidentally, on my way down to the visiting rooms on Nov. 7, I managed to see the boat on which you came as it steamed gracefully to harbour, beautiful in its bright colours. Even at a distance it looked a real prisoners' friend, and I became more anxious as it approached. You know why! I saw it again as it sailed back to the mainland. This time the picture was altogether different. Though it still retained its brightness, the beauty I had seen only a few hours before was gone. Now it looked grotesque and quite unfriendly. As it drifted slowly away with you, I felt all alone in the world and the books that fill my cell, which have kept me company all these years, seemed mute and unresponsive. Have I seen my darling for the last time, is a question that kept recurring.

22. FROM A LETTER TO ZINDZI MANDELA, DATED 1 DECEMBER 1970

It is on occasions such as this one that I fully understand how I am completely dependent on Mummy in almost everything I do. Ever since I was told that she and her friends had been more powerful forces operate. On such questions it would be equally misleading to place your trust on good men, no matter how highly placed they may be, where systems are involved, the goodness of individuals is very often unable to count. It's, however, a different story when you, Zeni, Maki, Kgatho, Mfundo, Mtsobse, Bagab, Pumla, Shamie and Ancute, Nombeko, Mpho and Ihabo and other young people become united by common ideas and when you follow up common plans. The old systems [the system as a whole must change] will be pushed aside and new ones arise [and will]. Only then will good men have the opportunity to serve their countrymen fully. Then mummy will not have to travel to [far] to see Daddy. I will be at home, where [some] will be. Together we shall sit around the fire and chat warmly and ~~tough~~ gaily. We may even invite the magistrate for dinner. *

Till then, please look after mummy, you and zeni. She is a brave person, but there are difficult times for her. She needs no pity, not even from you or me. But she deserves our full support, warm friendship and all our love. Look after her my darlings. See to it that she sees the specialists regularly, takes things easy and [pleasantly] keeps her mind occupied.

I have not forgotten that on the 23rd of this month you will be 10. In fact that's the main reason for writing this letter, to give you my love and special wishes. I hope mummy will be able to arrange a party which will be as bright as song, where your friends [gather and] will shout, as I shall also do, and say "Happy Birthday". I wish I could have written you a much shorter letter than this; not more than the 5½ word letter that you [written] wrote me, a letter where I would talk only of birthdays, food, nice dresses and your [?]. But a letter to you is also meant for zeni and mummy, for the whole family — a family [faced] affected with many problems; without regular income, enough food, that cannot afford payment of rent and a host of [other things] required by modern standard of living. These letters are the only means we have of keeping together, of affirming the ideals that inspire us and of reminding one another that tiduleuma liduleu. (Give mummy zeni and [nyanya] a big hug and warm kiss for me). Make sure that you personally see Maki and Kgatho and tell them to answer my letter.

Tons and tons of love and a million kisses

Affectionately,

Tata.

released, I lived in the hope that I would soon see her, and was excited as you become when you hear the bell of the ice-cream man ring, or when Mummy buys you a mini dress.

I tried hard to remain calm when Kgatho unexpectedly broke the painful news. Perhaps I would have done much better on the stage than in law or politics. I must have acted well because I succeeded in making one of my friends believe that Mummy's failure to come had not affected me. If only he knew! The truth is that my appearance had nothing to do whatsoever with the state of my feelings. I was badly wounded and shaken.

You and Zeni, and perhaps even Mummy, may be justified in thinking that the magistrate, who seemingly treated us with such pettiness and lack of feeling, is a cruel man. He himself probably has a wife and children, just as I have, and would certainly be aware of the hardship created by keeping Mummy and Daddy in forced separation for so long, and of denying us the pleasure of seeing each other. Yet I know that, as a person, he is far from being cruel. On the contrary, and within the limits imposed by certain traditions which have become accepted in our country, he is kind and courteous, and I consider him in all sincerity to be a gentleman. During the 9 years in which I practiced as an attorney I frequently appeared before him, and I found it a real pleasure to argue before a man I regarded as fair and just.

But even a man like the Chief Magistrate of mighty Johannesburg, South Africa's largest city, and Africa's richest town, has his hands firmly tied. He cannot do what he likes. His official duties may force him to do what his personal nature violently hates. Even junior officials in other departments may wield more power than him, and have the final say in regard to some of his important official duties. In matters of this kind it is never wise to single out individuals and lay blame on their shoulders. Such individuals may not themselves be responsible for the decisions they make. They may merely be the means through which more powerful forces operate. On such questions it would be equally misleading to place your trust on good men, no matter how highly placed they may be. Where systems are involved, the goodness of individuals is very often irrelevant. It is, however, a different story when you, Zeni, Maki, Kgatho, Mfundo, Motsobise, Bazala, Pumla, Thamie and Andile, Nombeko, Mpho and Thabo and other young people become united by common ideas and when you follow up common plans.[19] Then old systems will be pushed aside and new ones arise. The system as a whole must change. Only then will good men have the opportunity to serve their countrymen fully and well. Then Mummy will not have to travel to Cape Town to see Daddy. I will be at home, wherever home will be. Together we shall sit around the fire and chat warmly and gaily. We might even invite the magistrate for dinner. I don't know where we shall get the money to arrange the dinner. When I return I shall have forgotten almost everything about law and will have to do something else for a living, perhaps dig roads, clean drains or go down the coal pits with pick and shovel.

23. FROM A LETTER TO JOYCE SIKHAKHANE,
     DATED 1 JANUARY 1971[20]

Re roba matsoho for you and John![21] Is it true? Can you two really do this to me, take such momentous decisions without even as much as giving me a hint? I must have missed heaps of meat and pudding at the engagement party. To your wedding I would have been accepted just as I am, without having to sport a frock coat, starched shirt and top hat. What is even

---

19. Nomfundo (Mfundo) Mandela, Matso (Motsobise) and Bazala Biyana, and Thamie and Andile Xaba: cousins of Mandela's children. Nombeko Mgulwa: distant relation. Mpho and Thabo Ngakane: children of close family friends.
20. Joyce Sikhakhane, see People, Places and Events.
21. Re roba matsoho is a form of congratulation in Setswana.

more important to me, your wedding would have been one occasion in which I could have shined at last. I rehearse daily on a penny whistle; everyone around here calls it that though it cost R2.00. I'm still on the d.t.l.-stage but with more practice I could have tried Handel's Messiah on it on the great day.

24. CONVERSATION WITH RICHARD STENGEL

STENGEL: Did you have recurring nightmares when you were on Robben Island?

MANDELA: No, no, no. That I never had.

STENGEL: Oh, you didn't, okay.

MANDELA: No, I never had nightmares.

STENGEL: Okay. What would you say was your worst moment on Robben Island, when you felt the lowest?

MANDELA: Well, it's difficult . . . very difficult to pinpoint any particular moment as my worst moment, but the question of my wife being harassed and persecuted by the police, and sometimes being assaulted, and I was not there to defend her. That was a very difficult moment for me. And when I saw that she was being hounded from one job to the other by the police. They would go to the employer and say, 'By keeping this woman here you are starting trouble.'

STENGEL: But how did that make you feel? I mean, did you feel powerless? Did you feel angry?

MANDELA: Well, naturally there was an element of anger, but at the same time I tried to be cool about it, and remembered that this is the price we have to pay for being committed to the struggle. And it's something that disturbed *me* very much, and the feeling of frustration and helplessness *was* there, because there was nothing I could do about it.

STENGEL: What about . . . I've read before that sometimes you would come back to your cell at the end of the day and they would place press cuttings . . .

MANDELA: Yes, quite, they would do that.

STENGEL: Quite regularly?

MANDELA: Well, now and again, they did. Whenever there was some bad report about the family, they would put the cutting on my table. Very dirty.

STENGEL: And that would make you angry too, I suppose.

MANDELA: Yes, well one got used to the methods which they used, and decided to keep cool about it. But of course there was an element of anger against it, but one learned to be calm about these things.

STENGEL: Right. Well, I have a quote here from Mac Maharaj, who said about you, and this is relevant to what you were just saying, 'As he has been living through prison, his anger and hatred of the system has been increasing, but the manifestations of that anger have become less visible.'[22] Would you say that that's true?

MANDELA: Well, that certainly is correct in the sense that I am working now with the same people who threw me into jail, persecuted my wife, hounded my children from one school to the other . . . and I am one of those who was saying, 'Let us forget the past, and think of the present.'

25. CONVERSATION WITH RICHARD STENGEL ABOUT
    COMMUNICATION WITH OTHER SECTIONS IN PRISON

STENGEL: How did you communicate with people in the other sections?

MANDELA: Well, we smuggled letters . . . and Kathrada, Ahmed Kathrada, was in charge of that. But there were embarrassing situations, because one day I was standing with the warder;

---

22. Satyandranath (Mac) Maharaj, see People, Places and Events.

they were bringing in food, in drums, and the chaps from the kitchen are only allowed just to give us the drums through the door without entering our section. Now it was the *last* delivery of food for the day; it was in the evening, at sunset. So there was a young fellow . . . and he was *desperate* to pass on this letter, and as I was standing there receiving the food, he just took the letter and gave it to me. Now . . . by then, of course the warders respected me and I felt very small. I did not know what to do, not so much because of punishment, but because of the effect on this warder; especially because he was comparatively younger than myself, and I didn't want to abuse, you know, the respect . . . in which they held me . . . I was really tortured by that and I just walked away from him and I handed it to Kathrada and I found it *very* difficult to look at that young warder.

STENGEL: Because he saw?

MANDELA: He must have seen . . . because we were standing together and this young chap from the kitchen, just after delivering the drums, he just takes this thing and gives it to me. Because he was *desperate*, he had to *pass* the thing, you see, to get an urgent message.

STENGEL: And it was humiliating for the warder to witness this?

MANDELA: Well, it was humiliating and it was a breach of duty because he should have acted against that boy, against myself as well. He should have taken the letter, but out of respect, you know, he pretended as if he hadn't seen anything, didn't do anything. And that *really* humiliated me. To abuse your trust in that fashion. At the same time, I couldn't say to this youngster, 'Don't give it to me; take it back,' because if I had done so, the warder would have punished him. Would have charged him. But we *were* able to smuggle, very quietly.

26. FROM A LETTER TO TIM MAHARAJ, DATED 1 FEBRUARY 1971[23]

It has been said a thousand and one times that what matters is not so much what happens to a person than the way such person takes it. It may sound silly for me to burden you with what is a matter of more than common knowledge. Yet whenever it is my turn to be the victim of some misfortune, I forget precisely these simple things, and thereby let hell break loose upon me.

27. FROM A LETTER SMUGGLED FROM PRISON TO LAWYERS IN DURBAN, DATED JANUARY 1977

M/S Seedat, Pillay and Co, Durban
I intend instituting legal proceedings in the CPD [Cape Provincial Division] against the Dpt [Department] of Prisons for a declaration of rights and for an interdict restraining the prison authorities from abusing their authority and subjecting me and my fellow prisoners to political persecution and from committing other irregularities.

In this connection I should be pleased if you would act for me and brief Adv. [Advocate] G. Bizos of the Jhb [Johannesburg] Bar or any other barrister he recommends.[24] I hope you will be able to arrange a consultation at your earliest possible convenience either with a member of your firm or with counsel when the full facts on which the cause of action is founded will be placed before you.

If your firm is for any reason unable to come down for consultation, I would still like to retain your services but would be happy to have an interview with any other person you might send. Arrangement for payment of your fees and disbursements will be made directly with you or your representative at the consultation.

23. Tim Maharaj. Mac Maharaj's first wife. For Mac Maharaj, see People, Places and Events.
24. George Bizos, see People, Places and Events.

On Oct 7 1976 I wrote and asked the Commanding Officer, Col [Colonel] Roelofse, for permission to instruct my lawyers to institute proceedings. The request was refused and I had no option but to smuggle this letter out of prison.

On July 12, 1976 I wrote a 22 page letter to the Commissioner of Prisons and expressly drew his attention to the abuse of authority, political persecution and other irregularities committed by the C.O. [Commanding Officer] and his staff. A copy of this letter is still in my possession and I hope to hand it directly to you in due course. Meantime I would suggest that you ask him not to remove the document and other papers relevant to the contemplated proceedings from my custody.

Here is a summary of the letter: <u>Abuse of Authority.</u> Both Col Roelofse and Lt [Lieutenant] Prins, Head of Prison, have been systematically preaching racialism to fellow prisoners of different population groups in the single cell section where I live and trying to foment feelings of hostility amongst us.

<u>Improper interference with social relations.</u> After setting out the facts in support of this allegation I added, 'I now consider the untruthful explanations that are repeatedly made by the local officials about our correspondence and the so-called objection either to the contents of the letter or person who wrote it as a mere technique to deprive us of the legal right of preserving good relationships, between ourselves and our relatives and friends.'

<u>Censorship of outgoing mail.</u> As has often happened in the past, the birthday card I sent to my daughter in Dec. 75 did not reach her. Last Feb I wrote to my wife and regretted the fact. I also referred to photos my daughter repeatedly sent me and that had disappeared without trace. The C.O. objected to this paragraph. My daughter plays rugby and in another letter I advised her to pay attention to her diet. I was asked to remove the

M/s Seedat Pillay & Co, Durban // I intend
instituting legal proceedings in the CPD against the
Asst of Prisons for a declaration of rights & for an
interdict restraining the prison authorities from
abusing their authority & subjecting me & my fellow-
prisoners to political persecution & from committing
other irregularities // In this connection I should be
pleased if you would act for me & brief Addo & Bizos'
of the JHB Bar or any other barrister he recommends.
I hope you will be able to arrange a consultation at
your earliest possible convenience either with a
member of your firm or with counsel when the
full facts on which the cause of action is founded
will be placed before you // If your firm is for any
reason unable to come down for consultation, I
would still like to retain your services but would be
happy to have an interview with any other person
you might send. Arrangement for payment of your
fees & disbursements will be made directly with
you or your representative at the consultation. On Oct.
7, 1976 I wrote & asked the Commanding Officer, Col.
Roelofse, for permission to instruct my lawyers to
institute these proceedings. The request was refused &
I had no option but to smuggle this letter out of
prison. On July 12, 1976 I wrote a 22 page letter to the
Commissioner of Prisons & expressly drew his attention
to the abuse of authority, political persecution & other
irregularities committed by the C.O. & his staff. A
copy of this letter is still in my possession & I hope
to hand it directly to you in due course. Meantime
I would suggest that you ask him not to remove the
document & other papers relevant to the contemplated
proceedings from my custody. Here is a summary of
the letter: Abuse of Authority. Both Col Roelofse & Lt Rems,
Head of Prison, have been systematically preaching
racialism to fellow prisoners of different population

From a letter smuggled from prison to lawyers in Durban, dated January 1977, see pages
194–195, 197–204. The page above is actual size.

passage. My grandniece wished to study LL.B and I wrote and requested Mrs F. Kentridge of the JHB [Johannesburg] Bar to advise her on law as a profession for women. Lt. Prins first asked me to remove this particular paragraph and some wks [weeks] after I had handed in the altered letter I was then told that it would not be sent to her because the Dpt now objected to her person. I concluded, 'To prevent me from telling my wife that I sent my daughter a birthday card which did not reach her, that I always think of her and that the photos she had posted to me had disappeared is unreasonable and based neither on security considerations nor on the desire to maintain good order and discipline nor to promote my welfare. The same applied to my letter to Mrs Kentridge . . .'

<u>Censorship of Incoming Correspondence.</u> But the worst abuses in regard to the censoring of letters are committed in regard (to) incoming correspondence and, in this connection, the C.O. and his staff have gone rampant. The censoring is malicious and vindictive and, again, is actuated neither by considerations of security and discipline nor the desire to promote our welfare.

I regard it as part of a campaign of systematic political persecution and an attempt to keep us in the dark about what goes on outside prison even in regard to our own family affairs. What the C.O. is trying to do is not only to cut us off from the powerful current of goodwill and support that has ceaselessly flown in during the 14 yrs [years] of my incarceration in the form of visits, letters, cards and telegrams, but also to discredit us to our families and friends by presenting us to them as irresponsible people who never acknowledge letters written to them nor deal with important matters referred to them by the correspondents.

In addition, the double standards used in censoring letters is cowardly and calculated to deceive the public into the false impression that our outgoing letters are not censored. In the case of these we are requested to rewrite them whenever there is any matter to which the prison authorities object so as to remove any evidence that they have been heavily censored. Incoming ones are badly cut and scratched out as the censor pleases. Nothing will best convey to you the extent of the damage caused to the incoming mail more than actual inspection by you in person. Many of the letters from my wife consist of strips of incoherent information that are difficult to keep together even in a file.[25]

My wife has been in prison several times and not only knows the relevant Prison Rules well but also the sensitivity of your local officials to anything they might consider objectionable. She makes a conscious effort to confine herself to family affairs, yet hardly a single one of her letters escapes mutilation.

On Nov. 24, 1975 she wrote me a 5 page letter and only the remains of 2 pages finally reached me. The censorship policy adopted here is not followed even by your own officials in other jails. As you are aware my wife has recently served a 6 month sentence in Kroonstad.[26] Some of her letters were posted by the C.O. of that prison but heavily censored [at] that end.

But what I intensely detest is to force us to be parties to a practice based on plain falsehood. It is immoral for the C.O. to destroy or withhold letters from our families and friends and at the same time prevent us from telling them about what he does. I consider it callous to allow our people to continue wasting money, time, energy, goodwill and love by sending us letters and cards which the C.O. knows will never be given to us . . .

25. Prison censors often cut words, sentences and paragraphs that they found offensive out of the letters.
26. Winnie was sentenced for violating her ban by being in the company of another banned individual.

You ought to issue a public statement in which you clearly define the policy of your Dept and set out more particularly what you consider objectionable and the categories of persons who may not write or send us messages of goodwill.

Disappearance of letters in transit. The number of letters that disappear in transit is far too large to be explained on the basis of the inefficiency of the P.O. [Post Office] Dpt and from the unreasonable and persistent refusal of the C.O. to allow us to register our letters. I must draw the inference that their disappearance is not accidental.

Visits. Even here the measures taken by the C.O. in supervising conversations between prisoners and visitors go beyond security requirements. To put 4 or sometimes even 6 warders to one visitor and breathing or staring threatening[ly] at her is a blatant form of intimidation.

It is my duty to tell you that there is a widespread belief amongst my fellow prisoners that at these visits there is a listening device that records all conversations including confidential matters between husband and wife. If this be the case there is hardly any justification for the show of force now generally displayed during such visits.

Language qualifications of the Censors. The man who is directly in charge of censoring mail and magazines is W/O [Warrant Officer] Steenkamp who was previously in charge of the section. Although he may have passed Matric English he is certainly no more proficient in that language than I am in Afrikaans and I doubt if Sgt [Sergeant] Fourie is any the better.

Even the C.O. finds it difficult to express himself in English. In fact during the 14 yrs of my incarceration I have met no C.O. whose English is as poor as that of Col. Roelofse who commands a prison . . . where the overwhelming majority of prisoners are English-speaking and who know no Afrikaans.

<u>Ban on correspondence with political supporters.</u> Lt. Prins has now told me that we are not allowed to communicate with any people known to the Dpt to be our political associates nor to relatives of other prisoners irrespective of the contents of the letters.

<u>Telegrams and Easter cards.</u> The C.O. has introduced a new practice of not allowing us to see the actual telegrams sent to us. What happens now is that one is given a message scrawled on a piece of paper and without the date when the telegram was sent and received as well as other essential information. The current belief is that these telegrams are first referred for scrutiny to the security police before delivery to addressee and in order to cover up the resulting delay the C.O. has introduced this practice.

The people who send these telegrams pay more money in order to ensure speedy delivery of the message and it is a matter of public concern when a govt [government] dpt deliberately frustrates the smooth and efficient operation of a public service for which citizens pay a special fee.

<u>Money received for prisoners.</u> There is a general impression amongst prisoners that the C.O. and the Security Police are running a racket with our moneys. On May 31, 1976 Lt Prins sent a message to the effect that an amount of R30 was received from Mr and Mrs Matlhaku on Nov. 5, 1975. No explanation was given as to why this yr [year] he repeatedly told me that the money had not been received nor why the money was not shown as having been credited to my account in the statement supplied to me by the accounts section.

I must tell you that the negligent manner in which my complaints have been investigated and the lengthy delays involved in extracting simple information on what are essentially trust moneys is a matter of serious concern which you ought to investigate as soon as you can and clear the reputation of your Dpt at least in this particular respect.

Political discussions at the sittings of the Prison Board. It has been the practice for several yrs now at these sittings for its members to engage prisoners in political discussions. These discussions are used by the Board for the purpose of victimizing those who are opposed to the policy of separate development.

COP's [Commissioner of Prisons] failure to visit political prisoners on R.I. [Robben Island]. The abuses described above are aggravated by your failure to visit the island and to give us the opportunity of discussing these problems directly with you. A visit by other officials from H.O. [Head Office] whatever their rank may be, can be no substitute for a visit by the Head of the Dpt in person.

One of the main causes of the friction here is the link between this Dpt and the Security Police and one of the first steps in your attempt to address our grievances is to cut that link completely. Many prisoners regard the COP in regard to all matters concerning us as a mere figurehead and that the real boss is the chief of the S.P. [Security Police] who orders the COP not only what to do but how to do it.

I have been wondering whether I should continue to be party to a practice I consider unethical and which gives the impression that I still enjoy rights and privileges which have been so whittled away that they have become practically valueless.

But I still believe that you as Head of this Dpt who holds the rank of General will not allow [or] condone these underhand methods, and until your actual decision on the matter proves me wrong, I shall continue to act in the belief that you are not aware of what is going on in this prison.

It is futile to think that any form of persecution will ever change our views. Your Govt and Dpt have a notorious record for their hatred, contempt and persecution of the Black man, especially the African, a hatred and contempt which forms the basic principle of the country's laws. The cruelty of this Dpt in subjecting our people to the indecent practice of thawuza, according to which a prisoner was required to strip naked and display his anus to inspection by an official in the presence of others, the equally obscene practice of a warder poking a finger into a prisoner's rectum, of brutally assaulting them daily and without provocation was curbed by the Govt after it has erupted into a national scandal.

But the inhumanity of the average S.A. [South African] warder still remains; only now it has been diverted into other channels and has taken the subtle form of psychological persecution, a field in which some of your local officials are striving to become specialists. I have the hope that a man of your rank and experience will immediately grasp the gravity of this dangerous practice and take adequate measures to stop it.

It is pointless and contrary to the country's historical experiences to think that our people will ever forget us. Although 160 yrs have passed since the Slachter's Neck executions, 74 since the internment camps of the Anglo-Boer War and 61 since Jopie Fourie made his last speech.

I will certainly never believe you if you tell me that you have now forgotten the Afrikaner patriots, the men whose sacrifices helped to free you from British imperialism and to rule the country and for you in particular to become Head of this Dpt.

It is certainly unreasonable for any man to expect our people, to whom we are national heroes, persecuted for striving to win back our country, to forget us in our life-time and at the height of the struggle for a free SA. Your people are slaughtering mine today and not a century and a half ago. It is present SA that is a country of racial oppression, imprisonment without trial, of torture and harsh sentences and the threat of internment camps lies not in the distant past but in the immediate future. How can our people ever forget us when we fight to free them from all these evils?

In SA as in many other countries various issues divide prisoners and officials. I do not agree with the policy of the Dpt of which you are Head. I detest white supremacy and will fight it with every weapon in my hands. But even when the clash between you and me has taken the most extreme form, I should like us to fight over our principles and ideas and without personal hatred, so that at the end of the battle, whatever the result might be, I can proudly shake hands with you, because I feel I have fought an upright and worthy opponent who has observed the whole code of honour and decency. But when your subordinates continue to use foul methods then a sense of real bitterness and contempt becomes irresistible.

The letter ends here. It is a mere summary and some important facts have been left out.

With regard to the question of correspondence, it may well be that this Dpt is only entitled to object to the actual contents of a letter and not to the writer as such. But I have no access to the complete Prisons Act and Rules and Regulations and none whatsoever to the Service Orders. Perhaps you would like to investigate the matter.

I almost forgot to tell you that on Sept 9 the C.O. informed me that he had received [a] letter from the COP dated Aug 26 in which the latter stated that he was satisfied that the administration on this island was acting properly and that he could not investigate the complaints of individual persons kept in custody in the country's prisons. With this reply the COP has given his official blessing to the abuse of authority, systematic persecution and other irregularities mentioned in my letter of July 12.

Finally, I should like you to know that these instructions will only be cancelled by me either . . . under my signature or directly during an interview with a representative of your firm.

Yours sincerely
N R Mandela 466/64
January 1977

in the country's prisons. With this reply the COP has given his official blessing to the abuse of authority, systematic persecution & other irregularities mentioned in my letter of July 12/ I would. I should like you to know that these invasions will only be cancelled by me either ... under my signature or directly ...

interview with a representative of your firm.

Yours sincerely
NRMandela 466/64.
January 1977

From a letter smuggled from prison to lawyers in Durban, dated January 1977, see pages 203–204.

CHAPTER NINE

Accommodated Man

'Old and famous horses keel over like many that went before, some to be forgotten forever and others to be remembered as mere objects of history, and of interest to academicians only.'

....

From a letter to Archie Gumede, dated 1 January 1975, see page 209.

1. FROM A LETTER TO ARCHIE GUMEDE, DATED 1 JANUARY 1975

Old and famous horses keel over like many that went before, some to be forgotten forever and others to be remembered as mere objects of history, and of interest to academicians only.

2. FROM HIS UNPUBLISHED AUTOBIOGRAPHICAL MANUSCRIPT WRITTEN IN PRISON

(1) A story of one's life should deal frankly with political colleagues, their personalities and their views. The reader would like to know what kind of person the writer is, his relationships with others and these should emerge not from the epithets used but from the facts themselves. (2) But an autobiography of a freedom fighter must inevitably be influenced by the question whether the revelation of certain facts, however true they may be, will help advance the struggle or not. If the disclosure of such facts will enable us to see problems clearly and bring nearer our goal then it is our duty to do so, however much such revelations may adversely affect the particular individuals concerned. But frankness which creates unnecessary tensions and divisions which may be exploited by the enemy and retard the struggle as a whole, is dangerous and must be avoided. (3) The utmost caution becomes particularly necessary where an autobiography is written clandestinely in prison, where one deals with political colleagues who themselves live under the hardships and tensions of prison life, who are in daily contact with officials who have a mania for persecuting prisoners. Writing under such conditions the temptation is strong to mention only those things which will make your fellow prisoners feel that their sacrifices have not been in vain, that takes their minds away from the grim conditions in which they live and that makes them happy and hopeful. An essential part of that caution and fair play would be to have the widest possible measure of consultation with

your colleagues about what you intend to say about them, to circulate your manuscript and give them the opportunity of stating their own views on any controversial issue discussed so that the facts themselves may accurately reflect the standpoints of all concerned; whatever may be the comments of the writer on those facts. Unfortunately the conditions in which I have written this story, especially security considerations, made it impossible to consult any but a handful of my friends.[1]

3. FROM HIS UNPUBLISHED AUTOBIOGRAPHICAL MANUSCRIPT WRITTEN IN PRISON

(15) The spotlight has focused on a few well known figures amongst us such as Wilton Mkwayi, Billy Nair, Raymond Mhlaba, Ahmed Kathrada, Govan Mbeki and Walter Sisulu.[2] This is but natural because they are amongst our leading men in the country, admired by hundreds of thousands of people here and abroad for their courage and dedication. All of them are cheerful and optimistic and have been a source of inspiration to all my fellow prisoners. They are amongst those in prison who have helped to keep our members constantly aware of the noble tradition associated with the Congress Movement.[3] But this is only part of the story. Every [one] of our men is like a brick which makes up our organisation and there are men in the Main Section who, whilst we here deal with about 20 men, have handled greater and more delicate problems affecting several hundred men coming from all walks of life, the overwhelming majority of whom get no visits, no letters, have no funds to study, cannot read or write and who are constantly subjected to all the cruelties of prison life.

....

1. Mandela wrote the autobiography in secret and Ahmed Kathrada and Walter Sisulu would check it for factual inaccuracies. Mac Maharaj and Laloo Chiba would then transcribe the work in tiny writing onto thin sheets of paper.
2. Billy Nair, see People, Places and Events.
3. An alliance of anti-apartheid organisations made up of the ANC, SAIC, COD and the CPC.

4. FROM HIS UNPUBLISHED AUTOBIOGRAPHICAL MANUSCRIPT
   WRITTEN IN PRISON

Walter [Sisulu] and Kathy [Kathrada] share one common feature which forms an essential part of our friendship and which I value very much – they never hesitate to criticise me for my mistakes and throughout my political career have served as a mirror through which I can see myself. I wish I could tell you more about the courageous band of colleagues with whom I suffer humiliation daily and who nevertheless deport themselves with dignity and determination. I wish I could relate their conversations and banter, their readiness to help in any personal problem suffered by their fellow prisoners so that you could judge for yourself the calibre of the men whose lives are being sacrificed on the fiendish altar of colour hatred.

5. FROM A LETTER TO WINNIE MANDELA IN KROONSTAD PRISON,
   DATED 1 FEBRUARY 1975

Incidentally, you may find that the cell is an ideal place to learn to know yourself, to search realistically and regularly the process of your own mind and feelings. In judging our progress as individuals we tend to concentrate on external factors such as one's social position, influence and popularity, wealth and standard of education. These are, of course, important in measuring one's success in material matters and it is perfectly understandable if many people exert themselves mainly to achieve all these. But internal factors may be even more crucial in assessing one's development as a human being. Honesty, sincerity, simplicity, humility, pure generosity, absence of vanity, readiness to serve others – qualities which are within easy reach of every soul – are the foundation of one's spiritual life. Development in matters of this nature is inconceivable without serious introspection, without knowing yourself, your weaknesses and mistakes. At least, if for nothing else, the cell gives you the opportunity to look daily into your entire conduct, to overcome the bad and develop whatever is good in you. Regular meditation, say about 15 minutes a day before you turn in, can be very fruitful in this regard. You may find it difficult at first to pinpoint the negative features in your life, but the 10th attempt may yield rich rewards. Never forget that a saint is a sinner who keeps on trying.

6. FROM A LETTER TO MRS D B ALEXANDER, DATED 1 MARCH 1976

One of my favourite hobbies is to examine all the cards I've received during the previous year and only the other day, I was looking at the one you sent me last Dec[ember]. It contains only 4 printed words to which you added 3 in a clear and bold script. That economy in words is characteristic of all the seasonal messages I've received from you and yet they're full of warmth and inspiration and each time they come I feel younger than kleinseun [grandson] Leo.

7. FROM A LETTER TO ZAMILA AYOB, DATED 30 JUNE 1987

I once wrote to Zami during the early seventies what I considered to be a romantic letter; from a man who adored and worshipped his beloved wife. In the course of that letter I remarked that Zeni and Zindzi had grown beautifully and that I found it a real pleasure to chat with them. My beloved wife was furious and, when I reached the last line of her letter, I felt that I was very fortunate to be so far from her physically. Otherwise I would have lost my jugular vein. It was as if I had committed treason. She reminded me: 'I, not you, brought up these children whom you now prefer to me!' I was simply stunned.

My training and experience as a practicing lawyer in South Africa's biggest city, Johannesburg, sensitized me at an early age in my political career to what was going on inside the corridors of power in our country. This early experience was reinforced during my imprisonment on Robben Island.

At that time prison warders were by no means the best-educated section of the community. The majority was hostile to our aspirations and regarded every black prisoner as sub-human. They were intensely racist, cruel and crude in dealing with us.

There were notable exceptions amongst them, who patiently warned their colleague[s] that in other parts of the world, liberation movements frequently won against their oppressors and became themselves rulers. These progressive warders urged that prisoners should be treated strictly according to regulations and well, so that in due course [if] they won and became [the] government they should in turn treat whites well.

The ANC [African National Congress] has always stressed the principle that we were fighting not against whites as such, but against white supremacy, a policy that is fully reflected in the racial composition of the principal structures of the organisation and government nationally, provincially and [on] local levels.

Not all my fellow prisoners had had the opportunity to be acquainted with the affairs of government departments at that time. Some of the most influential amongst us seriously doubted whether dialogue with the apartheid regime was a feasible option.

9. CONVERSATION WITH RICHARD STENGEL ABOUT HIS
   PROMOTION TO A HIGHER GRADE IN PRISON[4]

STENGEL: So why were you the first?
MANDELA: Well, you know, it's just a question of good relationships with the authorities . . . Although they fought with us, I kept a good relationship because I wanted to be able to go [to them] . . . to discuss a problem. Because I was worried by people, both in the main section – people you have no contact with – and in our group, in our section; and they worried me about all sorts of problems, some very serious, which had to be solved and quite apart, you know, from the general problems of policy . . . and practice . . . And, therefore, I kept a good relationship with them, even with Aucamp and of course the Commissioner General Steyn . . . But I fought them on questions of principle, and when they did something wrong, I fought them.

10. FROM A CONVERSATION WITH RICHARD STENGEL ABOUT
    PRISON WARDERS

I don't want us to create the impression that *all* the warders were just animals, rogues, no. *Right* from the beginning, there were warders who felt that we should be treated correctly . . . Without boasting, you see, they normally came, especially during weekends and in the evenings, to talk to me. And . . . some of them were *really* good men. And expressed their views uncompromisingly about the treatment we were receiving. And, and we picked this up now, when we came to know the warders and the officers . . . that there was a *serious* argument amongst warders. Some saying, 'We can't afford to treat people like this.

....

4. Prisoners were classified according to four grades ranging from A to D; A-grade prisoners received the most privileges. On arrival, the political prisoners were grade D, meaning they could receive and write only one letter and see only one visitor every six months.

We must treat them decently. We must give them newspapers; we must give them radios.' And the others say[ing], 'No, if you do that, you are building up their morale. Don't do that.' They say, 'Even so, they'll still be on the Island.' And so that argument was going on. Now to see . . . this division amongst warders, we decided, after some time, to go on . . . a go-slow strike . . . we used to take about a *whole* morning, loading one load . . . They tried *everything* and we would not budge. But there was a chap called Sergeant Opperman, he would call us together and say, 'Gentlemen, it rained last night and the roads were washed away. I want lime so as to repair the roads. I want five loads today, lorry-loads. Can you help me?' Now, the fact that the chap called us together and addressed us as gentlemen, would, you know, make us feel that we should help this man and we would fill those five lorries, you see, hardly in an hour's time. And once he goes, we go back to [the] go-slow strike.

Now . . . *this* chap was not only courteous, but when he was on duty in the kitchen, we would get our rations . . . In the kitchen there was a *lot* of smuggling. Taking our meat, our sugar and so on. And *this* Sergeant would make sure that we [got] our ration[s]. So we respected him. Now there were *many* warders with that approach. And so although we had serious difficulties, there were bright moments where some warders would treat you, you know, as human beings.

11. CONVERSATION WITH RICHARD STENGEL

STENGEL: Some of the warders participated in political discussions with you?
MANDELA: Oh yes, yes. Oh quite a lot. Generally, you know, there were some sharp chaps and who were engaged in discussions. And as a result of those discussions, they became

very friendly to us – *very, very* friendly. Some of them, I'm friendly with them now, still.

STENGEL: And how did they start participating? They listened and then they started giving their opinions also?

MANDELA: Well, they asked us questions. As far as I was concerned, I never started a political discussion with any warder. I listened to them. You are more effective if you are responding to a person who wants to make enquiries. When the information is volunteered gratuitously, some people resent that and you are not effective. It's better to keep your distance. But when somebody asks, 'What exactly do you want?'; because that's how they normally asked: 'Just tell me, what do you want?' And then you explain. 'Well you have enough food and [you] worry about these things? Why create such difficulties, miseries for the country, attacking innocent people, murdering them?' And then you have a chance of explaining and saying, 'No, you don't know your own history. When you were oppressed by the English, you did exactly as we did. And that is the lesson of history.'

12. CONVERSATION WITH RICHARD STENGEL

STENGEL: . . . Mac Maharaj was talking about how you . . . in prison . . . used to represent other prisoners, and that was against regulations?

MANDELA: Yes, oh yes.

STENGEL: But eventually they allowed that?

MANDELA: Yes.

STENGEL: How did that happen?

MANDELA: No, by insisting and asserting your right. They had to accept. Because when a man fights, even the enemies, you know, respect you, especially if you fight intelligently . . . I say, '*This* is wrong; I have seen it. What are you going to do about it?

Whether I have a right, you know, to speak for other prisoners, a crime, an offence has been committed and what are you going to do? You're an officer: you have to do something about it. Very well, if you don't want to do so, give me permission to write to your head office. And if your head office doesn't assist me, I'll write to the minister of justice. If the minister of justice doesn't help me, then I will have exhausted the channels of complaint within the prison service. I'll go outside.' Now they feared that. They feared that . . . I was persistent, and there are cases where I took up the matter and eventually went to the minister of justice, and when *no* improvement happened, then I smuggled a letter out and reported the thing to the press. So when I went to them and I said, 'If you don't attend to this, I know what to do' . . . they feared because of previous experience. So in that way, you know, they allowed me to talk for other prisoners.

13. CONVERSATION WITH RICHARD STENGEL

STENGEL: Do you think that people of your generation though, still have a kind of deference towards the white man that will not exist in the younger generation? Even yourself, for example, is there some residual . . .

MANDELA: Inferiority to the white man?

STENGEL: Ja.

MANDELA: No, I don't think so . . . because especially when you have been in the liberation movement for so long and you have been in and out of jail . . . One of the purposes of the Defiance Campaign of 1952 was . . . to instill this spirit of resistance to oppression; not to fear the white man, the policeman, his jail, his courts . . . and at that time 8,500 people went to jail deliberately because they broke laws which were intended to humiliate us and to keep us apart, to reserve certain privileges for whites. We broke those laws and courted jail, and as a result of campaigns of that nature, you got our people now not to fear repression, to be prepared to challenge it. And if a man can challenge a law and go to jail and come out, that man is not likely to be intimidated, you see, by jail life, generally speaking. And, therefore, even in our older generation, there is no inferiority except that it may be said that we are more mature in handling problems. We know that contact is the best way of convincing somebody. Because most of these chaps, you see, haven't got the enlightenment, they haven't got the *depth* to be able to appreciate problems. And when you confront them with an argument very quietly, without raising your voice, [you do] not . . . seem to question [their] dignity and integrity. Let him relax and be able to understand your argument. Invariably, even the most hardened warders inside jail, when you sit down and talk to them, they crumble very badly, they crumble . . .

There was a chap, Sergeant Boonzaier, a very interesting chap . . . One day we had an argument and I said a few unpleasant things to him in the presence of other prisoners. But later, man, I thought I was too hard on him, because he's comparatively a young chap. He was in his twenties, but a very tough, aloof and cold chap, and he had made a mistake, obviously. But I thought my remarks were too severe, so the following day I went back to the office and I said to him, 'Look, I'm very sorry for what I said. It was not the proper thing to do. Even though you are wrong, but I'm sorry for what I said.' He says, 'You come back; you talk to me like that when you see your friends. You talk to me like that and then now you come privately crawling [*laughs*] . . . and ask for an excuse. You call those chaps that you swore at me in their presence.' And I had to call them and to say, 'No, he has got a good point because I pulled him up in your presence. And then I went to apologise to him privately and he wouldn't accept it, you see.' So he says, 'Well, then I accept it.' But even then, you see . . . there was no feeling of gratitude, of thanks to me, you know? . . . But he was still stuck-up [*laughs*] . . .

One of the things the warders fear is when . . . an officer of a higher rank comes to our section. They want to be there . . . to receive the officer . . . I see an officer coming from a distance. So I thought I should tip him and I said, 'Mr Boonzaier, Boonzaier, the colonel is coming.' He says, 'So? So what? He knows this place. He can come and walk alone. I'm not going to join him.' [*laughs*] . . . *Very* independent. He was an orphan. He told me his story and that is why I got so *ashamed* of what I had said . . . He was brought up in an orphanage and . . . one of the stories that he told me was that when they eat breakfast, or any other meal, they won't talk to each other because they *hate* their status. The fact that they had no parents, no parental love, and his bitterness, to me was due to that. And I respected the chap very much because he was a self-made chap, yes. And he was independent and he was studying. He was absolutely fearless . . . I think he left, he left prison, yes. That's why I talk so openly. Otherwise I wouldn't because it would affect him.

14. FROM A LETTER TO WINNIE MANDELA, DATED 26 OCTOBER 1976, AT THE WOMEN'S JAIL, WRITTEN ORIGINALLY IN ISIXHOSA AND TRANSLATED CLUMSILY INTO ENGLISH BY A PRISON OFFICIAL

There are times of happiness when I laugh alone by thinking of the opportunities I had as well as times of pleasure. But there is much time for meditation than [of] being busy with important matters. There are many things that attract attention – to chat with friends, to read different books, things that refresh the mind, writing letters to families and friends and revising those from outside. Thoughts come only when relaxing and surround one person, my permanent friends I know very

I wrote to the children just after your detention consoling them not to be worried about your absence from home. I also reminded them that you are experienced in facing difficulties at the same time wishing them good luck and success in the examinations. Although encouraging them, I am always concerned about your health, spending speelless nights rhinking about the children who are left alone the damage of property in the house, thinking of friends and the loss of such a good paying job, the loss of money paid for examinations and the anxiety of not knowing when we shall meet again. The firls told me that they visited you several times and that you seemed to be in good health. Such messages gives one courage.

This year I received two letters from ZINDZI and none from ZENI. I did not want to ask her about that when they were here for fear that she would be ashamed. Although I wrote to them in September I will do so again next month. It sounds well that ZEIN and BAHLE are still in good terms. ZINDZI said she parted with FIDZA. Her new friend is MAFUTHA OUPA. She said you will explain all about that for she could take the whole day and night to do that. I hope you will write about that. I always think of a place where they can spend the holiday sine you are not at home.

Although I am still without proof whether you received the letters of Sept. 1 and Oct. 1, as for the one of Aug. 1 I will always be expecting an answer to hear if you do receive my letters. In spite of what the contents of those letters might be, their main point love, sympathy, remembrance, respect and all that might be relevant to all that I had written therein. My main problem since I left home is my sleeping without you next to me and my waking up without you close to me, the passing of the day without my having seen you with that audible voice of yours. The letters I write to you and those you write to me are an ointment to the wounds of our separation.

As I am writing the book of that famous author about the desert country is not far from me. The spiritual draught has vanished and substituted by the rain that fell as I completed it. Your letter dated 19/9 is just arriving now. As I am speaking, all the springs of life are running. The tributaries are full of clean water, the lakes are full and all the grandeur of nature has returned to normal. At this minute all my thoughts are beyond the Vaal in Johannesburg in the room where you are my sister.

With love,

DALIBUNGA.

Mrs. Nobandla MANDELA, Female Section, Johannesburg Prison, P.O. Box 1133, Johannesburg (2000).

TRANSLATED FROM Xhosa to English by B/D/Sgt. RAPHADU.

CAPE TOWN.
1.11.1976.

From a letter to Winnie Mandela, dated 1 October 1976. For other extracts from this letter, see pages 219, 221. It was originally handwritten in isiXhosa but translated into English and typed up by a prison official.

well. The conscience is torn, respect and love multiply. That is the only wealth I possess.

15. FROM A LETTER TO ADVOCATE FELICITY KENTRIDGE, DATED 9 MAY 1976

I've been out of action for 16 yrs [years] now and my views may be outdated. But I've never regarded women as in any way less competent than men . . .

16. FROM A LETTER TO WINNIE MANDELA, DATED 2 SEPTEMBER 1979

You will be quite right to regard '79 as women's year. They seem to be demanding that society lives up to its sermons on sex equality. The French lady Simone Veil has lived through frightful experiences to become President of the European Parliament, while Maria Pintasilgo cracks the whip in Portugal. From reports it is not clear who leads the Carter family. There are times when Carter's Rosalynn seems to be wearing the trousers.[5] I need hardly mention the name of Margaret Thatcher. Despite the collapse of her world-wide empire and her emergence from the Second World War as a 3rd-rate power, Britain is in many respects still the centre of the world. What happens there attracts attention from far and wide.

Indira [Gandhi] will rightly remind us that in this respect Europe is merely following the example of Asia which in the last 2 decades has produced no less than 2 lady premiers. Indeed . . . past centuries have seen many female rulers. Isabella of Spain, Elizabeth I of England, Catherine the Great of Russia (how great she really was, I don't know), the Batlokwa queen, Mantatisi, and many more.[6] But all these became first ladies

5. Rosalynn Carter (1927–). Married to President Jimmy Carter.
6. Mantatisi (1780–1826). Regent of the Batlokwa (Sotho), 1813–26.

in spite of themselves – through heredity. Today the spotlight falls on these women who have pulled themselves up by their own bootstraps.

17. FROM A LETTER TO AMINA CACHALIA, DATED 27 APRIL 1980

How dare you torture me by reminding me of that pigeon meal! That is rubbing salt into a fresh wound. After 28 yrs [years] I still think nostalgically of that memorable day. Yes, you are quite right! It's time for another meal. Where and when? It no longer matters. That you still think about it, and that you ask such relevant questions is terrific enough. I am tempted to say: boil the damn pigeons and fly them over. If some men in JHB [Johannesburg] frequently order a meal from a Paris restaurant, why can't you manage it over a thousand miles? Of course, this is wishful thinking; You and I know very well that the meal would never reach the Atlantic. Last Dec[ember], our friend, Ayesha, from CT [Cape Town] sent me a Xmas meal fit for a monarch, unaware of the fact that there is no provision in this dpt [department] for such gestures.[7] What a treat it would have been to taste fresh and real curry prepared at home! Not only was the parcel returned to her, but some of the containers were smashed. What started off with a lot of goodwill and affection ended up in frustration and, it may well be, even in bitterness. I wrote her a comforting letter and can only hope that she felt a little better after getting it. But even as I scribble these hurried lines, the heart and the head, the blood and the brain are fighting each other, the one pining idealistically for all the good things we miss in life, the head resisting and guided by the concrete realities in which we live out our lives.

....

7. Dr Ayesha Arnold (d. 1987) was a friend in Cape Town whom Zeni and Zindzi stayed with when they visited Mandela in prison. She wrote to Mandela and sent him food.

MANDELA: I had a number of works by [C J] Langenhoven . . . *Christus Van Nasareth, Christ of Nazareth* [*Shadows of Nazareth*]. And the other one is *Loeloeraai* . . . That was a very clever book . . . written in the twenties . . . where a man from earth flew to the moon . . . And he then compares the conditions [on] the moon and the conditions on earth. Actually, it was a man from the moon who flew to the earth, and he describes the contrast between life on earth and life in [on] the moon, and how the streets there are paved with gold and so on, and how he flew back to his country . . .

STENGEL: Aha, and the reason you liked Langenhoven? Why did you like him?

MANDELA: Well, firstly he wrote very simply. And secondly, he was a very humorous writer, and of course part of his writing was to *free* the Afrikaner from the desire to imitate the English. His idea was to instil *national* pride amongst the [Afrikaners] and so I liked him very much. Yes . . . And then from the point of view of poetry, [D J] Opperman . . . His poetry was not really geared towards any particular idea of a political nature; it was just a question of literature, pure literature, which was rather *very* good.

19. FROM A LETTER TO WINNIE MANDELA, CARE OF BRIGADIER AUCAMP, PRETORIA PRISON, DATED 1 JANUARY 1970

A novel by [C J] Langenhoven, 'Skaduwees van Nasaret' [*Shadows of Nazareth*] depicts the trial of Christ by Pontius Pilate when Israel was a Roman dependency and when Pilate was its military governor. I read the novel in 1964 and now speak purely from memory. Yet though the incident described in the book occurred about 2000 years ago, the story contains a moral whose truth is universal and which is as fresh and

January 1, 1970

Dade we thu,

A novel by Langenhoven, "Skaduwees van Nasaret" (Shadows of Nazareth) depicts the trial of Christ by Pontius Pilate when Israel was a Roman dependancy & when Pilate was its military governor. I read the novel in 1964 & now speak purely from memory. Yet though the incident described in the book occurred about 2000 years ago, the story contains a moral whose truth is universal & which is as fresh & meaningful today as it was at the height of the Roman Empire. After the trial Pilate writes to a friend in Rome to whom he makes remarkable confessions. Briefly this is the story as told by him & for convenience, I have put it in the first person:

As governor of a Roman province I have tried many cases involving all types of rebels. But this trial of Christ I shall never forget! One day a huge crowd of Jewish priests & followers, literally shivering with rage & excitement, assembled just outside my palace & demanded that I crucify Christ for claiming to be king of the Jews, at the same time pointing to a man whose arms & feet were heavily chained. I looked at the prisoner & our eyes met. In the midst of all the excitement & noise he remained perfectly calm, quiet & confident as if he had millions of people on his side. I told the priests that the prisoner had broken Jewish & not Roman law & that they were the rightful people to try him. But in spite of my explanation they stubbornly persisted in demanding his crucifixion. I immediately realised their dilemma. Christ had become a mighty force in the land & the masses of the people were fully behind him. In this situation the priests felt powerless & did not want to take the responsibility of sentencing & condemning him. Their only solution was to induce imperial Rome to do what they were unable to do.

At festival time it has always been the practice to release some prisoner & as the festival was then due, I suggested that this prisoner be set free. But instead, the priests asked that Barabas, a notorious prisoner, be released & that Christ be executed. At this stage I went into court & ordered the prisoner to be brought in. My wife & those of other Roman officials occupied seats in the bay reserved for distinguished guests. As the prisoner walked in my wife & her companions instinctively got up as a mark of respect for Christ but soon realised that this man was a Jew & a prisoner, whereupon they resumed their seats. For the first time in my experience, I faced a man whose eyes appeared to see right through me, whereas I was unable to fathom him. Written across his face was a gleam of love & hope, but at the same time he bore the expression of one who was deeply pained by the folly & suffering of mankind as a whole. He gazed upwards & his eyes seemed to pierce through the roof & to see right beyond the stars. It became clear that in that court room authority was not in me as judge, but was down below in the dock where the prisoner was.

My wife passed me a note in which she informed me that the previous night she had dreamt that I had sentenced an innocent man whose only crime was that of messiah to his meaningful today as it was at the height of the Roman Empire. After the trial, Pilate writes to a friend in Rome to whom he makes remarkable confessions. Briefly this is the story as told by him and, for convenience, I have put it in the first person:

As governor of a Roman province I have tried many cases involving all types of rebels. But this trial [of] Christ I shall never forget! One day a huge crowd of Jewish priests and followers, literally shivering with rage and excitement, assembled just outside my palace and demanded that I crucify Christ for claiming to be king of the Jews, at the same time pointing to a man whose arms and feet were heavily chained. I looked at the prisoner and our eyes met. In the midst of all the excitement and noise, he remained perfectly calm, quiet and confident as if he had millions of people on his side. I told the priests that the prisoner had broken Jewish, and not Roman law and that they were the rightful people to try him. But in spite of my explanation they stubbornly persisted in demanding his crucifixion [sic], immediately realised their dilemma. Christ had become a mighty force in the land and the mass[es] of the people were fully behind him. In this situation the priests felt powerless and did not want to take the responsibility of sentencing and condemning him. Their only solution was to induce imperial Rome to do what they were unable to do.

At festival time it has always been the practice to release some prisoners and as the festival was then due, I suggested that this prisoner be set free. But instead, the priests asked that Barabas, a notorious prisoner, be released and that Christ be executed. At this stage I went into Court and ordered the prisoner to be brought in. My wife and those of other Roman officials occupied seats in the bay reserved for distinguished guests. As the prisoner walked in my wife and her companions instinctively got up as a mark of respect for Christ, but soon realised that this man was a Jew and a prisoner, and whereupon they resumed their seats. For the first time in my experience, I faced a man whose eyes appeared to see right through me, whereas I was unable to fathom him. Written across his face was a gleam of love and hope; but at the same time he bore the expression of one who was deeply pained by the folly and suffering of mankind as a whole. He gazed upwards and his eyes seemed to pierce through the roof and to see right beyond the stars. It became clear that in that courtroom authority was not in me as a judge, but was down below in the dock where the prisoner was.

My wife passed me a note in which she informed me that the previous night she had dreamt that I had sentenced an innocent man whose only crime was that of messiah to his people. 'There before you, Pilate, is the man of my dream; let justice be done!' I knew that what my wife said was quite true, but my duty demanded that I sentence this man irrespective of his innocence. I put the note in my pocket and proceeded with the case. I informed the prisoner what the charge was against him, and asked him to indicate whether or not he was guilty. Several times he completely ignored me and it was clear that he considered the proceedings to be utter fuss, as I had already made up my mind on the question of sentence. I repeated the question and assured him that I had [*sic*] authority to save his life. The prisoner's gleam dissolved in a smile and for the first time he spoke. He admitted that he was king and with that single simple answer he totally destroyed me. I had expected that he would deny the charge as all prisoners do, and his admission brought things to a head.

You know, dear friend, that when a Roman judge tries a case in Rome, he is guided simply by the charge, the law and the evidence before the court, and his decision will be determined solely by these factors. But here in the provinces, far away from Rome, we are at war. A man who is in the field of battle is interested only in results, in victory and not justice and the judge is himself on trial. So it was, that even though I well knew that this man was innocent, my duty demanded that I give him the death sentence and so I did. The last time I saw him he was struggling towards Calvary amidst jeers, insults and blows, under the crushing weight of the heavy cross on which he was to die. I have decided to write you this personal letter because I believe that this confession to a friend will at least salve my uneasy conscience.

This in brief is the [story] of Jesus and comment is unnecessary; save to say that Langenhoven wrote the story . . . to arouse the political consciousness of his people in a South Africa where and at a time when, in spite of the formal independence his people enjoyed, the organs of government, including the judiciary, were monopolised by Englishmen. To the Afrikaner, this story may recall unpleasant experiences and open up old wounds, but it belongs to a phase that has passed. To you and I, it raises issues of a contemporary nature. I hope you will find it significant and useful, and trust it will bring you some measure of happiness.

20. FROM A LETTER TO WINNIE MANDELA, DATED 26 OCTOBER 1976, AT THE WOMEN'S JAIL IN JOHANNESBURG, AND TRANSLATED FROM ISIXHOSA INTO ENGLISH BY A PRISON OFFICIAL

I have just read a book by our famous writer about the Karoo and some other areas. It reminded me of the times when I went through those places by air, rail and road. I saw it again on passing through Botswana on my way back from Africa. But of all the deserts I don't think there is one fearful as the Sahara where there are heaps and heaps of extensive masses of sand visible even when in the air. I never saw a single tree nor a patch of grass.

So dry it was in the desert that there was not a drop to quench my thirst. The letters from you and the family are like dew and summer rains and all the national beauty that refreshes the mind and makes one feel confident. Since you were detained I only received one letter from you dated Aug. 22. Up to now I don't know anything about the affairs at home, the person in the house, the paying of rent and telephone account, the maintenance of the children and costs or [if] there is hope that you will be reinstated in your work after release. Before I receive your letter explaining these things I will never be settled . . . As I am writing, the book of that famous author about the desert country is not far from me. The spiritual [drought] has vanished and [been] substituted by the rain that fell as I completed it. Your letter dated 19/9 is just arriving now. As I am speaking, all the springs of life are running. The tributaries are full of clean water, the lakes are full and all the grandeur of nature has returned to normal.

21. FROM A LETTER TO ZINDZI MANDELA,
   DATED 10 FEBRUARY 1980

The other day I was going through the notes I took from <u>Black As I Am</u>.[8] Unfortunately, the actual book is no longer in my possession, and although I can now read the collection a little more carefully, I do not have the advantage of studying each poem with the help of the accompanying photographs. Nevertheless, when I first saw the anthology, I took the necessary precaution that may help me to remember the associated picture whenever I dealt with a particular poem.

---

8. *Black As I Am* was a collection of poems published when Zindzi was sixteen years old and dedicated to her parents.

A Tree Was Chopped Down
By Zindzi Mandela

A tree was chopped down
and the fruit was scattered
I cried
because I had lost a family
the trunk, my father
the branches, his support
so much
the fruit, the wife and children
who meant so much to him
tasty
loving as they should be
all on the ground
the roots, happiness
cut off from him

Reading 'a tree was chopped down' with the picture of the dry tree above it clear in my mind, and with the shanties and mountain range in the background, I was immediately fascinated by the symbolism of contradictions that clearly looms from the lines. It is perhaps this type of contradiction that is inherent in almost every aspect of life. In nature and society these contradictions are in the centre of every phenomenon and can stimulate the urge for serious thinking and real progress.

Without the lines below, the tree would look less than ordinary. Hardly anybody would even notice it. It seems to have been struck by lightning during the stone age and its sap to have been drained by a thousand vampires. If inanimate objects could ever become ghosts, that tree would easily have been one.

Age or disease have destroyed it. It can no longer trap the energy of sunlight nor draw the vital water supplies from the soil below. Its branches and its leaves, its beauty and dignity that once caught the eye of nature lovers and game of all kinds have disappeared. The tree is no more than firewood on roots. It is as barren as an iron-stone and few people will easily believe that at some [time] in the course of its history it could bear fruit.

Yet the metaphor has turned that same dead spectacle into a living object of tremendous meaning, more significant than a young and healthy tree in a fertile and well-watered valley; with a range as wide as that of David's sling of Biblical fame. There must be few things in nature that are so dead and deadly at one and the same time as that wretched looking tree. But in verse it ceases to be an insignificant object in a local area and becomes a household possession, part of world art that helps to cater for the spiritual needs of readers in many countries. The skilful use of the metaphor makes the tree the centre of a conflict that is as old as society itself; the point where two worlds meet: The one that was and the other that is; the symbol of a dream house raised to the ground, of hopes shattered by the actual reality in which we live out our lives.

Good art is invariably universal and timeless and those who read your anthology may see in those lines their own aspirations and experiences. I wonder what conflicts in Mum's thoughts and feelings must have been aroused by the anthology. Happiness and pride must have been galore. But there must be moments when your pen scratches the most tender parts of her body, leaving it quivering with sheer pain and anxiety, all of which would turn her bile ever more bitter.

The chopping down of the tree and the scattering of the fruit will remind her of the loving peach tree that stood next to our bedroom window and its harvest of tasty peaches. Her dreams must have been haunted by the picture of a merciless wood-cutter whose trade is to demolish what nature has created and whose heart is never touched by the lament of a falling tree, the breaking of its branches and the scattering of its fruits.

Children on the ground and out of reach! I immediately think of the late Thembi and the baby Makaziwe I [the first] who succeeded him and who has slept at Croesus [cemetery] for the last 3 decades. I think of you all in the wretchedness in which you have grown and in which you now have to live. But I wonder whether Mum has ever told you of your brother who died before he was born. He was as tiny as your fist when I left you. He nearly killed her.

I still remember one Sunday as the sun was setting. I helped Mum out of bed to the toilet. She was barely 25 then and looked loving and tasty in her young and smooth body that was covered by a pink silk gown. But as we returned to the bedroom she suddenly swayed and almost went down. I noticed that she was also sweating heavily and I discovered that she was more ill than she had revealed. I rushed her to the family doctor and he sent her to Coronation Hospital where she remained for several days. It was her first dreadful experience as a wife [and] the result of the acute tension brought on us by the Treason Trial which lasted more than 4 yrs. 'A tree was chopped down' reminds me of all these harsh experiences.

But a good pen can also remind us of the happiest moments in our lives, bring noble ideas into our dens, our blood and our souls. It can turn tragedy into hope and victory.

22. FROM A LETTER TO WINNIE MANDELA, DATED 26 APRIL 1981

I continue to dream, some pleasant, others not. On the eve of Good Friday you and I were in a cottage on the top of a hill overlooking a deep valley with a big river coursing the edge of a forest. I saw you walk down the slope of the hill not as erect in your bearing as you usually are and with your footsteps less confident. All the time your head was down apparently searching for something a few paces from your feet. You crossed the river and carried away all my love, leaving me rather empty and uneasy. I watched closely as you wandered aimlessly in that forest, keeping close to the river bank. Immediately above you there was a couple which presented a striking contrast. They were obviously in love and concentrating on themselves. The whole universe seemed to be on that spot.

My concern for your safety and pure longing for you drove me down the hill to welcome you back as you recrossed the river on your way back to the cottage. The prospect of joining you in the open air and in such beautiful surroundings evoked fond memories and I looked forward to holding your hand and to a passionate kiss. To my disappointment I lost you in the ravines that cut deep into the valley and I only met you again when I returned to the cottage. This time the place was full of colleagues who deprived us of the privacy. I so wanted to sort out many things. In the last scene you were stretched out on the floor in a corner, sleeping out depression, boredom and fatigue. I knelt down to cover the exposed parts of your body with a blanket. Whenever I have such dreams I often wake up feeling anxious and much concerned, but I immediately become relieved when I discover that it was all but a dream. However, this time my reaction was a mixed one.

23. FROM A LETTER TO AMINA CACHALIA, DATED 3 MAY 1981

Now and again there have been rumours that my health has broken down and that I am on my last legs. The latest of these rumours must have shaken the family and friends. It is true that a treacherous disease may be eating away at the vital organs of the body without the victim becoming aware of it. But up to now I have felt simply tremendous . . .

24. FROM A LETTER TO ZINDZI MANDELA, 1 MARCH 1981

Often as I walk up and down the tiny cell, or as I lie on my bed, the mind wanders far and wide, recalling this episode and that mistake. Among these is the thought whether in my best days outside prison I showed sufficient appreciation for the love and kindness of many of those who befriended and even helped me when I was poor and struggling.

25. FROM A LETTER TO THOROBETSANE TSHUKUDU, DATED 1 JANUARY 1977[9]

Fourteen yrs [years] is a long period in which setbacks and good fortune have gone hand in hand. Beloved ones have aged rapidly as a result of all kinds of physical and spiritual problems too terrible to mention, bonds of affection tend to weaken whilst the idealist recites the maxim: absence makes the heart grow fonder, children grow old and develop outlooks not in line with the wishes of pa and mum. When absent parties eventually return they find [a] strange and unfriendly environment. Dreams and time schedules prove difficult to fulfill and when misfortune strikes fate hardly ever provides golden bridges.

But significant progress is always possible if we ourselves try to plan every detail of our lives and actions and allow the intervention of fate only on our own terms.

26. FROM A LETTER TO WINNIE MANDELA, DATED 9 DECEMBER 1979

Distortions have misled many innocent people because they are weaved around concrete facts and events which those who still have a conscience would never deny. Habits die hard and

---

9. Thorobetsane Tshukudu was a made-up name for Adelaide Tambo (Tshukudu was her maiden name), see People, Places and Events. Mandela didn't want to alert the authorities that he was writing to the Tambos, who were in exile in the UK, and the letter was sent care of Winnie.

they leave their unmistakable marks, the invisible scars that are engraved in our bones and that flow in our blood, that do havoc to the principal actors beyond repair, that may confront their descendants wherever they turn, depriving them of the dignity, cleanliness and happiness that should have been theirs. Such scars portray people as they are and bring out into the full glare of public scrutiny the embarrassing contradictions in which individuals live out their lives. Such contradictions are in turn the mirror which gives a faithful representation of those affected and proclaim 'whatever my ideals in life, this is what I am'.

Our life has its own built-in safeguards and compensations. We are told that a saint is a sinner who keeps on trying to be clean. One may be a villain for ¾ of his life and be canonised because he lived a holy life for the remaining ¼ of that life. In real life we deal, not with gods, but with ordinary humans like ourselves: men and women who are full of contradictions, who are stable and fickle, strong and weak, famous and infamous, people in whose bloodstream the muckworm battles daily with potent pesticides. On which aspect one concentrates in judging others will depend on the character of the particular judge. As we judge others so we are judged by others. The suspicious will always be tormented by suspicion, the credulous will ever be ready to lap up everything from oo-thobela sikutyele,[10] while the vindictive will use the sharp axe instead of the soft feather duster. But the realist, however shocked and disappointed by the frailties of those he adores, will look at human behaviour from all sides and objectively and will concentrate on those qualities in a person which are edifying, which lift your spirit [and] kindle one's enthusiasm to live.

----

10. *Oo-thobela sikutyele* is an isiXhosa phrase meaning one who takes advantage of you if you are vulnerable or gullible.

As you know, I was baptised in the Methodist Church and was educated in Wesleyan schools – Clarkebury, Healdtown and at Fort Hare. I stayed at Wesley House. At Fort Hare I even became a Sunday School teacher. Even here I attend all church services and have enjoyed some of the sermons . . . I have my own beliefs as to the existence or non-existence of a Supreme Being and it is possible that one could easily explain why mankind has from time immemorial believed in the existence of a god.

I'm sure you know that so-called European civilization was largely influenced by the ancient civilization of the Greeks and the Romans. Yet despite their advanced scientific knowledge in many fields, the Greeks had no less than 14 gods. You have heard of the names of some of them – Apollo, Atlas, Cupid, Jupiter, Mars, Neptune, Zeus, etc. A poll was recently taken in England to find out the number of people who believed in god and, if I remember my facts correctly, less than 30 per cent of the total population were found to be believers. I'm making no comment on the matter one way or the other except to say that, from experience, it's far better, darling, to keep religious beliefs to yourself. You may unconsciously offend a lot of people by trying to sell them ideas they regard as unscientific and pure fiction.

28. FROM A LETTER TO ZINDZI MANDELA, DATED 25 MARCH 1979

About the same time a priest told us about a Nepalese who had powers similar to those of the son of Satan. According to the priest, the Nepalese killed cats, dogs and pigs just by looking at their eyes. He also claimed that he could dispose of human beings with equal ease. The priest also told us that a Christian Minister in that country informed the Nepalese that the power of God was greater than evil in man's heart. He then challenged the Nepalese to a trial of strength. The story goes on that on an appointed day the Minister and his elders confronted the Asian and also beseeched the Almighty to give them strength to demonstrate the superiority of the Xian [Christian] faith. The outcome was the conversion of the Nepalese to Xianity [Christianity].

My one difficulty about that sermon is that I don't like miracles that always occur in distant lands; especially if they are not capable of scientific explanation. This tale is difficult to believe even though told from the pulpit. However, if it is intended to depict [the battle] of good against evil, of justice over cruelty, then we accept the symbolism.

29. FROM A LETTER TO PRINCESS ZENANI LA MANDELA DLAMINI, DATED 25 MARCH 1979[11]

But the habit of attending to small things and of appreciating small courtesies is one of the important marks of a good person.

30. FROM A CONVERSATION WITH RICHARD STENGEL ABOUT WHETHER BLACK CONSCIOUSNESS PRISONERS ON ROBBEN ISLAND FELT THE ANC (AFRICAN NATIONAL CONGRESS) PRISONERS WERE TOO MODERATE[12]

No, I don't think so, but quite a number of them joined us, and people had wrong conceptions about the ANC, because the first thing a politician does is to be aggressive towards the enemy. But that is all right, may be all right, but you want to educate people and to convert them to your point of view, and we did that with the warders in prison. And you can't do that by being aggressive. By being aggressive you drive them away,

---

11. Zenani (Zeni) Mandela, see People, Places and Events. Married Prince Thumbumuzi (Muzi) Dlamini, a son of King Sobhuza of Swaziland, in 1977.
12. The Black Consciousness Movement was an anti-apartheid movement targeting black youth and workers, see People, Places and Events.

and you make them fight back too, whereas a softer approach, especially when you are confident of a case, brings about results far more than aggression.

31. CONVERSATION WITH RICHARD STENGEL

STENGEL: Over the weekend you told a parable, a parable of the sun and the wind?

MANDELA: Oh, I see, yes.

STENGEL: I thought that was a very lovely story and I thought that maybe we could use it somewhere in the book.

MANDELA: Yes.

STENGEL: Could you retell it right now?

MANDELA: Yes, what was important is to make sure that the message of peace went down deeply in the thinking and approach of our people . . . I was . . . contrasting the strength of peace over and above that of force and I told the incident . . . of an argument between the sun and the wind, that the sun said, 'I'm stronger than you are' and the wind says, 'No, I'm stronger than you are.' And they decided, therefore, to test their strength with a traveller . . . who was wearing a blanket. And they agreed that the one who would succeed in getting the traveller to get rid of his blanket would be the stronger. So the wind started. It started *blowing* and the *harder* it blew, the *tighter* the traveller pulled the blanket around his body. And the wind blew and blew but it could not get him to discard the blanket. And, as I said, the *harder* the wind blew, the *tighter* the visitor tried to hold the blanket around his body. And the wind eventually gave up. Then the sun started with its rays, very mild, and they increased in strength and as they increased . . . the traveller felt that the blanket was unnecessary because the blanket is for warmth. And so he decided to relax it, to loosen it, but the rays of the sun became stronger and stronger and eventually he threw it away. So by a gentle method it was possible to get the traveller to discard his blanket. And this is the parable that through peace you will be able to convert, you see, the most determined people, the most committed to the question of violence, and that is the method we should follow.

CHAPTER TEN

Tactics

'The ideals we cherish, our fondest dreams and fervent hopes may not be realised in our lifetime. But that is besides the point. The knowledge that in your day you did your duty, and lived up to the expectations of your fellow men is in itself a rewarding experience and magnificent achievement.'

....

From a letter to Sheena Duncan, dated 1 April 1985, see page 243.

1. FROM A LETTER TO THE REV FRANK CHIKANE,
   DATED 21 AUGUST 1989[1]

Victory in a great cause is measured not only by reaching the final goal. It is also a triumph to live up to expectations in your lifetime.

2. FROM A LETTER TO SHEENA DUNCAN, DATED 1 APRIL 1985[2]

The ideals we cherish, our fondest dreams and fervent hopes may not be realised in our lifetime. But that is besides the point. The knowledge that in your day you did your duty, and lived up to the expectations of your fellow men is in itself a rewarding experience and magnificent achievement.

3. FROM A LETTER TO PROFESSOR SAMUEL DASH,
   DATED 12 MAY 1986[3]

You cannot unlock the gates of this prison so that I can walk out as a free man, nor can you improve the conditions under which I have to live. But your visit has certainly made it easy for me to bear all the grimness that has surrounded me over the past 22 years.

4. FROM HIS UNPUBLISHED AUTOBIOGRAPHICAL MANUSCRIPT
   WRITTEN IN PRISON

I am also aware that massive efforts have been made here and abroad for my release and that of other political prisoners, a campaign which has given us much inspiration and shown us that we have hundreds of thousands of friends. Next to my

<hr>

1. Frank Chikane (1951–). Cleric, anti-apartheid activist, writer and public servant. Member of the ANC.
2. Sheena Duncan (1932–2010). Anti-apartheid activist. Leader of Black Sash, a white women's anti-apartheid organisation. Mandela wrote this letter to her on the thirtieth anniversary of the founding of Black Sash.
3. Samuel Dash (1925–2004). Board member of the League of International Human Rights. Chief counsel to the Senate Watergate Committee. Dash was the first American to interview Mandela in prison, in 1985.

wife's affection and that of the family as a whole, few things have inspired me more than the knowledge that in spite of all that the enemy is doing to isolate and discredit us people everywhere never forget us. But we know the enemy very well – they would like to release us from a position of strength and not of weakness and this is an opportunity they have missed forever. However inspiring it is to know that our friends are insisting on our release, a realistic approach clearly shows that we must rule out completely the possibility that such a demand will succeed. But I am highly optimistic, even behind prison walls I can see the heavy clouds and the blue sky over the horizon, that however wrong our calculations have been and whatever difficulties we still must face, that in my lifetime I shall step out into the sunshine, walk with firm feet because that event will be brought about by the strength of my organisation and the sheer determination of our people.

5.   FROM A LETTER TO HILDA BERNSTEIN, DATED 8 JULY 1985

Talking about progress, the mind goes back to '62 when I listened to the experiences of Ben Bella's colleagues, which were very informative.[4] In some of these discussions I faced youngsters, some barely in their twenties, but who spoke as veterans and with authority on vital issues on which, to say the least, I was a mere amateur. I almost blushed with shame and asked myself why we were so far behind in this regard. But now things have changed, and it is a source of inspiration to know that SA [South Africa] is producing determined young people whose level of awareness is remarkably high. If your knees are becoming stiff, your eyes dim and your head is full of silver, you must take comfort in the knowledge that your own contribution is an important factor in this ferment.

....

4.   Mandela is referring to his military training in Morocco in 1962.

6. FROM A LETTER TO LORD NICHOLAS BETHELL,
    DATED 4 JUNE 1986[5]

But I must say that it is a matter of grave concern to sit on the sidelines and be a mere spectator in the tragic turmoil that is tearing our country apart, and that is generating such dangerous passions. It may well be that the days when nations will turn mighty armies into powerful peace movements, and deadly weapons into harmless ploughshares are still years away. But it is a source of real hope that there are today world organisations, governments, heads of state, influential groups and individuals who are striving earnestly and courageously for world peace.

7. FROM A LETTER TO HILDA BERNSTEIN, DATED 8 JULY 1985

The mind keeps on churning out these and other long-forgotten events, some involving close friends who are no more. It disturbs us that in most of these cases it was not possible for us to pay our last respects to them, or even to send messages of sympathy to their beloved ones – Moses and Bram, Michael and JB, Duma and Jack, Molly and Lilian, MP and Julian, George and Yusuf. The list is very long and I cannot hope to exhaust it here. But the brutal manner in which Ruth [First] died shocked and embittered us beyond words and, almost three years since that tragic event, the wounds have not completely healed. As you will readily concede, few of her friends were not at one time or other bruised by her sharp tongue. But none will deny that she was a fully committed and highly capable person whose death was a severe setback to us all.

---

5. Lord Nicholas Bethell (1938–2007). British politician, historian and human rights activist. Member of both the European parliament and assembly. He interviewed Mandela at Pollsmoor Prison in 1985.

8. CONVERSATION WITH RICHARD STENGEL ABOUT WHEN HE
RETURNED TO PRISON AFTER HIS PROSTATE OPERATION IN
NOVEMBER 1985

STENGEL: So were you surprised when they took you to that cell by yourself?

MANDELA: No . . . the Commanding Officer was then Brigadier Munro, he came to fetch me, and along the way from the hospital to the jail he said, 'No we are not taking you back to your friends now, to your colleagues.[6] You are going to stay alone.' I said, 'Why?' He said, 'I don't know, I've just been given those instructions from the head office.'

STENGEL: But you had not asked to be [transferred]?

MANDELA: No, no, no, oh no. I had not asked, but of course *once* they did that, I decided that I was going to *use* it to start negotiations and because it would be a *sensitive* affair . . . The propaganda of the government in the elections has always been that 'We will never talk to the ANC [African National Congress]' . . . It's a terrorist organisation of people who are bent on murder and destruction of property. So to make a move, the element of confidentiality had to be there, and when I was staying alone I could maintain that element of confidentiality. And so although I *missed* my friends, and I didn't want to be separated from them, I then decided that . . . I was going to use that opportunity and that's what I did. And I told my colleagues that we should make no issue about this matter. I didn't tell them of course that I was going to use it. *If* I had told my friends that I was going to use it for the purpose of starting negotiations, we would not have been negotiating now. They would have *rejected* it. So what I decided to do was to start negotiations *without* telling them, and then confront them with a *fait accompli*.

....

6. Mandela had been sharing a communal cell with Walter Sisulu, Raymond Mhlaba, Andrew Mlangeni and Ahmed Kathrada.

the deepening political crisis in our country has been a matter of grave concern to me for quite some time, and I now consider it necessary in the national interest for the African National Congress and the Government to meet urgently to negotiate an effective political settlement.

At the outset I must point out that I make this move without consultation with the ANC. I am a loyal and disciplined member of the ANC, and my political loyalty is owed primarily, if not exclusively, to this organisation and, in particular, to our Lusaka headquarters where the official leadership is stationed, and from where our affairs are directed.

In the normal course of events I would put my views to the organisation first, and if these views were accepted, the organisation would then decide on who were the best qualified members to handle the matter on its behalf, and on exactly when to make the move. But in my current circumstances I cannot follow this course, and this is the only reason why I am acting on my own initiative, in the hope that the organisation will, in due course, endorse my action.

I must stress that no prisoner, irrespective of his status or influence, can conduct negotiations of this nature from prison. In our special situation negotiation on political matters is literally a matter of life and death which requires to be handled by the organisation itself through its appointed representatives. The step I am taking should, therefore, not be seen as the beginning of actual negotiations between the Government and the ANC. My task is a very limited one, and that is to bring the country's two major political bodies to the negotiating table.

I must further point out that the question of my release from prison is not an issue at least at this stage of the discussions, and I am certainly not asking to be freed. But I do hope that the Government will, as soon as possible, give me the opportunity from my present quarters to sound the views of my colleagues, inside and outside the country, on this move. Only if this initiative is formally endorsed by the ANC will it have any significance.

I will touch presently on some of the problems which seem to constitute an obstacle to a meeting between the ANC and the Government. But I must emphasise right at this stage that this step is not a response to the call by the Government on ANC leaders to declare whether or not they are nationalists,
/ and to...

Handwritten draft of a letter proposing talks between the ANC and the government, c.1985.

My comrades in prison were men of honesty and principle. Bearing in mind how some revolutionaries elsewhere in the world had betrayed [the] struggle on the eve of victory or soon thereafter, they were suspicious of individual initiative. If my comrades had known beforehand about my plan to talk to the government, their concern about one man who was isolated from them doing so would have been understandable. The headquarters of the organisation [African National Congress] was in Zambia where the leaders who conducted the struggle were stationed. Only they . . . knew the strategic moment to make the move. The ANC never deviated from the principle that liberation of our country would ultimately be brought about through dialogue and negotiation.

Nevertheless I approached the government without even telling my fellow prisoners. It was during these talks that Dr Niël Barnard, head of the apartheid Intelligence Service, proposed that their team had decided to start confidential discussions with Thabo Mbeki, adding that from their sources, he was one person who was in favour of negotiations.[7]

I objected to this proposal on the ground that such talks could never be secret, seeing that they would take place in a foreign country, I pointed out that they should contact the President or the Secretary General of the ANC, Oliver Tambo or Alfred Nzo respectively.[8] I added that to start such unauthorized talks might ruin the future of a talented young man's political career. I thought that Barnard had accepted my advice.

I was therefore shocked when I later discovered that Barnard had ignored my advice and contacted Thabo Mbeki.

....

7. Dr Lukas (Niël) Barnard, see People, Places and Events. Thabo Mbeki, see People, Places and Events.
8. Alfred Baphetuxolo Nzo, see People, Places and Events.

But the latter was wise enough and refused to engage in clandestine talks without the consent of the organisation. He reported to the President who authorized him and his friend, Jacob Zuma, to meet Barnard.[9]

10. CONVERSATION WITH RICHARD STENGEL ON THE TALKS ABOUT TALKS IN THE 1980S[10]

STENGEL: And you kept telling them that the armed struggle is one in reaction to what the government had initially done, and that since there was no room for peaceful or constitutional protest that was left.

MANDELA: Yes.

STENGEL: What was their response to that?

MANDELA: Well, they couldn't answer that question, of course. At first they adopted the normal attitude that violence is just criminal action which they could not tolerate. And the point I was making was that the *means* which are used by the oppressed to advance their struggle are determined by the oppressor himself. Where the oppressor uses peaceful methods, the oppressed will *also* use peaceful methods, but if the oppressor uses force the oppressed will also retaliate in force. That was my argument . . . But a *question* which they raised, which I felt was very reasonable . . . was 'We have been throughout the year making public statements that we will never negotiate with ANC [African National Congress]; *now* you say we should negotiate. We are going to lose *credibility* with our people. How do we overcome that? We can talk to you and perhaps our people can accept that, but we can't talk to the ANC as such because it would be a complete *radical*

---

9. Jacob Gedleyihlekisa Zuma (1942–). President of South Africa (2009–).
10. Mandela wrote to Minister of Justice Kobie Coetsee in 1985, to request a meeting to begin discussing the possibility of talks between the government and the ANC.

departure from the policy that we have put forward before. We will *lose* credibility.' That is the question that they asked.

And I found it a bit difficult to *meet* that question, and *I* said to them, '*You* have been applying apartheid. You have said blacks should be taken back, you know, to the countryside. You have changed that now. You had the pass system as, what-you-call, one of your major policies, and you have repealed the pass laws. You have not lost credibility . . . The question of negotiations must be looked at from that point of view. You must be able to tell your people that there can be no solution [to] this question without the ANC.' That was my approach. But it was a difficult question to answer because it was true.

STENGEL: So, and the other issues that they wanted to discuss with you, was also the issue of group rights: how can we protect the interest of the white minority?

MANDELA: Yes, Yes.

STENGEL: What did you explain to them about that during those discussions? . . .

MANDELA: I referred them to my article in 1956, in a journal called *Liberation*, where I wrote . . . [that] the Freedom Charter is not a blueprint for socialism.[11] In so far as Africans are concerned, it is actually a blueprint for capitalism because Africans would have . . . the opportunity, which they have *never* had before, of owning property wherever they want, and capitalism will flourish amongst them as never before. *That* was the theme I put forward.

---

11. The Freedom Charter, see People, Places and Events.

11. CONVERSATION WTH RICHARD STENGEL ABOUT
   CONSTANTIABERG MEDI-CLINIC, WHERE HE WAS TREATED
   FOR TUBERCULOSIS

STENGEL: What was Constantiaberg like?

MANDELA: Oh, very good. In fact, the first day I was taken there, Kobie Coetsee came to see me *very* early in the morning and then they brought my breakfast. The first day I arrived, they didn't know the diet that was prescribed for me . . . a cholesterol-free diet, which meant I should take no eggs, no bacon. But this particular morning they brought two eggs and a lot of bacon and then cereal, [*chuckles*] and then the *Major*, who was in charge of me in [Pollsmoor Prison] said, 'No, Mandela, you can't eat this food – it's against the instruction of the doctor.' I said, 'Today I am prepared to die; I am going to eat it.' [*laughs*] Yes, I hadn't had eggs and bacon for a *long* time.

12. CONVERSATION WITH RICHARD STENGEL ABOUT HIS MOVE
   FROM CONSTANTIABERG MEDI-CLINIC TO VICTOR VERSTER
   PRISON IN DECEMBER 1988

MANDELA: I [was] already used to the habits of warders . . . And [on] this particular occasion I could *see* [from] the move-ment that *something* was going to happen, there was something extraordinary . . . The Major, who was in charge, was very tense and quite *irritable*, and there were a lot of consultations amongst the warders and there was *vigilance* in preventing anybody from coming into my ward, allowing only . . . the nurse that was supposed to be on duty . . . and I could see something was afoot but I didn't know what it was. Eventually, in the evening, the Major came in and said, 'Mandela, prepare yourself. We are taking you to Paarl.'[12] And I said, 'What for?'

---

12. Victor Verster Prison is located between Paarl and Franschhoek in the Western Cape, see People, Places and Events.

He says, 'Well, that is where you are going to be now.' And at nine o'clock we left with a big escort . . . It was dark when we arrived and we went into this big bedroom . . . but it had a lot of insects. Of course . . . I'm used to insects because that is a *wild* place, wild in the sense of liking it, you know? If you like nature, you will be *happy* in that place. But it had a *lot* of insects, some I had never seen before – a wide variety, rich variety of insects, and . . . centipedes, you see, that move around . . . I had a lot of those things.

STENGEL: In your bedroom?

MANDELA: Yes, in the bedroom . . . mostly in the bedroom. And in the morning I would sweep them out, and there were also mosquitoes. But I slept very nicely. *Then* the following day in the afternoon, Kobie Coetsee, the minister of justice, came and . . . wanted to know how this building was – the house – [and] went from [room] to [room] inspecting it. We went outside inspecting the security walls, and he says, 'No, these security walls must be raised' . . . He was very careful and he . . . wanted to make sure that . . . I was comfortable, and he also brought me some nice, *very* expensive wines . . . He was *very* kind, very gentle, and then he told me . . . 'No, we'll move you here. This is a stage between prison and release. We are doing so because we hope you'll appreciate it. We want to introduce some confidentiality in the discussions between ourselves and yourself.' And I appreciated that. That's what happened.

STENGEL: And did you feel in between being free and being in prison when you were there? . . .

MANDELA: Well, one felt it, because what they did was to fence the place apart from the security wall, and [made it so] that there was *plenty* of [space for] movement; I could move . . . in the area, on the grounds. The warder, who was doing the catering for me, Warrant Officer Swart,[13] would come at 7 a.m. and leave at 4 [p.m.]. No keys. I could stay outside as long as I want. And then when he [left] for his house, there would be warders on guard duty for the night, and I had a swimming pool . . . And so I was very relaxed in this area. The only thing was that I was surrounded by barbed . . . wire and a security wall; otherwise I was free . . .

[Swart] was prepared to cook *and* wash the dishes. But . . . I took it upon myself, to break the tension and a possible resentment on his part that he has to serve a prisoner by cooking and then washing dishes, and I offered to wash dishes and he refused . . . He says that is his work. I said, 'No, we must share it.' Although he insisted, and he was genuine, but I *forced* him, literally forced him, to allow me to do the dishes, and we established a *very* good relationship . . . A *really* nice chap, Warder Swart, a *very* good friend of mine . . . In fact, man, just give – just give me a plain sheet of paper because I must phone the commissioner of prisons and just phone him again, man.

13. FROM A CONVERSATION WITH RICHARD STENGEL ABOUT WHAT HE LEARNED IN PRISON

I am not in a position to identify any single factor which I can say impressed me, but firstly there *was* the policy of the government which was ruthless and very brutal and you have to go to jail to discover what the real policy of a government is . . . behind bars . . . But at the same time one immediately discovers that not all warders are beasts. Of course that is the main policy and the average warder is a brutal man, but nevertheless there were good fellows, human beings, and who treated us *very* well and who tried within the regulations and

13. Jack Swart was a prison warder who cooked for Mandela at Victor Verster Prison.

sometimes a little . . . outside the regulations, outside the regulations, who tried to make us feel at home.

And then there was the question of the *militancy* of the prisoners. One would have expected with the *harsh* conditions that existed, especially in the sixties . . . our people, you know, to be cowed down. Not at all, they fought right from the beginning, and some of the people who led those fights were . . . hardly known, who are still hardly known even today . . . And you found, you know, the *resistance*, the ability of the human spirit to resist injustice *right* inside prison. And . . . you learn that you don't have to have a degree to have the qualities of a leader, the qualities of a man who wants to fight injustice wherever he is . . . There were many men who could take a . . . militant stand . . . who would prefer punishment and even assault, rather than to give in . . . In the section in which we were, you had people who were literate, widely read, travelled overseas, and it was a pleasure to speak to them . . . When you sat down and had a discussion with them you felt that you had learned a lot.

14. FROM A CONVERSATION WITH RICHARD STENGEL ABOUT THE POLICE'S HARASSMENT OF WINNIE MANDELA

They had been harassing Comrade Winnie for the twenty-seven years I had been away, [and] what I criticised was the *element* of propaganda and publicity they gave to it . . . [When] Comrade Winnie . . . landed in Jan Smuts [International Airport] after seeing me, there was an unusually large press corps and they asked questions relating to the case, and then Comrade [Winnie] got into the car . . . and drove to Orlando. She had a bus which accommodated some of [her] supporters. *Along* the way to Soweto the police *stopped* . . . the bus, searched it and seized it. Now that was unnecessary. It was just a way of giving publicity to the country and the world . . . They could have . . . quietly and in a dignified way investigated and even [taken] the bus if they thought it was their duty to seize it . . . But they didn't do that . . . Secondly . . . when they . . . went to raid . . . the house they brought the SABC [South African Broadcasting Corporation], and the *whole* raid was shown [on television]. It was about 3 a.m . . . and my wife was shown there in [her] nightgown and my daughter . . . Some of the chaps were stripped naked in the back rooms . . . So there was a great deal of publicity. It was no longer just a police investigation, it was a propaganda affair. And that is what I criticised.

15. FROM A LETTER TO CHIEF MANGOSUTHU BUTHELEZI, DATED 3 FEBRUARY 1989

One of the most challenging tasks facing the leadership today is that of national unity. At no other time in the history of the liberation movement has it been so crucial for our people to speak with one voice, and for freedom fighters to pool their efforts. Any act or statement, from whatever source, which tends to create or worsen divisions is, in the existing political situation, a fatal error which ought to be avoided at all costs . . . The struggle is our life and, even though the moment of victory may not be at hand, we can nevertheless make that struggle immensely enriching or absolutely disastrous. In my entire political career few things [have] distressed me as to see our people killing one another as is now happening.[14]

---

14. Members of the ANC and the Inkatha Freedom Party (IFP) were engaged in a deadly battle for supremacy in parts of the country.

16. CONVERSATION WITH AHMED KATHRADA ON WHETHER
HE HAD ENDORSED A SPEECH BY WINNIE MANDELA ABOUT
'NECKLACING' – BURNING PEOPLE ALIVE BY LIGHTING
PETROL-SOAKED TYRES AROUND THEIR NECKS

KATHRADA: You see there is this question of you . . . where you are supposed to have approved of the 'necklace speech' of Winnie.

MANDELA: Gee whiz.

KATHRADA: . . . Anthony Sampson has . . . sent me a transcript of a conversation . . . Now we don't know who made these notes . . .[15] 'NM approved of WM's necklace speech. He said that it was a *good* thing as there has not been one black person who has attacked WM. He however had some reservations on WM's attack on Rex Gibson of the *Star* because Gibson had published a powerful defence on the speech a few days earlier' . . .

MANDELA: I expressly condemned the thing.

KATHRADA: [Sampson] says, 'Regarding the contentious matter of Madiba's alleged comments on Winnie's "necklace speech" I thought you should see the document in which my remarks are based since this is apparently authentic and is in a public archive. I do not think I can ignore it, *but*, of course, I can state that the president firmly contradicts it. But it would be useful to explain or speculate how this misunderstanding came about.'

MANDELA: But how can he not take us into trust? Who is it that kept these archives? . . . There is nothing of the sort. I condemned the thing *unreservedly* . . .

KATHRADA: . . . I have also done it . . .

MANDELA: Absolutely untrue.

---

15. The notes were made by Mandela's lawyer, Ismail Ayob, and were located in the ANC archives at the University of Fort Hare.

17. CONVERSATION WITH RICHARD STENGEL ABOUT STUDYING
    IN PRISON

STENGEL: Was that enjoyable in prison, to be studying law, or did it seem distant from what you were going through at the time? Or distant from the struggle?

MANDELA: No, it *was*. Law – I'm very much interested in law. But I was *too* busy on Robben Island. I made no progress *whatsoever* in studying. First year I was all right, second year I was all right, but the final year, I just didn't have proper time to study because of the political problems, and I think I failed three times, the final. It is only . . . when I went to Pollsmoor [Prison] that I got a chance of . . . concentrating, especially when I was alone. Then I knew, right from the beginning, that I would pass. But apart from that, you know, I abandoned – I literally abandoned it.

18. FROM A CONVERSATION WITH RICHARD STENGEL

In the ANC [African National Congress], in addressing any particular problem, we normally start from opposite poles and debate the matter thoroughly . . . then reach a consensus which makes our decisions very strong. Generally speaking, on the island, Comrade [Harry] Gwala led one group with a particular approach and . . . because of his knowledge, his ability, his experience, he was able to influence a large number of our comrades.[16] But on almost every issue we eventually reach a consensus. And we were grateful for the fact that we had looked at the matter from *all* angles . . . On the question, for example, [of] the relationship between the ANC and the [Communist] Party, he was inclined to *blur* the distinction, and many of our debates were due to that fact. That whereas some of us wanted

---

16. Harry (Mphephethe) Themba Gwala (1920–95). Teacher, politician and political prisoner. Member of the SACP. Member of MK.

to keep the difference very wide, very clear, he tended to blur it. And there was perhaps some reason for that in prison because we wanted to speak with one voice. But still, it was not an accurate approach because the Party and the ANC have *always* been totally different even though they cooperated.

19. FROM A CONVERSATION WITH RICHARD STENGEL

Well, I used to like reading, as you know, during those days, before I was really busy . . . It was one of the things I miss now, you know, which I enjoyed in prison . . . I could wake up, have a bath, wait for the hospital doctor . . . then have breakfast, *then* I was . . . free to sit down and study . . . That what-you-call scene of Kutozov [in *War and Peace*], discussing whether they should defend Moscow or not, that was beautiful. When *everybody* was saying we *cannot* abandon the capital, his concern was that . . . the Russian army should be saved for winter because . . . Napoleon's army would never be able to meet the Russian army during winter . . . 'I'm not concerned with buildings; that's just emotion. I'm concerned with saving my army from destruction.' And that was the attitude of [Zulu king] Shaka, too.[17] Shaka, when fighting . . . retreated against an attack by one of the tribes, and when they came to the Royal Kraal, then . . . his counsellors said, 'No, let's now resist; let's stand.' He says, 'Why should I defend buildings? . . . Buildings can be destroyed today and built tomorrow, but an army which is destroyed, it will take years to build.' . . . [He] retreated, but made sure that along the way there was not a single morsel of food which the enemy could get – drove away their stock, carried away their mealies [maize] and millet, beans and so on. Made sure that there was no food at all. *Then* . . . this enemy

17. Shaka ka Senzangakhona (1787–1828). King of the Zulus, 1816–28.

army got tired and hungry . . . When they were retreating, he followed them – *very* close – and then . . . the enemy would stand . . . wanting a conflict to finish the threat. But he wouldn't, he wouldn't attack. When they stood he would stop and when they advanced he would retreat.

But eventually the enemy withdrew. They were now hungry, and when they slept . . . [Shaka] sent [his] men to mix amongst them because the uniform was the same . . . and at dead of night Shaka's men would *stab* the chap next to him and then cry, you know, and you say . . . the wizard: 'Umthakathi's attacking me,' *and* everybody gets up, you see? So they didn't sleep; he kept them awake and preparing to attack them when they are tired, you know, hungry, you know? So that went on, you see . . . until they reached . . . a big river where . . . there was one crossing and . . . the enemy had to break its ranks, in order to cross. When *half* of them had crossed, he then *charged*, and attacked them and wiped them out . . . then crossed, to wipe out the remainder. So he had tactics, you see, like those of Kutuzov against Napoleon.

20. CONVERSATION WITH AHMED KATHRADA

MANDELA: I could have made a lot of money when I was in Victor Verster. You know, two newspapers, totally different . . .
KATHRADA: Ah.
MANDELA: . . . came to take a picture of me and one promised me half a million.
KATHRADA: That appeared in the papers.
MANDELA: Is that so?
KATHRADA: No, no, wait a bit or was [Warder Christo] Brand telling me? But I knew of that.
MANDELA: *Half* a million!
KATHRADA: Ja. Oh ja. No, Brand told us.

MANDELA: So I say, 'No, I wouldn't agree to that thing.'

KATHRADA: Ja.

MANDELA: I said no.

KATHRADA: But wasn't that while you were in the clinic [Constantiaberg Medi-Clinic]?

MANDELA: Hey?

KATHRADA: Wasn't it while you were in the clinic?

MANDELA: The *other* one was while I was in the clinic.

KATHRADA: Ja.

MANDELA: But the other one was at Victor Verster. I say, 'Look man, I'm negotiating, and for *these* people to see that I've abused my position here . . .

KATHRADA: Ah.

MANDELA: . . . it would destroy my credibility. I can't do that.' They say, 'Half a million rand.'

KATHRADA: Ja.

MANDELA: . . . As poor as I am with children and grandchildren, you know?

KATHRDA: Ah.

MANDELA: And I didn't want to think because I thought if I stopped and [thought] I would be tempted.

KATHRADA: Ja.

MANDELA: And I said, 'No, no, no.' I didn't want, I don't want [it] at all, and I became abrupt and loud, you see, because I thought also there was, you know, the bugging instruments.

KATHRADA: Ja.

MANDELA: Because we were inside the . . . building, in the lounge.

KATHRADA: Ah.

MANDELA: And I said, 'No, no, no, no, no. I don't want to consider that. I'm negotiating, you see. Perhaps if, some other time if I was not engaged in negotiations, I could think about it. Not now!' And I was *very* abrupt.

KATHRADA: Ah.

MANDELA: Then they said, 'Well, what about 750,000?' I said, 'You can give me 750 *million*.'

KATHRADA: Ah.

MANDELA: I won't take it. So I just turned it down. And *then* when I was at the, what-you-call, at the clinic, *another* one. This one was a million.

KATHRADA: Ja. That was *Time* magazine, I think.

MANDELA: Ah, I think you're right.

KATHRADA: Ja.

MANDELA: Yes. So I refused, and poor, you know, to be poor is a terrible thing.

KATHRADA: No, I have also written about that when you suffer deprivation in jail.

MANDELA: Yes.

KATHRADA: You are tempted . . .

MANDELA: That's right.

KATHRADA: . . . by *many* things.

MANDELA: Absolutely.

KATHRADA: Ja.

MANDELA: Absolutely. Even, you know, outside, you know, just have to *get* the habit, you know, of going to *report* to your fellows, when you have been offered something.

21. FROM A LETTER TO NURSE SISTER SHAUNA BRADLEY, DATED 21 AUGUST 1989[18]

One morning I listened to a radio sermon in which the preacher was giving advice on how to face problems. He pointed out that troubles are always of a temporary nature and that, depending on a person's approach, they are often followed by happier moments.

---

18. Shauna Bradley was a nurse at Constantiaberg Medi-Clinic.

STENGEL: People say, 'Nelson Mandela's great problem is that he's too willing to see the good in other people.' How do you respond to that?

MANDELA: Well that's what many people say. That has been said right from my adolescence and I don't know . . . There may be an element of truth in that. But when you are a public figure you have to accept the integrity of other people until there is evidence to the contrary. And when you have no evidence to the contrary, and people do things which appear to be good, what reason have you got to suspect them? To say that they are doing good because they have got an ulterior motive? It is until that evidence comes out that you then either deal with that point, with that instance of infidelity, and forget about it. Because that's how you can get on in life with people. You have to recognise that people are produced by the mud in the society in which you live and that therefore they are human beings. They have got good points, they have got weak points. Your duty is to work with human beings as human beings, not because you think they are angels. And, therefore, once you know that this man has got this virtue and he has got this weakness you work with them and you accommodate that weakness and you try and help him to overcome that weakness. I don't want to be frightened by the fact that a person has made certain mistakes and he has got human frailties. I can't allow myself to be influenced by that. And that is why many people criticise [me].

And then in a position which I hold, your main task is to keep different factions together and therefore you must listen very carefully when somebody comes to explain a problem to you, the difficulty of working with others. But you, at the same time, you must, whilst listening and addressing that problem, realise that the *dominating* factor is that you must keep the organisation together. You can't divide the organisation. People must be able to come to you . . . so that you can exercise the role of keeping the organisation together.

23. FROM A CONVERSATION WITH RICHARD STENGEL

People will feel I see too much good in people. So it's a criticism I have to put up with and I've tried to adjust to, because whether it is so or not, it is something which I think is profitable. It's a good thing to assume, to act on the basis that . . . others are men of integrity and honour . . . because you tend to attract integrity and honour if that is how you regard those with whom you work. And one has made a great deal of progress in developing personal relationships because you [make] the basic assumption . . . that those you deal with are men of integrity. I believe in that.

CHAPTER ELEVEN

Calendar Time

An entry from a desk calendar in which Mandela notes that on 21 July 1976 there was a 'Raid'.

Mandela kept a series of desk calendars on Robben Island and in Pollsmoor and Victor Verster prisons, which run from 1976 to 1989. Together with the notebooks, they are the most direct and unmediated records of his private thoughts and everyday experiences. He did not make entries every day. In fact, there are sometimes weeks where he made none at all, which explains some of the gaps in dates that appear in the selection that makes up chapter 11. Of the entries that do exist, the most important and most interesting have been brought together in this chapter. Even though these entries represent a small percentage of the total, the overall tenor of the calendars has not been altered substantially. The inclusion of some entries may seem strange. It should be borne in mind, however, that taken-for-granted necessities in the outside world were actually precious luxuries in prison. Milk for tea, for example, was an event. So, too, were visits and letters. And the single word 'Raid' masks a deeper menace.

....

18 AUGUST 1976

Received information on arrest of Zami.

C.O. [Commanding Officer] denies that birthday card came

23 AUGUST 1976

Informed by W/O [Warrant Officer] Barnard that birthday card withheld

8 DECEMBER 1976

Begin reading 'Bury my heart' Dee Brown: sent letter U[niversity of] London[1]

....

1. *Bury My Heart at Wounded Knee*, Dee Brown (published 1970).

23 DECEMBER 1976

Zindzi's birthday

17 JANUARY 1977

Gossiping about others is certainly a vice, a virtue when about oneself.

20 JANUARY 1977

Dreamt of Kgatho falling into ditch and injuring leg

21 FEBRUARY 1977

Raid by approximately 15 warders under W/O Barnard

2 MARCH 1977

Heavy tremor at 6.55 am[2]

25 MARCH 1977

Dreamt of Kgatho, George, I and others racing up a field with green crop and coming down a hill at full gallop. Kgatho falls and is assisted. I wake up as I run to him.

25 APRIL 1977

Journalists, photographers and TV representatives visit island and take photographs of prisoners' cells and buildings[3]

4 JUNE 1977

Zami and Zindzi see me for 1½ hrs. Advise that deportation to Brandfort occurred on 16.5.77[4]

---

2. An earthquake had occurred on the mainland, causing most damage in the town of Tulbagh.
3. The government invited twenty-five journalists to Robben Island to dispel rumours about the mistreatment of political prisoners.
4. Following Winnie's imprisonment in 1976, she was banished from Johannesburg to Brandfort in the Free State in 1977.

11 JULY 1977
Razor blade

22 AUGUST 1977
Letter re shaving cream and 2 cold creams handed in

7 NOVEMBER 1977
Major Zandburg advises that K.D. [Kaiser Matanzima] wishes to visit Madiba [himself] on 2.12.77. Madiba replies that visit must be postponed[5]

29 DECEMBER 1977
2 100ml. Mentadent tooth paste
6 large Vinolia soap
1 large Vaseline hair oil
1 kg Omo [washing powder]

11 MARCH 1979
DDD Syndrome: debility, dependancy, dread

27 APRIL 1979
Minister Jimmy Kruger visits Island accompanied by G. du Preez. We chat for about ± 15 minutes.[6]

9 MAY 1979
Consultation with Dr A.C. Neethling, eye-specialist.

Eyesight excellent. Virus infection, but will soon clear no need for new spectacles

....

5. Mandela and the other imprisoned Rivonia trialists had decided that, due to Matanzima's support of the Bantustan scheme, Mandela should not meet with him.
6. James Kruger (1917–87). Politician. Minister of Justice and Police, 1974–79. President of the Senate, 1979–80.

20 MAY 1979

Virus again active starts from left eye to the right one

21 MAY 1979

Right eye singularly painful and red

22 MAY 1979

In the afternoon commence with Albucid drops

23 MAY 1979

I dream coming home at night with doors wide open and Zami asleep in one bed and in the other chdn [children], possibly Zeni and Zindzi. Many school children outside. I embrace Zami and she orders me to bed.

24 MAY 1979

Start using Albucid 30% eyedrops midday

1 JUNE 1979

'It's easy to hope, it's the wanting that spoils it.'

2 JUNE 1979

In a sick country every step to health is an insult to those who live on its sickness

The purpose of freedom is to create it for others

3 JUNE 1979

Zami and Zazi for 1 hr.[7] Zami in red jersey and head gear

Zazi in coat similar to mine

----

7.   Zaziwe (Zazi) is Zenani's daughter, Mandela's granddaughter.

12 JUNE 1979

[In Afrikaans] Gnl. Roux came. Spoke with Brig. Du Plessis.

14 JUNE 1979

21st wedding anniversary

14 JULY 1979

Zeni, Zindzi and Zamaswazi visit for 45 minutes[8]

Zamaswazi has cold and yells frequently

6 AUGUST 1979

Minister L le Grange visits the prison accompanied by C.O.P. [Commanding Officer of the Prision] Du Preez[9]

15 SEPTEMBER 1979

Acting Paramount Chief Bambilanga visits me 1.30 hrs[10]

9 OCTOBER 1979

Interview with Mr A.M. Omar re state vs Sabata Dalindyebo.

17 OCTOBER 1979

Weight without clothes 75 kg

20 OCTOBER 1979

Interview with Zindzi for ±1 hr.

Zindzi looks beautiful and cheerful. Staying with Anne [*sic*] Tomlinson

---

8. Zamaswazi (Swati) is Zenani's daughter, Mandela's granddaughter.
9. Minister of Law and Order Louis le Grange. Du Preez was commissioner of prisons.
10. Albert Bambilanga Mtirara. Ruler of AbaThembu.

Zindzi returns for ±45 minutes. Again looks bright and cheerful. Chat on books and publisher Mike Kirkwood.

5 NOVEMBER 1979

Hospitalised: Minor op. removal of torn tendon on right heel; performed by Dr Breitenbach.

Dream Zindzi and I visit Bara [Baragwanath Hospital] at night. Asked why I instructed a certain lawyer instead of another.

17 NOVEMBER 1979

Zami sees me for ±2 hrs. Pale blue dress – put on reasonable weight and looking really elegant

19 NOVEMBER 1979

POP and stitches removed by Sgt Kaminga. Rather large ossicle removed from right heel by Dr Breitenbach. Anaesthetic Dr C Moss

3 DECEMBER 1979

Letter re purchase [of] slippers addressed to Major Harding

25 DECEMBER 1979

1 hr visit from Zami: Xmas groceries from Pmburg [Pietermaritzburg].

26 DECEMBER 1979

45 minute visit from Zami and Swati. Promises to send 20 photos

3 JANUARY 1980

Reading 'Black as I am': Zindzi's 55 poems. 'Black and Fourteen' to be published shortly

To NM in his imprisonment and Nomzamo Mandela in her sentence of silence for the suffering they do for all of us.[11]

10 JANUARY 1980

New blade

13 JANUARY 1980

Milk for Tea

See above.

26 JANUARY 1980

Visited by Zami for ± 45 minutes. She complains that Madiba looks tired.

13 MARCH 1980

Swati's 1st birthday

11. The dedication in *Black As I Am*.

19 MARCH 1980

Received Zami's telegram re Lily's [Lilian Ngoyi] death

20 MARCH 1980

Sent condolence telegram (urgent) to Edith Ngoyi[12]

14 MAY 1980

Mrs Helen Suzman MP comes with Gen. Roux.[13] Interview for ±1 hr.

See above.

23 MAY 1980

Consultation with Dr. A.L. Maresky pronounces me in good condition. Heart better than the last time he examined me.

12. Lilian Ngoyi's daughter.
13. Helen Suzman, see People, Places and Events.

Dreamt returning home late at night, almost at dawn. Embraced sickly Zami as she enters the backdoor of our Orlando home. Zeni is about 2 yrs and has swallowed a razor blade which she vomits out. I spank her for it.

25 MAY 1980

Dream about Zami, Zeni and Zindzi. Zeni is about 2 yrs. Zindzi asks me to kiss her and remarks that I am not warm enough. Zeni also asks me to do so.

See above.

8 JUNE 1980

Zami returns cheerful in blue garment.

9 JUNE 1980

Balance R41.44

24 JUNE 1980

Sgt Kamminga takes blood pressure 180/90

30 JUNE 1980

Examined by Dr Kaplan BP. 120/80 weight taken 78 kg.
Also read to me Dr Maresky report on cardiograph.

12 JULY 1980

Zami, Zindzi and Zobuhle fail to turn up because of rough
weather

13 JULY 1980

Zami, Zindzi and Zobuhle turn up on extended visit[14]

Announcement of death of Sir Seretse Khama

24 AUGUST 1980

Buthi and Kgatho,[15] the first time I see Kgatho with tie on.

7 SEPTEMBER 1980

250g Nescafe R4.10
Mustard Sauce 54 cents
Trims 45
Coconut cookies 54
Sandwich spread 71
Marmite 55
Fray Bentos 55
Game lemon 26
Cake mixture 250g 38

---

14. Zobuhle is Zoleka Mandela (1980–). Zindzi's daughter and Mandela's granddaughter.
15. Buthi (means 'brother', although not necessarily a blood brother). A male relation of Mandela's from
his home town.

14 SEPTEMBER 1980

Zami and Oupa. Zami in maroon dress and a gold plated pendant looks lovely. Oupa in a suit (black) with white stripes[16]

10 OCTOBER 1980

73, 000 people sign petition for the release of N.M.

11 OCTOBER 1980

Prisoners' Day[17]

27 OCTOBER 1980

Documents removed without my consent by W/O Pienaar

3 NOVEMBER 1980

M-Drive in Zimbabwe: The Free-M[andela] at the University of Zimbabwe has collected 600 signatures petitioning for his release

Clifford Mashiri the organiser

28 NOVEMBER 1980

[In Afrikaans] As long as the Afrikaners think they are the super race and have a right to force solutions on others, the future will remain bleak.

Concept of Bantu Education carries with it a stigma.[18] No system, however improved, will ever be accepted as long as it is a racially separate one

....

16. Oupa Seakamela. Zindzi's partner at the time.
17. The official Day of Solidarity with South African Political Prisoners was designated by the United Nations General Assembly in 1976.
18. The Bantu Education Act of 1953 legalised the separation of races in educational institutions.

25 DECEMBER 1980

Zami, Zindzi and Zobuhle visit RI [Robben Island] for ±1 hr. Both dressed in light gear. Promised to pose for Ayesha [Arnold]: Commemoration in Dbn [Durban]. Nehru Award[19]

Tape of Indira Gandhi's address did not arrive

22 JANUARY 1981

Primrose oil lowers blood pressure, cholesterol level and overweight

18 FEBRUARY 1981

Princess Anne 23 951
Jack Jones 10 507   } Chancellor of London University
N.M. 7 199

N.Ms supporters included senior don: Prof Barbara Hardy and current affairs commentator Jonathan Dimbleby[20]

1 APRIL 1981

Mandela documentary: BBC producer Frank Cox, who made the TV drama documentary on editor Donald Woods's escape from SA [South Africa], is planning a TV drama documentary on N.M. [Nelson Mandela] for filming in June.

Casting for white and black South African actors starts in June. The programme will run for 50 minutes and will be part of a series of 3 on the subject of human rights. The programme will be filmed on a mock-up Robben Island somewhere in Britain

....

19. Mandela was awarded the Jawaharlal Nehru Award for International Understanding by the Government of India in 1979.
20. Mandela was nominated for the position of chancellor of the University of London in 1981.

3 APRIL 1981

Bishop [Desmond] Tutu speaks in Committee Room of House of Commons at culmination of Release M campaign.[21] Present Michael Foot,[22] David Steel.[23] Petition endorsed by 94 MPs, 25 peers, 30 leading churchmen including 19 bishops, and 98 professors, 500 organisations representing estimated 12,000,000

5 MAY 1981

IRA [Irish Republican Army] martyr Bobby Sands dies

10 MAY 1981

Zami and Swati ±10am: Swati bangs on glass partition shouting, 'Open, open!' Finally she cries and is finally removed by Mda's sister

17 MAY 1981

Number of prisoners who are studying

Std V	29
JC	102
Matric	127
Degree	59
Diploma	17
Total	334

30% of them do not sit for the examination

5 AUGUST 1981

Dr Ekwueme (Alex) Vice-President of Nigeria receives the freedom of Glasgow on behalf of NM from the Lord Provost Mr Michael Kelly. The scroll conferring the honour known as

21. Archbishop Desmond Tutu, see People, Places and Events.
22. Michael Foot (1913–2010). British Labour Party leader and writer.
23. David Steel (1938–). British politician and leader of the Liberal Party, 1976–88.

the Burgess Ticket will be kept safely in Govt House in Lagos. 'When M gains his freedom in, I hope, the not too distant future, he will be able to come to Lagos to receive it.'

Morris Lemba Mangaba
9.2.59.

May Mei Mai Mai Mayo					
Sunday Sondag Dimanche Sonntag Domingo	17	Unity Secretarial Services, P.O. BOX 6134, JHB. In English. number of prisoners who are studying			
Monday Maandag Lundi Montag Lunes	18	std V de mature	29 102 127	30% of them do not sit for	
Tuesday Dinsdag Mardi Dienstag Martes	19	Degree Diploma	39 17	the examination	
Wednesday Woensdag Mercredi Mittwoch Miércoles	20	Total	334		

See page 279.

15 AUGUST 1981

Zami and Zobuhle: I kiss Zobuhle against partition glass and speak to her by telephone. She fusses around and makes conversation with Zami absolutely impossible. We decide she should not return the following day.

19 AUGUST 1981

Anthony Bobby Tsotsobe, 25
Johannes Shabangu, 28
David Moise
sentenced to death by Judge Theron (Charl).[24] 'Long live the spirit of the toiling masses of SA, long live the spirit of international mankind, long live NM; long live Solomon Mahlangu!'[25]

24. Anthony Bobby Tsotsobe, Johannes Shabangu and David Moise were all members of MK.
25. Solomon Mahlangu (1956–79). Member of MK. He was hanged.

26 SEPTEMBER 1981

Zami spends her 45th birthday with us. Reports intensive harassment of herself and family by SAP [South African Police] re Zindzi's passport and Mabitsela's living at home.[26]

Zeni and Zindzi leaving for Rio de Janeiro, USA and Madrid on 9.10.81

19 NOVEMBER 1981

[Griffiths] Mxenge murdered[27]

14 DECEMBER 1981

Commanding Officer informs me that Zami involved in car accident in Mt. Ayliff. Sustained serious neck, shoulder and rib injury. Also a 14 yr old Madikizela girl. Hospitalised in Kokstad. Might be transferred to Durban. Telegram of good wishes immediately dispatched.

28 DECEMBER 1981

Zami's banishment to Brandfort and house-arrest there renewed for another year

6 JANUARY 1982

Bomb blast in Soweto and rocked the Orlando Community Hall about 9 pm, shattered windows of neighbouring houses, cracked walls: second blast in the area

30 JANUARY 1982

Zami's left hand still in plaster. She looks quite unwell. New cast put by Bloemfontein orthopaedic surgeon, Dr Shipley. Will see him on Feb. 10 and if no improvement might operate.

---

26. Mabitsela was M K Malefane. Member of MK. He was staying at Winnie's house.
27. Mlungisi Griffiths Mxenge (d. 1981). Anti-apartheid activist, human rights lawyer and political prisoner. Member of ANC. He was murdered by the security police.

See page 281.

31 JANUARY 1982

Zami returns wearing sunglasses. Will post photos of Thembi's wedding on Monday morning.

26 MARCH 1982

Tom Lodge: 'Black Resistance Politics in S.A 1948–1981'

[Mandela is suddenly moved to Pollsmoor Prison on the mainland on 30 March 1982]

24 APRIL 1982

Zami visits me at Pollsmoor, accompanied by Mr Allister Sparks but he is not allowed to come in.[28]

---

28. Allister Sparks (1933–). Writer, journalist and political commentator.

25 APRIL 1982

Zami returns again accompanied by A.S. She looks very well. Plans to return next month.

5 MAY 1982

Packet of Bisto [powdered gravy] given to kitchens by Adj [Adjutant] Terblanche with instruction that one teaspoon be used on Wednesdays only. First teaspoon used

12 MAY 1982

One teaspoon of Bisto used for second time

17 MAY 1982

Amalgamated Union of Engineering Workers (London) is to give R1800 to Zami so that she can visit Madiba. Zami was able to visit Madiba last month, thanks to the generosity of a Dorset woman, Mrs Marjorie Ruck

26 JUNE 1982

Zami in fawn coat reports on death threats and attempt to bomb the combi [minibus]: accompanied by Mabitsela but he did not enter cubicle

1 AUGUST 1982

Birthday card to Ayesha [Arnold]

7 AUGUST 1982

Maki (intended visit applied for on 30th April). Maki did come for one hour and staying at Cowley House

8 AUGUST 1982

Maki for 30 minutes. Two front teeth pulled out and one on the side.

17 AUGUST 1982

[In Afrikaans, presumably from a newspaper cutting] A letter bomb has claimed the life of Ruth First: Ruth First, an official of the banned ANC [African National Congress] died in Maputo after a letter bomb exploded in her hands. The incident happened at the university's Centre for African Studies where she worked, according to the official news agency, Angop. The other people in the vicinity included the Centre's director Mr Aquino de Braganca, who was injured in the explosion, said a family member of his family. Apparently one of Pres. Samora Machel's advisors said he was not seriously injured.

Books by her: 177 days, The Barrel of a Gun, a study of military rule in Africa, A Biography of Olive Schreiner, and A Study of Modern Libya [possibly *Libya: The Elusive Revolution*].

21 AUGUST 1982

King Sobhuza dies at the age of 83[29]

25 SEPTEMBER 1982

Zami wearing an outfit, present from Kenya's Ngugi[30]

2 OCTOBER 1982

Dream of Zami and me eating from one dish . . . After only a few spoons I left to attend to some urgent business, hoping to return soon and continue eating out of the common dish. Alas, I was delayed for several hrs and became acutely worried over your reaction and anxiety. It was a medley of dreams. Hobdozela falling down a steep bank into a river with a member of family on his back.

---

29. Ngwenyama Sobhuza II (1899–1982). King Sobhuza of Swaziland. Zenani's father-in-law.
30. Ngugi wa Thiong'o (1938–). Kenyan author.

2 DECEMBER 1982

Breyten Breytenbach released from Pollsmoor Prison[31]

4 JANUARY 1983

Former British Liberal Party leader, Mr Jeremy Thorpe met Zenani while on a business trip to Swaziland.[32] Mr Thorpe, who is promoting a plan to built low-cost houses with highly compressed grasses, discussed Zami's house arrest and her hubby's imprisonment.

7 JANUARY 1983

Zami raided by police in 3 hr search by 6 police vehicles in presence of Helen Suzman M.P., and Peter Soal M.P.[33] Served with summons for allegedly breaking a <u>banning</u> order. They confiscated posters, books, documents and bed spread. Also photographed 6 patients attending mobile health clinic.

31 JANUARY 1983

Sowetan. 31.1.83: Security Police took her bed cover – senators plan to replace it. Powerful members of the U.S. Congress will replace the bedspread SA Security policemen seized from Mrs W.M. [Winnie Mandela] recently. The new bedspread will be presented to the wife of the ANC [African National Congress] leader as a symbol of Congressional concern over civil rights abuses in SA.

2 FEBRUARY 1983

Admitted to Woodstock Hospital

31. Breyten Breytenbach (1939–). Writer and painter. Imprisoned in Pollsmoor Prison for seven years under the Terrorism Act.
32. John Jeremy Thorpe (1929–). British Liberal Party leader.
33. Peter Soal (1936–). Johannesburg city councillor and MP.

3 FEBRUARY 1983

Operation conducted on the back of head and on right-hand toe.

5 FEBRUARY 1983

Zindzi looks bright and cheerful

14 FEBRUARY 1983

W/O Van Zyl takes out stitches in head wound

15 FEBRUARY 1983

Sister Ferreira, Woodstock Hospital, takes out stitch in big toe: Dr Stein points out that report from medical laboratories indicates that there was no sign of malignancy in the toe.

21 MARCH 1983

Ancient Olympia: Jailed black SA leader, N.M, was made an honorary citizen of the Greek village

22 MARCH 1983

The Anti-apartheid Committee Movement and the UN Committee Against Apartheid yesterday published a declaration carrying more than 4 000 signatures urging the release of ANC leader, NM.

24 MARCH 1983

A.N.C. leader to get award: City College of N.Y. [New York] has awarded N.M. doctorate in law for 'unselfish commitment to principles of freedom and justice'. Dr Bernard Harleston, president of varsity. 'Award will be made in June.'

29 MARCH 1983

Zami invited to attend opening of Parliament in Bonn on 29 March by Die Grunenim [*sic*]. Sowetan reports. The street in

Camden, North London, where the anti-apartheid movement has its new headquarters is to be renamed Mandela Street in honour of the imprisoned leader of the ANC. It is currently called Selous Street after the British explorer who helped Cecil John Rhodes bring Rhodesia under colonial rule.[34]

25 APRIL 1983

Mandela resolution: A liberal democrat has asked Congress to proclaim NM, the jailed leader of the ANC and his wife W, honorary United States citizens. Mr Crocket was supported by 12 of his House of Representative Colleagues when he introduced his joint resolutions – Mr Crocket.[35] A resources centre for information on Southern Africa, which, it is believed, will be the only one of its kind, is being planned to commemorate the work of Ruth First, who was killed by a letter bomb in Maputo last yr [year]. The main aim of the centre initially to be based at a British university will be to collect on microfilm all the historical, economic and sociological material on Southern Africa held in universities and institutions around the world.

21 MAY 1983

UDF [United Democratic Front] formed to fight govt's [government's] constitutional proposals – TIC, CUSA, SAAWU, SOWETO CIVIC ASSOCIATION and others.[36] 32 organisations – more than 150 delegates and observers adopted declaration forming UDF and pledging to fight the constitutional and reform proposals. Dr I. Mohammed chairman.

4 JUNE 1983

Herald: Dublin City Councillors have decided to erect a bust

---

34. Selous Street was named after Frederick Courtney Selous (1851–1917).
35. George W Crockett, Jr (1909–77). Member of the US House of Representatives, 1980–91.
36. Transvaal Indian Congress, Council of Unions of South Africa, South African Allied Workers' Union.

of NM to mark his 'remarkable contribution to freedom'. Originally the request was to have him made a freeman of Dublin, but some councillors felt this would not be appropriate as he could not be present to carry the honour.

9 JUNE 1983
Simon Mogoerane, Jerry Masololi and Marcus Motaung hanged in Pretoria Central Prison[37]

14 JUNE 1983
Advocate Ismail Mahomed and attorney Ismail Ayob – legal consultation on living conditions in Pollsmoor Maximum Security Prison

1 JULY 1983
Mrs Helen Suzman MP visits the section accompanied by Brig[adier]s Munro and Bothma. We acquaint her with our grievances and show her the yard and the single rooms under construction. Informed her that it was an honour to be awarded a doctorate by University of Brussels.

3 DECEMBER 1983
Weight stripped 76.8kg
Height 1,78m
about 5'10"

13 DECEMBER 1983
Archbishop Huddleston, president of AAM [Anti-Apartheid Movement], has unveiled a plaque in Leeds, Yorkshire, officially naming gardens in front of the city's civic hall after jailed ANC leader, NM. The plaque, made of slate, describes M as 'symbol

....

37. All members of MK who were executed for high treason.

of resistance to apartheid in SA' and records a statement made by him. The unveiling ceremony followed a meeting in the City Hall at which several people spoke of M. A message from U.N. Secretary General Mr Javier Perez de Cuellar was also read.

16 JANUARY 1984
Planted carrots, beetroots and peanuts[38]

18 JANUARY 1984
Planted tomatoes in 2 separate trays

19 FEBRUARY 1984
Suppl. [supplementary] results delivered
2 visits with Zami from 8.45 am: dressed in white maxi with beautiful beadwork round the neck. She and Oupa to drive to Umtata tomorrow.

28 FEBRUARY 1984
Brig. Munro informs that K.D. [Matanzima] desires to meet me and Walter [Sisulu]. We remind K.D. of R.I [Robben Island] decision that the time is not appropriate for such a meeting.

1 MARCH 1984
Further meeting with Brig. Munro when I requested permission to write to OR [Oliver Tambo] and Govan [Mbeki] re proposed visit by K.D.[39]

7 MARCH 1984
CT. [*Cape Times*] reports that Zami will report to Madiba offer of release from KD.

....

38. Mandela grew vegetables on the rooftop at Pollsmoor Prison.
39. Archibald Mvuyelwa Govan Mbeki, see People, Places and Events.

8 MARCH 1984

Zami wearing a dark brown maxi and matching headgear reports on proposal from Daliwonga [Matanzima]. 2 visits of 40 minutes each.

CT carried further reports. [Kobie] Coetsee states release not even under consideration.

10 MARCH 1984

CT. Madiba sees wife again and gives her response to KD's offer.

12 MARCH 1984

CT. Leader of ANC, NM, rejects offer: he would defy any attempt to release him and restrict him to the Transkei: determined to return to his home in Soweto and will not stay in Transkei.

15 MARCH 1984

Madiba records sell well. Record calling for the release of NM has made a big impression on pop charts after only one week. 'Free NM' by the Specials – a multi-racial group – is No. 4 on Capitol Radio charts and no. 68 on the national charts.[40]

22 MARCH 1984

The sum of R49,40 sent to Time for renewal.

E.C.G. performed by Dr Le Roux – satisfactory – Trace of blood in urine. HBP 140/90

1 MAY 1984

Cape Times 1/5: The highly articulate Mrs M[andela]; who cannot be quoted under SA law because she is a banned person, held forth at length without mincing her words and she was heard and seen in May

....

40. 'Free Nelson Mandela' was a protest song written by Jerry Dammers of The Specials (released on the single *Free Nelson Mandela / Break Down the Door*, 1984).

Zami and Zeni: have contact visit for the first time. 2 visits

18 JUNE 1984

Sowetan: Cuban President Fidel Castro has awarded one of Cuba's most prestigious medals to NM, the leader of the banned ANC who has been in SA jail for 22 yrs. The Order of Playa Giron (Bay of Pigs) was given to Mr Alfred Nzo, the G[eneral] Secretary of the ANC who is visiting Cuba. Mr Jesus Montane, deputy member of Cuba's Politburo, said 'M is the inspirational example of the indomitable spirit of resistance.'

23 JUNE 1984

Maki and Dumani for 40 minutes[41]

16 JULY 1984

Cape Times. In a brief reference to ANC leader, NM, who is serving a life sentence in prison, Mr [Allan] Hendrickse said it was time he was freed.[42] 'If he has done wrong, then he has certainly served his sentence,' he said.

18 JULY 1984

Subscription for the 'Star' renewed for 6 months with effect from 84/03/03
Subscription R95.28

5 AUGUST 1984

Zami returns and takes 2 visits of 40 minutes each; brought by Marietjie.[43] Zami reports that Shenaz has written several letters which I did not receive.[44]

----

41. Dumani Mandela. Makaziwe Mandela's son and Mandela's grandson.
42. Allan Hendrickse (1927–2005). Minister, teacher and Labour Party politician.
43. Marietjie van der Merwe. Wife of Harvey van der Merwe, a friend of Mandela's.
44. Shenaz Meer. Daughter of Fatima Meer, see People, Places and Events.

12 AUGUST 1984

Sunday Express Review: Joubert Malherbe: Jimmy Cliff has vowed not to return to SA until it has majority rule.[45] He said this during the annual NM festival at Crystal Palace Bowl in South London last week.

About 5,000 people streamed into the theatre to be treated to the sounds of Cliff, SA ace trumpeter, Hugh Masekela, a number of African bands, and the hard-hitting British reggae outfit, Aswad, who wound up the show

28 AUGUST 1984

Blood in urine. Another specimen taken by Maj Burger

30 AUGUST 1984

BP taken by Major Burger 140/80

5 SEPTEMBER 1984

Balance R560.77 Consultation with Dr Loubscher, urologist, tested urine confirmed presence of blood: X-rayed by Messrs Basson, Pienaar, etc. diagnose some kidney disorder but not certain of its identity: Further examination at Volkshospital [*sic*] tomorrow.

6 SEPTEMBER 1984

Put under scanning machine at Volkshospital [*sic*]. Discovered cyst on right kidney as well as on liver; that on kidney purely watery; in liver may be calcified. Further investigation in hospital arranged.

----

45. Jimmy Cliff (1948–). Jamaican ska and reggae singer.

12 SEPTEMBER 1984

Admitted at Woodstock Hospital for investigation of renal problems

1 NOVEMBER 1984

BP 170/100 taken by Sister du Toit

Cape Times: How the ANC switched to policy of armed struggle. Andrew Prior. Dpt of Political Studies

14 NOVEMBER 1984

Sol Plaatje, SA Nationalist 1876–1932 (By Brian Willan)[46]

12 DECEMBER 1984

Results: failed all 6 subjects[47]

31 JANUARY 1985

Commanding officer supplies me at 12.15 am with copy of President Botha's speech. At 3.15 I have 40 minute consultation with 4 comrades from roof.

1 JANUARY 1986

Col Marx drives me out to the prison gardens. Spend 1½ hours inspecting the layout. Interesting bird life. Later joined by my 4 colleagues from the roof in my quarters where we had some snacks for about 1 hr.

4 JANUARY 1986

Driven out to the gardens by Lt. [Lieutenant] Barkhuizen. Spend 1 hr and bring back whole bag of tomatoes.

....

46. *Sol Plaatje: South African Nationalist*, Brian Willan (published 1984). Solomon Tshekisho Plaatje, see People, Places and Events.
47. Mandela is referring to his study for his law degree.

6 JANUARY 1986
1.11.85 weight 72 kg, Height 1,80 meters[48]

12 JANUARY 1986
Driven out to the gardens by Lt. Barkhuizen and spend an hr [hour] seeing various fields. Brig Munro gives instructions for us to keep away from the highway for security reason.

14 JANUARY 1986
Shifted to next door cell as own cell is being painted

23 JANUARY 1986
Informed that the application for plug, hot plate and electric kettle turned down, as well as request for permission to send book presents to doctors associated with the operation. See film 'Sophie's Choice'[49]

24 JANUARY 1986
Driven out by Brig Munro to the gardens after lock-up and then through western Tokai past a sprawling vineyard that stretches out to the foot of the mountain, past houses with wealth shining through the brick walls.

28 JANUARY 1986
Seen library films 1) Terrorists and Hostages; 2) Students in Moscow 3) Position of Maori women 4) Animation

....

48. Mandela's height measures two centimetres taller than the previous measurement in December 1983, suggesting a lackadaisical attitude by the guards measuring him.
49. *Sophie's Choice* (released 1982).

1 FEBRUARY 1986

Three-hr consultation with George [Bizos]. Will apply for consultation with all of us on 14.2. Request for him to shake hands with others refused.

5 FEBRUARY 1986

Zeni's birthday celebrated by opening tin of mutton
40 minute interview with Tyhopho [Walter Sisulu]

7 FEBRUARY 1986

See 4 reels of Amadeus.[50] Exciting story but the ending struck me as somewhat flat

12 FEBRUARY 1986

Spent a little over 2 hrs with [Raymond Mhlaba] Ndobe on the occasion of his 66th birthday. Have lunch together and shared a Xmas cake. Requested him to discuss with the other comrades our instructions to George Bizos.

21 FEBRUARY 1986

Had 80 minutes special visit from Zami and Zindzi. Minutes after the end of the family, visited by Brig. Munro. Spent another ±45 minutes with very important personage, Gen Obasanjo.[51] Prior to this saw film: 'Boetie gaan grens toe'[52] [*Brother Goes to the Border*].

5 APRIL 1986

Xhamela [Walter Sisulu] and I witnesses to the marriage of Dideka and Ndobe which was solemnized by Bishop Sigqibo

....

50. *Amadeus* (released 1984).
51. Olu$egun Obasanjo (1937–). General of the Nigerian Army. President of Nigeria, 1999–2007. He was one of seven in the Eminent Persons Group, who were sent by the Commonwealth to investigate apartheid South Africa.
52. Possibly *Boetie Gaan Border Toe* (released 1984).

Dwane assisted by Rev Mpumlwana in the presence of Mrs Sallie, Brig Munro and W/O Gregory[53]

Muzi and Zeni visit for 80 minutes

8 APRIL 1986

Zami and NoMoscow pay 40 minute visit and report death of Sabata the previous day.[54] Zami to inform the family and to try to collect body from Lusaka.

15 APRIL 1986

Seen the tragic film 'Paul Jacob and Nuclear Gang' plus 'Electric Boogie' a baffling new dance.[55]

18 APRIL 1986

Seen film 'Missing' and the short 1974 Lions match against Springboks which Lions won by 12-3.

5 MAY 1986

Mrs Helen Suzman MP and Mr Tiaan van der Merwe visit me from 9.30 to 11.55.[56] Have a wide-ranging conversation on political issues.

6 MAY 1986

Brig Munro informs me that Gen. [General] Venter would like to get more precise information re Bambilanga and Daliwonga[57]

16 MAY 1986

Interview with all members of E.P.G [Commonwealth Eminent Persons Group]

53. James Gregory (1941–2003). Warder, censor and author of *Goodbye Bafana* (published 1995).
54. NoMoscow. Senior wife of King Sabata and mother of King Buyelekhaya. King Sabata Jonguhlanga Dalindyebo died in exile in Zambia.
55. *Paul Jacobs and the Nuclear Gang* (released 1978). *Electric Boogie* (released 1983).
56. Tiaan van der Merwe. Progressive Federal Party MP.
57. Daliwonga is K D Matanzima.

28 MAY 1986

'I know why the caged bird sings' by Maya Angelou
Library Film

....

See above.

16 JUNE 1986

Dreamt of Zami having become an attorney. She appears in a
case against Mandela and Tambo, takes judgment by default.
NM arrives in court to apply for rescission of judgment and I
call her into court

17 JUNE 1986

W/O Gregory informs me in arrogant manner that the letter he
misplaced is gone and that there is absolutely nothing he can

do about it. He also states that nobody, whatever his position, can threaten him.

18 JUNE 1986
Had discussion with Maj Van Sittert re W/O Gregory. Major promises to take up matter as soon as W/O Gregory is available

18 AUGUST 1986
Rev Peter Storey devotional prelude on 'The Monday'[58]

Film of Muhammad Ali in Germany, also 'The Nerds take Revenge' and a short[59]

19 AUGUST 1986
Rev Peter Storey on forgiveness

20 AUGUST 1986
Rev Peter Storey on the Lord's Prayer

25 AUGUST 1986
BP taken by Major Burger 140/80

Rev Brian Johanson . . . on 'standing'

26 AUGUST 1986
Rev Brian Johanson on 'walking'

27 AUGUST 1986
Rev Brian Johanson on 'sitting'

....

58. Reverend Peter Storey. Methodist minister.
59. *Revenge of the Nerds* (released 1984).

4 SEPTEMBER 1986

Father Michael Austin of Johannesburg. On how to live like Christ

BP 120/70 taken by Major Burger

5 SEPTEMBER 1986

Father Michael Austin: Loyola said if somebody told him that he was about to die he would continue to play cards

10 SEPTEMBER 1986

Zondo (Sibusiso), Sipho Bridget Xulu and Clarence Lucky Payi executed[60]

1 OCTOBER 1986

Provided with television set. Whole programme upset watching tel[evision] from 4 pm – 6.45 pm

8 OCTOBER 1986

Supplied with new and better antenna

10 OCTOBER 1986

Meeting with Daliwonga, accompanied by H.T. Mpunzi, Transkei Consul and Nelson Mabunu[61]

19 OCTOBER 1986

President Samora Machel dies in air crash on the border between SA and Mozambique

....

60. Members of MK who were executed on 9 September 1986.
61. Nelson Title Mabuna (d. 1996). Imbongi. (An imbongi is a traditional praise poet.)

20 OCTOBER 1986

Radio announces the death of Samora Machel, President of the Republic of Mozambique. The Minister of Defence and Minister of Transport and Deputy Minister of Foreign Affairs

11 DECEMBER 1986

Post Zindzi's birthday card. Dreamt of Jimmy and Connie.[62] Jimmy visits Zami and me and we invite him to come to spend holiday with us. Also dreamt asking Mr Sidelsky to get me a job

26 DECEMBER 1986

Spent the day with colleagues at their premises and enjoyed a lovely lunch

27 JANUARY 1987

[In Afrikaans] Not satisfied with the evidence about the missing letter to Zami. It was not a photostat. The post office promises to sent a photostat in the meantime

18 FEBRUARY 1987

1 reel of 50 m dental floss.

Start receiving 1 litre a day of fresh milk.

20 FEBUARY 1987

BP. 120/80.

23 FEBRUARY 1987

Celebrate Thembi's birthday with a piece of rich fruit cake and peanuts

....

62. Dr James (Jimmy) Lowell Zwelinzima Njongwe (1919–76). Medical doctor and anti-apartheid activist. Cape president of the ANC. Constance (Connie) Njongwe (1920–2009). Nurse and anti-apartheid activist. Wife of Dr James Njongwe.

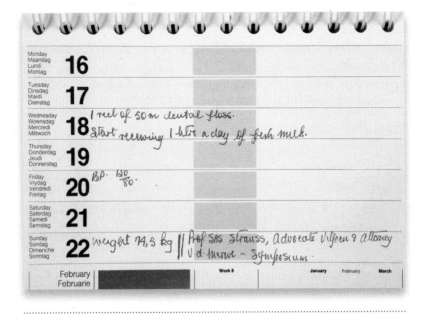

Monday Maandag Lundi Montag	**16**		
Tuesday Dinsdag Mardi Dienstag	**17**		
Wednesday Woensdag Mercredi Mittwoch	**18**	1 reel of 50 m dental floss. Start receiving 1 litre a day of fresh milk.	
Thursday Donderdag Jeudi Donnerstag	**19**		
Friday Vrydag Vendredi Freitag	**20**	BP. 120/80.	
Saturday Saterdag Samedi Samstag	**21**		
Sunday Sondag Dimanche Sonntag	**22**	weight 74,5 kg	Prof SAS Strauss, Advocate Viljoen & attorney V d merwe – Symposium.

| February
Februarie | | Week 8 | | January | February | March |

See page 300.

4 APRIL 1987

Examined by Dr Marshall: trouble with the right eye. Can see nothing

8 APRIL 1987

Consultation with Prof J Van Rooyen, Tygerberg [Hospital], finds hole in retina and operates on right eye and recommends new reading lenses. To see us again in a fortnight

20 APRIL 1987

Visited by my 4 comrades from Women's Section of the prison for 2 hrs[63]

63. Walter Sisulu, Raymond Mhlaba, Andrew Mlangeni and Ahmed Kathrada were now being held in the women's section of Pollsmoor Prison.

22 APRIL 1987

Jim Fish of the BBC announces the resignation of Joe Slovo as MK [Umkhonto we Sizwe] Chief of Staff. A comment by John Barratt.[64]

Consult Prof Van Rooyen, Tygerberg. Puts additional laser shots on right eye, to see me again in month's time

23 APRIL 1987

Interview with C.O.P [commissioner of prisons] Gen. Willemse, re harassment of family.

9 JULY 1987

Dakar Conference between ANC and group of South Africans begins.

14 JULY 1987

Consulted Dr De Haan, Ear, Nose and throat specialist re pain in right jaw joint. Examination reveals no observable abnormalities other than a slight swelling of a duct in the right ear and possibly unrelated to the pain.

6 AUGUST 1987

Ayesha [Arnold]'s birthday: At 9.20 am Sgt. [Sergeant] Brand informs me of the death of Ayesha. Immediately handed in telegram for dispatch to Ameen and the children.

19 AUGUST 1987

Weight 67 kg: body mass without clothes
New razor blade

----

64. John Barratt (1930–2007). National director of the South African Institute of International Affairs, 1967–94.

20 AUGUST 1987

Measurement of cell 6,4 metres x 5,4 metres

22 AUGUST 1987

An hr interview with Kathy [Ahmed Kathrada] on his birthday

7 SEPTEMBER 1987

Attempt to avoid taking plain sugar in all kinds of food and drink

12 SEPTEMBER 1987

My sister, Mabel, pays 40 minute visit. Gave her R120,00[65]

26 SEPTEMBER 1987

Celebrated Zami's birthday with mutton breyani plus butter beans and a piece of rock fruit cake

27 DECEMBER 1987

Harvey advises that our new house in Soweto has been bombed and damaged. Saw Tyhopho [Walter Sisulu] for 40 minutes.

5 JUNE 1988

Consultation with Dr Shapiro on pain under right collar bone and on left foot. X-ray reveals no abnormalities, but there's blood in urine. Suggest examination by urologist. Weight 72¼ kg

12 AUGUST 1988

Admitted to Tygerberg Hospital after 10 p.m. Examined by Prof Rossenstrauch

....

65. Nontancu Mabel Timakwe (née Mandela) (1924–2002).

See page 303 and below.

13 AUGUST 1988

Examined by Prof. De Kock, Head of Internal medicine.
Diagnose T.B. and pleural effusion

17 AUGUST 1988

Visited by Rev Anthony Simons

24 AUGUST 1988

Weight 71 kg: Matron Elaine Kearns goes on leave as from
25.8.88
New pyjamas and sleepers

25 AUGUST 1988

Weight 70,3 kg

27 AUGUST 1988

Weight 71,5 kg. Sister De Waal goes on holiday

10 SEPTEMBER 1988

Examined by Dr Stock. Brings along hazel nuts. Home supplies bag of peanuts

11 SEPTEMBER 1988

Examined by Dr Stock: Observations taken by Sister E Kearns (no relation of matron). E Kearns of Tygerberg. Sister Letitia Johnson taking observations in the evening. Sister Marlene Vorster brings chocolate cake.

12 SEPTEMBER 1988

Weight 69,5 kg

14 SEPTEMBER 1988

Sister Killassy Pam, E. leaves on week's holiday

20 SEPTEMBER 1988

Examined by Dr Stock. Matron Tee announces that she would fly to London to visit her sick sister

22 SEPTEMBER 1988

Weight 70 kg. Four blood specimen[s] taken by Major Kleinhans.

Dr Stock did not turn up. Dr Stock turns up about 5 pm. Received report that I have started coughing again. I assure him that I was not coughing.

26 SEPTEMBER 1988

Weight 71 kg. Dr Stock examines me as usual
Visited the 'garden' for ±45 minutes. Misty and cold

27 SEPTEMBER 1988

Examined by Dr Stock, as usual

Nurse Kay celebrated her 21st birthday on 25.9.88 Visited by
Sister Bradley

28 SEPTEMBER 1988

Prison outfit brought over

15 OCTOBER 1988

Examined by Dr Stock as usual. Examined also by Prof De Kock

Visited by Zami, Leabie, Zindzi, Zozo and Zondwa[66]

17 OCTOBER 1988

Sat for exam in Military Law

Dr Stock examines at about 5.30 pm

22 OCTOBER 1988

Dr Stock examines me as usual. Prescribes two pairs of long
elastic socks and Cepacol

24 OCTOBER 1988

Weight 71 kg. Dr Stock examines me: Got 500 g peanuts; 100g
brazils; 100g almonds. Dr Strauss, Chief Superintendent of

....

66. Nomabandla (Leabie) Piliso (née Mandela) (1930–97). Zozo is Zindzi's daughter and Mandela's
granddaughter, Zoleka, and Zondwa is Zindzi's son and Mandela's grandson, also known as Gadaffi
(1985–).

Tygerberg, visits me.

3 NOVEMBER 1988

Examined by Dr Stock. Major Marais advises that request to purchase clothing has been granted. Weight 71 kg

19 NOVEMBER 1988

Examined by Dr Stock. Sister Ruth Skosana takes fortnight's leave

21 NOVEMBER 1988

Weight 73 kg. Sister Ray leaves for 3 weeks holiday to Johannesburg. Examined by Dr Stock

30 NOVEMBER 1988

Examined by Dr Stock. Returns twice to report on results of blood test and on condition of Sister Julie Morgan. Tests disclose viral meningitis.

7 DECEMBER 1988

Examined by Dr Stock

Transferred from Constantiaberg Clinic about 9.30 pm to Paarl [Victor Verster Prison]

8 DECEMBER 1988

Private X 6005 South Paarl. Prison 1335/88

Examined by Dr Schoening. 7624-41011 (02211)

23 DECEMBER 1988

Spent 7 hrs with Pollsmoor comrades

25 DECEMBER 1988

Visited by Zami, Zindzi, Zozo and the 2 Zondwas[67]

2 JANUARY 1989

Visited by Brig T.T. Matanzima from ± 1915 am [*sic*] to 1.30 pm.

Agreed to see the 2 contending parties in the Thembu succession dispute.

17 JANUARY 1989

Zami and Zindzi pay visit from 11 am to 1.15 pm. Had lunch together

25 JANUARY 1989

Visited the X-ray firm of Ormond and Partners at City Park. On return journey drove past Langa, Gugulethu, Crossroads, Khayelitsha, Strand, Beaufort West, Du Toit Pass [*sic*], Grabouw, Elgin and Frenchoek [*sic*]. R9,70 to Sgt Gregory

27 JANUARY 1989

T.B. treatment ended

24 FEBRUARY 1989

Visited by Mr Sidelsky for 40+ minutes. His wife and daughter, Ruth, not allowed in. Barry a minister of religion in Israel. Colin in commerce in SA (estate agent).[68] R9.70 given to Sgt Gregory

12 MARCH 1989

Received so far 674 birthday cards from Cape Democrats.

....

67. One Zondwa is Zindzi's son. The other is Zondwa Malefane, son of M K Malefane.
68. Lazar Sidelsky's children.

15 MARCH 1989

Visited by Tyhopho from 11.15 to 2 pm

16 MARCH 1989

Examined by Prof. M.B. Van Rooyen. Right eye deteriorating but op not indicated. Passed through Wellington, Worcester, Rawsonville, Tulbagh through Du Toit [*sic*] tunnel. Re-examination by Dr Van Seggelin. Also visited Pollsmoor [Prison].

17 MARCH 1989

Visited by Bri Bri [Wilton Mkwayi] from 11.15 am to 1.30 pm. Liquifilm.

24 MARCH 1989

Visited by Mandla from 11.30 am to 1.30 pm.[69] Brought Sakharov Award. Scroll and cheque and medal

25 MARCH 1989

Visited by Wonga [K D Matanzima], Mafu and their wives.[70] R400 from Wonga and R200 from Mafu. Picked up a further R5 from bathroom.

26 MARCH 1989

Visited by Mandla from 11.10 am to 12.50 pm. Given him R400 in addition to the R90 given to him on 24.3.89

30 MARCH 1989

Visited by Mrs Engelbrecht and Mr Nel from First National Bank, Paarl. Letter to Shenge [Mangosuthu Buthelezi] handed

....

69. Mandla Mandela (1974–). Makgatho's son and Mandela's grandson.
70. Mafu is Mafu Matanzima.

in for posting today. Amended in terms of request from prison authorities.

21 APRIL 1989

57 birthday cards issued by the Labour Party in London handed in.

31 MAY 1989

Zami arrives at gate unexpectedly. Request she should come with Zindzi.

8 JUNE 1989

Visited by Amina and Yusuf Cachalia for 3 hrs.

9 JUNE 1989

Visited by Gen. W. [Willemse] and exchanged views on an important matter.

14 JUNE 1989

Visited by Mike Rossouw.

Advised to have no visits until 24th of this month

15 JUNE 1989

Visited by Xhamela [Walter Sisulu] for about 1½ hrs.

20 JUNE 1989

Advised that the plan has fallen through.

26 JUNE 1989

Visited by Gen. Willemse and another from 9.am to 11.45.

4 JULY 1989

Crucial meeting with Min K.C. [Kobie Coetsee]

5 JULY 1989

Meeting with very important person – no politics discussed.

B.P. 7 am 170/100   3.45 pm 160/90.

11 JULY 1989

BP. 7 am 180/90   2.30 pm 210/90

Visited by G.W. [General Willemse] and 2 others. Visited by Chief MB Joyi and his brother for ±3 hrs

13 JULY 1989

BP. 7 am 160/80   3.45 pm: 170/90

Visited by Mrs Helen Suzman.

14 JULY 1989

Visited by Kathy [Kathrada], Mpandla [Mlangeni], Mokoni [Motsoaledi], Ndobe [Mhlaba] and Xhamela [Sisulu].

18 JULY 1989

BP 170/80   7 am 71st birthday. Visited by Zami and all the children and grandchildren save Zeni family and Isaac.

19 JULY 1989

Drove out from 10.15 am to 3.45 pm.

2 AUGUST 1989

Visited by comrades from Pollsmoor and Robben Island for 5 hrs

3 AUGUST 1989
Visited by Fatima [Meer] from 9.15 am to 3.45 pm

4 AUGUST 1989
Visited by Mrs Stella Sigcau from 10 am to 3.30 pm[71]

8 AUGUST 1989
Visited by Chiefs Zanengqele Dalasile and Phathekile Holomisa

10 AUGUST 1989
Visited by Mamphela Ramphele for 3 hrs.[72]

11 AUGUST 1989
Meeting for 3 hrs with Oscar Mpetha at Pollsmoor.[73]

12 AUGUST 1989
Report that OR had stroke, flown to London.

Zeni and children fail to turn up.

13 SEPTEMBER 1989
Visited by Kgatho, Zondi, Mandla and Ndaba[74]

20 SEPTEMBER 1989
BP. 7 am 165/90   3.45 pm 160/80
Mr F.W. de Klerk inaugurated as new State President[75]

....

71. Princess Stella Sigcau (1937–2006). Prime minister of the Transkei, 1987, and a cabinet minister in post-apartheid South Africa.
72. Mamphela Ramphele (1947–). Academic, doctor and anti-apartheid activist.
73. Oscar Mafakafaka Mpetha (1909–94). Anti-apartheid activist, trade unionist and political prisoner.
74. Ndaba Mandela. Makgatho's son and Mandela's grandson.
75. Frederik Willem (F W) de Klerk, see People, Places and Events.

10 OCTOBER 1989

BP. 180/90 Announcement of intended release of Tyhopho and others.[76]

Visited by Kgatho 7.15 to 8.30 am

Visited by Ministers Coetsee and Dr G Viljoen.[77]

11 OCTOBER 1989

Chest and leg xrays by Dr Kaplan. Climbed Paarl Rock.

13 OCTOBER 1989

Visited by Jeff Masemola from 10.45 to 4 pm[78]

16 OCTOBER 1989

Visited by Rochelle[79]

18 OCTOBER 1989

Visited by 7 relatives and friends from Thembuland.

19 OCTOBER 1989

Visited by four relatives and friends: Zami delivers note

26 OCTOBER 1989

Spoke to Cyril and Murphy[80]

---

76. Walter Sisulu, Raymond Mhlaba, Ahmed Kathrada, Andrew Mlangeni, Elias Motsoaledi, Jeff Masemola, Wilton Mkwayi and Oscar Mpetha were released five days later from Johannesburg Prison.
77. Gerrit Viljoen (1926–2009). Minister of Constitutional Development. He provided a framework for the government's discussions with the ANC.
78. Jafta (Jeff) Kgalabi Masemola (1928–90). Political activist and political prisoner. Member of the PAC.
79. Rochelle Mtirara. Mandela's granddaughter by tradition.
80. Cyril Ramaphosa and Murphy Morobe.

29 OCTOBER 1989
National welcome rally for the 7 released prisoners plus Govan [Mbeki]

31 OCTOBER 1989
Visited by Zami, Zindzi and baby from 9 am to 5 pm.

10 NOVEMBER 1989
Visited by 5 Robben Islanders from 11 am to 4 pm.

28 NOVEMBER 1989
Mary Benson's 70th Birthday[81]

13 DECEMBER 1989
Met State President F.W. de Klerk for 2 hrs 55 m

29 DECEMBER 1989
BP 7 am 160/90   8.30 am 140/80   4 pm 160/80

Visited by Laloo Chiba, Reggie Vandeyar and Shirish Nanabhai[82]

30 DECEMBER 1989
Spoken to Xhamela and Ntsiki[83]

31 DECEMBER 1989
BP 7 am 155/80   3.45 pm 140/80
Trouser size 87R/34R
Style   8127

---

81. Mary Benson (1919–2000). Writer and anti-apartheid activist.
82. Reggie Vandeyar and Shirish Nanabhai were members of MK who became political prisoners.
83. Ntsiki is Albertina Sisulu.

Mandela's stay in the house in Victor Verster Prison was a time of transition between imprisonment and freedom. Dated 13 January 1990, this is the very last diary entry he made while in prison.

Flock of ducks walks clumsily into the lounge and loiter about apparently unaware of my presence. Males with loud colours, but keeping their dignity and not behaving like playboys. Moments later they become aware of my presence. If they got a shock they endured it with grace. Nevertheless, I detect some invisible feeling of unease on their part. It seems as if their consciences are worrying them, and although I feared that very soon their droppings will decorate the expensive carpet, I derive some satisfaction when I notice that their consciences are worrying them. Suddenly they squawk repeatedly and then file out. I was relieved. They behave far better than my grandchildren. They always leave the house upside down.

8.00	Flock of ducks walks clumsily into the lounge
8.30	and loiter about apparently unaware of my
9.00	presence. Males with loud colours, but keeping
9.30	their dignity and not behaving like play-
10.00	boys. Moments later they become aware of
10.30	my presence. If they got a shock they
11.00	endured it with grace. Nevertheless, I detect
11.30	some invisible feeling of unease on their
NOON	part. It seems as if their consciences
1.00	are worrying them, and although I feared
1.30	that very soon their droppings will decorate
2.00	the expensive carpet, I derive some
2.30	satisfaction when I notice that their
3.00	consciences are worrying them. Suddenly
3.30	they squawk repeatedly and their file
4.00	file out. I was relieved. They
4.30	behaved far better than my grandchild-
5.00	ren. They always leave the house upside
5.30	down

NIGHT APPOINTMENTS

14 Sunday   **15** Monday

See page 316.

PART FOUR

Tragicomedy

The years after Nelson Mandela's release from prison were extremely cluttered for him. He was preoccupied with organising the African National Congress, conducting negotiations, preparing for the elections, governing as president, travelling the world as the most celebrated leader of his age, and all the while coping with the pain of his divorce from Winnie. A private man even in his private life, he found it difficult to talk about personal relationships. His time was seldom his own. This is reflected in the series of notebooks he kept during the period. Aside from the lengthy 'minutes' he wrote during meetings, the entries are a staccato representation of day-to-day events.

The period 1990–94 was one of blood and fear in South Africa. Thousands died in political violence. Massacres, like those at Sebokeng, Boipatong and Bisho, were common. Throughout, there was a palpable fear of a right-wing, military-backed coup. Pragmatism drove the negotiations and the policy of reconciliation. The conversations Mandela had with Richard Stengel and Ahmed Kathrada for his authorised book projects took place at the same time that he was either keeping the country together (before April 1994) or actually running it (from May 1994). One day he witnesses the brutal effects of violence with his own eyes; the next, he is in quiet and studied contemplation of the past. While he probably enjoyed the conversations and often chuckled or laughed (on one occasion he looked down and said '[I have] reversed my socks'), he also yawned fairly frequently and once complained that he could not keep his eyes open.

Nelson Mandela's remembrance of his prison years is not without nostalgia. The routine. The camaraderie. The lessons learned. The time for reading and study. The time for writing letters. For contemplation. In a twist of irony, though, he has remained, in a sense, a prisoner. Frequently over the years since his release he has teased visitors and guests with the comment that he is still not free, while pointing a finger at his personal assistants: 'And these are my jailers.'

CHAPTER TWELVE

From a Polecat to a Miracle

'We do not underestimate the enemy and in past conflicts against superior odds it has fought courageously and received the admiration of all. But then they had something to defend – their independence. Now positions are reversed – they are a minority of oppressors heavily outnumbered here at home and isolated in the entire world. And the result of the conflict will certainly be different.'

....

Excerpt from his unpublished autobiographical manuscript written in prison, see page 325.

We do not underestimate the enemy and in past conflicts against superior odds it has fought courageously and received the admiration of all. But then they had something to defend – their independence. Now positions are reversed – they are a minority of oppressors heavily outnumbered here at home and isolated in the entire world. And the result of the conflict will certainly be different. The wheel of life is there and national heroes throughout our history from Autshumayo [*sic*] to [Chief Albert] Luthuli, in fact the entire people of our country have been working for it for more than 3 centuries. It is clogged with dry wax and rust but we have managed to make it creak and move backwards and forwards and we live in the hope and confidence that one day we'll be able to turn it full circle so that the exalted will crumble and the despised be exalted, no – so that all men – the exalted and the wretched of the earth can live as equals.

2. CONVERSATION WITH RICHARD STENGEL ABOUT HIS SPEECH-
   MAKING STYLE

STENGEL: Sometimes people do criticise you for not being a more rousing speaker.
MANDELA: Well, in a climate of this nature, when we are trying to reach a settlement through negotiations you don't want rabble-rousing speeches. You want to discuss problems with people soberly, because the people would like to know *how* you behave or how you express yourself, and then they can have an idea of how you are handling important issues in the course of those negotiations. The masses like to see somebody who is responsible and who speaks in a responsible manner. They *like* that, and so I avoid rabble-rousing speech. I don't want

to incite the crowd. I want the crowd to understand what we are doing and I want to *infuse* a spirit of reconciliation to them.

STENGEL: Would you say your speaking style is different now than in the old days before you went to prison?

MANDELA: Well, I have mellowed, very definitely, and as a young man, you know, I was very *radical* and using high-flown language, and fighting everybody. But now, you know, one has to lead and . . . a rabble-rousing speech therefore is not appropriate . . .

3. FROM THE UNPUBLISHED SEQUEL TO HIS AUTOBIOGRAPHY

Leaders fully appreciate that constructive criticism within the structures of the organisation, however sharp it may be, is one of the most effective methods of addressing internal problems, of ensuring that the views of each comrade are carefully considered, that if a comrade is to express his views freely there must be no fear of marginalization or, even worse, of victimization.

It is a grave error for any leader to be oversensitive in the face of criticism, to conduct discussions as if he or she is a schoolmaster talking to less informed and inexperienced learners. A leader should encourage and welcome [a] free and unfettered exchange of views. But no one should ever question the honesty of another comrade, whether he or she is a leader or ordinary member.

4. FROM THE UNPUBLISHED SEQUEL TO HIS AUTOBIOGRAPHY

One should never forget the main aim in a debate, inside and outside the organisations, in political rallies, in Parliament and other government structures, is that we should emerge from that debate, however sharp our differences might have been, stronger, closer and more united and confident than ever before. The removal of differences and mutual suspicion within one's organisation, between one's organisation and adversaries, but total focus on the implementation of the basic policy of one's organisation, should always be our guiding principle.

5. FROM A CONVERSATION WITH RICHARD STENGEL ABOUT HIS SEPARATION FROM WINNIE MANDELA

No I would [not] go into details except just to state that I had to separate from her on personal grounds.

6. FROM A NOTEBOOK

Number of deaths in Sannieville, Krugersdorp
18 people were killed in broad daylight at the funeral of [Sam] Ntuli[1]
    All the evidence stretching over the past 2 years shows that the NP [National Party] and the regime know who the killers are, and why they are killing innocent and defenceless men, women and children, and who pays them for doing so. Why is Battalion 32 not sent there

7. FROM A NOTEBOOK – THOUGHTS ON NEGOTIATING

    1) Start with negotiation
    2) Political prisoners must be released before Xmas

    Capture the thoughts and feelings of this audience in the eloquent language of art – in this particular case of vibrant music and animated dancing they are like raindrops from the blue sky

....

1. Sam Ntuli (d. 1991). Assassinated member of the ANC. Mourners were murdered by gunmen at his funeral in Katlehong, East Rand.

and the developing world.

4

Aids.

Aids is a major problem to be tackled by the entire world. To deal with it requires resources far beyond the capacity of one continent. No single country has the capacity to deal with it.

An aids epidemic will destroy or retard the economic growth throughout the world. A world wide multi-faceted strategy in this regard is required.

5.

The continent of Africa is well aware of the importance of environment. But most of the continent's problems on environment are simply the product of poverty and lack of education. Africa has no resources or skills to deal with desertation, deforestation, soil erosion and

---

From a notebook, see page 329.

8. FROM A NOTEBOOK

Think through brain not blood

9. FROM A NOTEBOOK

AIDS is a major problem to be tackled by the entire world. To deal with it requires resources far beyond the capacity of one continent. No single country has the capacity to deal with it.

An AIDS epidemic will destroy or retard economic growth throughout the world. A world wide multi-faceted strategy in this regard is required.

10. FROM A NOTEBOOK

The continent of Africa is well aware of the importance of the environment. But most of the continent's problems on [the] environment are simply the product of poverty and lack of education. Africa has no resources or skills to deal with desertation [sic], deforestation, soil erosion and pollution.

None of these issues should be treated separately as if the world is not a single world. The position is worsened by the rich countries which are exploiting the poverty of the people of Africa, and dumping toxic waste on the continent. They give them money; literally bribe them to expose the population to all the dangers of pollution.

11. FROM A NOTEBOOK

A cardinal point that we must keep constantly in mind, the lodestar which keeps us in course, as we negotiate the uncharted twists and turns of the struggle for liberation is that the breakthrough is never the result of individual effort. It is always a collective effort and triumph.

12. FROM THE UNPUBLISHED SEQUEL TO HIS AUTOBIOGRAPHY

During my political career, I have discovered that in all communities, African, Coloured, Indian and Whites, and in all political organisations without exception, there are good men and women who fervently wish to go on with their lives, who yearn for peace and stability, who want a decent income, good houses and to send their children to the best schools, who respect and want to maintain the social fabric of society.

13. FROM A NOTEBOOK

21.9.92
Troika, investigation, mass actions – feeling
Indictment, concern for economy, social fabric of blacks
Boardroom should be swept before we meet at 1 pm

14. FROM A NOTEBOOK

In future you must come early
Stronger movement for unity
Case to disgrace certain organisations
Attack a young man who is unable to defend himself
Review
Admission
100 of thousands
Humphrey – video
Will consult chiefs
Chiefs must not be members of political organisations
[December 1991]

15. FROM A DRAFT LETTER TO GRAÇA MACHEL, c.1992[2]

Losing your luggage, especially on your way abroad, must have been a painful experience. I do not want to think of the embarrassment and inconvenience you suffered among strangers in foreign countries. Fortunately you told me about it almost at the end of your visit, to that extent my distress was eased by the knowledge that you would soon be back, and join the children.

They must have missed you very much and, in spite of your and Zina's assurance I found it difficult to be comforted . . . To your brother you are becoming very special and a lot of thinking and feeling was centred on you. Visiting two capitals must have been somewhat strenuous, but you are a remarkable person, and you have enormous capacity to take such a workload in your stride.

I think of you.

16. FROM A NOTEBOOK DURING POLITICAL NEGOTIATIONS AT CODESA (CONVENTION FOR A DEMOCRATIC SOUTH AFRICA)[3]

1) Suggestion for stopping violence
2) Can we remain indifferent to the slaughter and continue to talk to regime?
3) Would pulling out of Codesa not be shortest way to breakthrough?
4) Would withdrawal

---

2. Graça Machel, see People, Places and Events.
3. CODESA was a multi-party negotiating forum which started on 21 December 1991 at the World Trade Centre in Johannesburg.

17. FROM A NOTEBOOK

20.8.92

Meeting with 3 regions of Natal[4]
Violence: no of deaths

March	140 died
April	91
May	79
June	82
July	133
Aug	52

Over 700 people died
7 000 refugees in Midlands
Ngwelezana and Stanger
Attacks by small groups of armed men – attacks houses in strongholds of ANC. Main targets ANC and alliance.
Intimate [sic] role of security forces.
Pump gun – using pellets.
Attacks of people only from ANC events.
Existence of hit squads –
June – 119 people died from hit-squads
45 occurred in Natal

18. FROM A NOTEBOOK

26.8.92
Whoever runs [the] country he will want a good economy.
2 mnths [months] – economy going down.
To retrieve economy will be extremely difficult.

....

4. Violence between supporters of the Inkatha Freedom Party (IFP) and the ANC led to thousands of deaths in KwaZulu-Natal from 1985 to 1995.

19. FROM A NOTEBOOK

I was in prison when she [Ruth First] was assassinated felt almost all alone. Lost a sister in arms.
It is no consolation to know that she live[s] beyond her grave. This commemoration
A Jewish woman from a well-to-do family broke ranks with her privileged comm[unity]

20. FROM A DRAFT LETTER TO PRESIDENT F W DE KLERK, c.1992, ON THE EVE OF THE BISHO MASSACRE[5]

To be sent to Mr F.W. de Klerk by 7.30 am
I refer to our conversation earlier this evening, and I confirm that what you conveyed to me is inconsistent with the contents of your letter of 4 September 1992.

In that letter you refer expressly to actions being planned in the Ciskei on 7 September 1992. You then state that your Government has no objection to peaceful demonstrations which take place within the parameters of the National Peace Accord and the guidelines of the Goldstone Commission.[6]

For this reason, you pointed out; you do not question the key objectives of the organizers of the planned march as have been defined.

You further point out that you are doing everything possible to help in the arrangement of an agreement between all those involved which will ensure that the planned action takes place peacefully. You then appeal to me to ensure that the ANC [African National Congress] gives its cooperation in this regard. I readily assured you of our cooperation.

---

5. Twenty-eight ANC supporters were shot dead by soliders on 7 September 1992, during a protest march where 70,000 ANC supporters tried to enter a sports stadium in Bisho, Ciskei.
6. The National Peace Accord, negotiated by South African political organisations in 1991, aimed to prevent violence. The Goldstone Commission was established to investigate political violence and intimidation.

All these statements and assurances concerned what is planned inside, and not outside, the Ciskei.

Our entire position today has drastically shifted. Nowhere in the above-mentioned letter did you even hint that, while you were soliciting our cooperation, you were at the same time deploying troops on the Ciskeian borders, erecting road blocks and declaring unrest areas, all of which . . . to your knowledge, create tensions.

Equally disturbing is the fact that this evening you state, contrary to your letter of 4 September, that you will not interfere in the internal affairs of the Ciskei. These contradictions are unfortunate and tend to strengthen then the perception that you and I are not negotiating in good faith. I urge you to honour our agreement of 4 September, and not to do anything which may damage the climate for peaceful negotiations for which we have all worked so hard to create.

I further confirm that we do not recognise the Bantustans, and accordingly do not consider ourselves bound by the decisions of its courts. We hope that all the parties concerned will help to diffuse the volatile situation and allow the demonstrations to proceed as planned.

The march will be led by our Secretary-General, Cyril Ramaphosa, Chris Hani, Gertrude Shope, Ronnie Kasrils, Raymond Suttner, Tony Yengeni and others.[7]

Yours sincerely,

Nelson Mandela
President, ANC.

....

7. Matamela Cyril Ramaphosa (1952–). Thembisile (Chris) Hani, see People, Places and Events. Gertrude Shope (1925–). Ronnie Kasrils (1938–). Dr Raymond Suttner (1945–). Tony Yengeni (1954–). ANC leaders.

CONVERSATIONS WITH MYSELF

21. FROM A NOTEBOOK

Our strength lies in discipline.
Right to peaceful demonstration
It was criminal.
Forces for democracy.
Not of revenge. Keep in state of readiness
Whatever we do must be within the peace process. We cannot allow ourselves to be accused of violating peace process.

22. FROM A NOTEBOOK

Our present position on this aspect is the same as that of the Federal Republic of Germany, which contains in its constitution a clause on nationalization as one of the options the Government might employ in case of need. That option has not been exercised in that country for decades.

South African economy is in a parlous state.

23. FROM A NOTEBOOK, c.1993

In the period we are all going into we have to consider moving away from our past – must change our approach.

In such a situation all people become concerned about the future. What's going to happen to me, wife and chldn [children]. Every country needs a police force which protects its, their values.

We . . . who have been struggling have to change.

We come from an environment which saw police force as hostile. You come from a background where Govt [goverment] used you to defend interests of ruling party. No doubt many of you joined force to serve State and people. But ruling party made itself synonymous with that state.

Now moving to a state where all of us want to be part of state – police force can now protect people.

Best thing is that those who were in police force and outside police force do it together.

There is no doubt that ANC [African National Congress] is going to be major party in Govt. We want to avoid mistake of the past, we do not want police to be defenders of the ANC. That does not mean that you are neutral to police as individuals.

Police force are neutral to party politics, but defenders of democracy.

Address their concrete concerns.

Obviously there are going to be changes. The experience of running a p. [police] force exists in this current phase.

Ideally all changes must include members of police force and those not members. Whatever changes are done are done with their involvement.

This is approach we are taking I. G. of N [Interim Government of National] – Unity – champion.

Appealing to them to become part of that process of change – in particular change of police force. That way they will make sure that ANC addresses their concerns.

24. FROM THE UNPUBLISHED SEQUEL TO HIS AUTOBIOGRAPHY

In 1959 [Chris] Hani had enrolled at Fort Hare University and attracted the attention of Govan Mbeki. Govan played a formative role in Hani's development. It was here that Hani encountered Marxist ideas and joined the already illegal and underground South African Communist Party. He always emphasized that his conversion to Marxism also deepened his nonracial perspective. Hani was a bold and forthright young man and did not hesitate to criticise even his own organisation when he felt it was failing to give leadership. He recalled that:

'Those of us in the camps in the Sixties did not have a profound understanding of the problems. Most of us were very young, in our early twenties. We were impatient to get into action. "Don't tell us there are no routes," we used to say. "We must be deployed to find routes. That's what we were trained for."'

25. FROM A TELEVISED ADDRESS TO THE NATION AFTER CHRIS HANI WAS ASSASSINATED BY JANUSZ WALUŚ ON 10 APRIL 1993[8]

Tonight I am reaching out to every single South African, black and white, from the very depths of my being.

A white man, full of prejudice and hate, came to our country and committed a deed so foul that our whole nation now teeters on the brink of disaster.

A white woman, of Afrikaner origin, risked her life so that we may know, and bring to justice, this assassin.[9]

The cold-blooded murder of Chris Hani has sent shock waves throughout the country and the world. Our grief and anger is tearing us apart.

What has happened is a national tragedy that has touched millions of people, across the political and colour divide.

Our shared grief and legitimate anger will find expression in nationwide commemorations that coincide with the funeral service . . .

Now is the time for all South Africans to stand together against those who, from any quarter, wish to destroy what Chris Hani gave his life for – the freedom of all of us.

Now is the time for our white compatriots, from whom messages of condolence continue to pour in, to reach out with an understanding of the grievous loss to our nation, to join in the memorial services and the funeral commemorations.

8. Chris Hani, see People, Places and Events.
9. Mandela is referring to Hani's neighbour, who recorded Waluś's licence-plate number and called the police.

Now is the time for the police to act with sensitivity and restraint, to be real community policemen and women who serve the population as a whole. There must be no further loss of life at this tragic time.

This is a watershed moment for all of us.

Our decisions and actions will determine whether we use our pain, our grief and our outrage to move forward to what is the only lasting solution for our country – an elected government of the people, by the people and for the people.

We must not let the men who worship war, and who lust after blood, precipitate actions that will plunge our country into another Angola.

Chris Hani was a soldier. He believed in iron discipline. He carried out instructions to the letter. He practised what he preached.

Any lack of discipline is trampling on the values that Chris Hani stood for. Those who commit such acts serve only the interests of the assassins, and desecrate his memory.

When we, as one people, act together decisively, with discipline and determination, nothing can stop us.

Let us honour this soldier for peace in a fitting manner. Let us rededicate ourselves to bringing about the democracy he fought for all his life: democracy that will bring real, tangible changes in the lives of the working people, the poor, the jobless, the landless.

26. FROM THE UNPUBLISHED SEQUEL TO HIS AUTOBIOGRAPHY

Hani put the last years of his life [into] tirelessly addressing meetings throughout the length and breadth of South Africa: village gatherings, shop stewards councils and street committees. He [lent] all his authority and military prestige to defend[ing] negotiations, often speaking patiently to very [sceptical] youths, or committees suffering the brunt of Third Force violence . . . Clive Derby-Lewis admitted that they had hoped to derail negotiations by unleashing a wave of race hatred and civil war. It is a tribute to the maturity of South Africans of all persuasions, and it is a tribute to the memory of Hani, that his death, tragically but factually, finally brought focus and urgency to our negotiated settlement.

27. FROM A NOTEBOOK

14.5.93

1.
Priority is commitment to oppressed.
Will fall or rise depending on our success or failure to address their needs, to accommodate their aspirations.
Specifically we must get them houses and put to an end informal settlements; end unemployment, school crisis, lack of medical facilities.

2.
Fears of minorities about future.

3.
Threat from right wing not from black surrogates.

28. FROM A CONVERSATION WITH RICHARD STENGEL

You see, Chris Hani was a hero amongst our people, especially to the youth, and there was anger at his death. We had to do something to channel away that anger, and the only thing we could do was to have demonstrations throughout the country so that the people could find expression for their anger. If we had not done so the right wing and these sinister elements would have succeeded in drawing the country [in]to a racist war and incalculable loss of human lives and bloodshed . . . But because of the steps that we took we prevented that, and in spite of . . . isolated incidents of violence, those demonstrations went on very well . . . We frustrated the objective of the people who killed Hani.

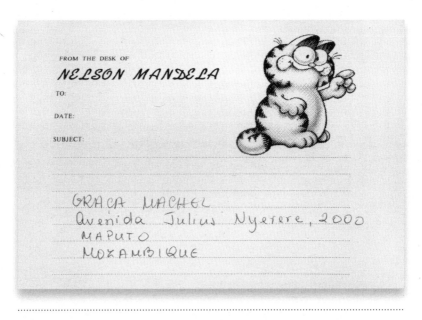

FROM THE DESK OF

NELSON MANDELA

TO:

DATE:

SUBJECT:

GRACA MACHEL
Avenida Julius Nyerere, 2000
MAPUTO
MOXAMBIQUE

Mandela notes the address of Graça Machel (who was later to become his third wife) on his personalised notepaper.

29. FROM A NOTEBOOK

I met Graça Machel in Johannesburg on no less than three different occasions. She always was polite, discrete and understanding. But in Maputo, where she was Minister of Education and Culture for 14 years, and where she still remains Member of Parliament in charge of International Affairs, I met a totally different Graça, firm and authoritative even though courteous and charming. I had enormous respect for President Chissano.[10]

30. FROM A NOTEBOOK, c.1993

I will leave at 7 am tomorrow for Pieterm[aritzburg] + will return on Sunday evening. Some third force elements, believed to be State Security Service, have in that area, recently killed an alarmingly large number of innocent civilians, including children going to school. The massacre started a day before the start of the peace talks in Johannesburg. We suspect that these elements want our people to continue to slaughter one another [with] the ultimate aim of stopping negotiations. Our investigations show serious discrepancies between the police version of what happened and ours.

31. FROM A NOTEBOOK, c.1993

Writing letters to friends used to be one of my favorite hobbies and each letter gave me a lot of pleasure. Pressure of work now makes it impossible for me to engage in this hobby. Apart from typed formal letters from the President's office, I cannot remember ever writing any message similar to this letter since February 1990.

32. FROM A DRAFT LETTER TO GRAÇA MACHEL

The situation in Angola is causing great concern.

Now on a personal note: Mr Samaranch, President of the International Olympic Committee, has invited me to a health farm in Switzerland for a check-up and treatment presumably for about 7 days; Although I know very little about such health

---

10. Joaquim Alberto Chissano (1939–). President of Mozambique, 1986–2005.

centres, I have agreed to go. You probably know better in this regard than me and I would be happy to get your advice.

Meeting the girls for the first time made me hesitant to discuss certain ideas with them, at least with Olivia. I wanted to find out about her schooling. Being your daughter a lot is expected of her both inside and outside Mozambique. The upgrading [of] high academic qualifications would certainly put her in a better position to serve Mozambique and its people. If she is interested in going to High School or university you and I can then discuss the matter further. It may perhaps be wise not to mention the matter to her until we have exchanged views.

I went back to the office on 8th March and plunged immediately into work with the first engagement being at 7 am and leaving the office at 5 pm. Yesterday <u>I started at 6.45 am but was back home by 2 pm. We are trying to limit my office work to mornings only.</u> Today I again started at 6.45 am. Had lunch with Board of Directors of Liberty Life Insurance Company and other leading businessmen and I was back home at 3.45 pm.

When friends go abroad we tend to feel lonely even though we have never actually lived with them. There's always a conflict between reality and feeling, between the brain and the blood.

33. FROM A CONVERSATION WITH RICHARD STENGEL

Well, it was clear that something was happening because there was an unacceptably high incidence of violence in which people were killed. And the arrests and convictions, you see, were few and far between, and it was clear that there was connivance on the part of the security forces. Some of the incidents indicated that the police themselves were involved, the police, the army. Because if you went to the townships – talked to the people there, they had no doubt that the police are *highly* instrumental in this . . . Yesterday I went to the Vaal, to Sebokeng, and then in the course of my speech I said that the police are very much involved . . .'[11] I went to the hospital first and saw the people, the patients there who were shot but escaped death. I saw them, and one of them, a young lady, a young girl, said that she was shot by a white man in a bakkie [pick-up truck], yes . . . So I say, 'Well this is the first time I hear of this.' She says, 'No, I could see the white man very clearly, and when he shot me.' And because the press as well as the TV and radio have been saying, 'Four black men' . . . and this young lady says, 'No there was a white man.'

34. FROM A NOTEBOOK

On the dropping of the voting age below 18 . . . it is clear from the explanation given by Cde [Comrade] Cyril [Ramaphosa] yesterday morning that the N.C. [Negotiating Committee] does not endorse my proposal as I thought, and that the organisation as a whole has not accepted that proposal.[12]

A statement on major policy matters should not be made without being processed and cleared, no matter what the status of a comrade is.

The statement must be an acute embarrassment to the policy making structures of the organisations, and to the membership as a whole . . .

35. FROM THE UNPUBLISHED SEQUEL TO HIS AUTOBIOGRAPHY

At meetings of the ANC [African National Congress], I often stressed that I did not want weak comrades or puppets who

---

11. On 26 March 1990 twelve people were killed and three hundred injured when police opened fire on a group of ANC protestors in Sebokeng, thirty miles from Johannesburg.
12. In 1993 Mandela proposed to reduce the voting age from eighteen to fourteen. The idea was rejected by the ANC Executive Committee.

would swallow anything I said, simply because I was President of the organisation. I called for a healthy relationship in which we could address issues, not as master and servants, but as equals in which each comrade would express his or her views freely and frankly, and without fear of victimization or marginalization.

One of my proposals, for example, which generated a lot of sound and fury, was that we should reduce the voting age to fourteen, a step which had been taken by several countries elsewhere in the world. This was due to the fact that in those countries, the youth of more or less that age were in the forefront of their revolutionary struggles. It was that contribution which induced their victorious governments to reward them by giving them the right to vote. Opposition to my proposal from members of the National Executive Committee was so vehement and overwhelming that I retreated in order. The Sowetan newspaper dramatised the issue in its cartoon column when they showed a baby in napkins voting. It was one of the most graphic manners of ridiculing my idea. I did not have the courage to insist on it again.

36. FROM A NOTEBOOK

Leadership falls into 2 categories
    a) Those who are inconsistent, who[se] actions cannot be predicted, who agree today on a [matter] and repudiated it the following day.
    b) Those who are consistent, who have a sense of honour, a vision.

37. FROM A NOTEBOOK

The leader's first task is to create a vision.
His second is to create a following to help him implement the

vision and to manage the process through effective teams. The people being led know where they are going because the leader has communicated the vision and the followers have bought into the goal he had set as well as the process of getting there.

38. FROM THE UNPUBLISHED SEQUEL TO HIS AUTOBIOGRAPHY

It is a phenomenal leader who can succeed in exile to keep united a vast multiracial organisation with divergent schools of thought, with a membership deployed in distant continents, and a youth seething with anger at the repression of their people; a [youth] who believe that anger alone without resources and proper planning can help to overthrow a racist regime.

OR [Oliver Tambo] achieved all this. To political and common law prisoners inside the country, to foreign freedom fighters, diplomats, Heads of State, OR was acknowledged as a shining example of a smart and balanced leader who was sure to help restore the dignity of the oppressed people and put their destiny in their hands.

39. FROM THE UNPUBLISHED SEQUEL TO HIS AUTOBIOGRAPHY

OR's [Oliver Tambo] death was like the falling of a giant oak tree which had stood there for ages dominating and beautifying the entire landscape, and attracting everything around it, people and animals alike. It was the end of an era of a leader . . . with strong religious convictions, an accomplished mathematician and musician who was peerless in his commitment to his people.[13]

---

13. Oliver Tambo, who had returned to South Africa in 1991 after three decades in exile, died of a stroke on 24 April 1993.

40. FROM A CONVERSATION WITH RICHARD STENGEL ON THE DEATH OF OR (OLIVER) TAMBO

I felt very lonely indeed and seeing him lying there I couldn't believe that he was dead. It was a tragedy.

41. FROM A DRAFT LETTER TO GRAÇA MACHEL

Some people become national or international assets in their own humble way.

I have spent some time thinking about the other day, the things you advised me on. I hope you will understand it is never easy for those directly involved in a matter to reflect objectively, since they are invariably influenced by emotion rather than logic. I am, however working out a plan to accommodate some of your concerns, and will report to you in due course.

It will be an unfortunate mistake on your part to keep on harping on the fact that your advice may be misconstrued as interfering in matters which do not concern you. Your views have been sound and, as usual, I am confident that what I am going to say will not make you swollen-headed. But I know of some person very close to me, in fact, a sister, who is becoming an international asset in her own humble way, who has visited our country several times, and also some overseas countr[ies].

42. FROM A CONVERSATION WITH RICHARD STENGEL ON HIS INTERVIEW WITH PLAYWRIGHT ARTHUR MILLER

Well, I can't remember now the details except that I was told by our Department . . . of Information and Publicity that the BBC would like to send Arthur Miller to come and see me. I was, of course, keen to see him because he is an international figure of immense courage and ability and it was an honour for me to be interviewed by him . . . We spent about four hours together

. . . My impressions of him were confirmed: that this was a remarkable man. He knew what to ask. Like all truly great men, he did not throw his weight about; he tried as much as possible to make me feel comfortable in the presence of greatness [*laughs*] . . . I really was happy to meet him, to meet Arthur. He is really an impressive man.

43. FROM A NOTEBOOK, c.1993

On the eve of my departure to US [United States] and UN [United Nations] from South Africa over a score of people were shot dead on a highway outside Johannesburg.

Once again the police failed to protect the people going about their ordinary daily routine, and failed to pick up the trail of the killers.

And yet there has been a clear pattern to these attacks going back for three years. In those three years over 10 000 people have been slaughtered, with only a few of the perpetrators apprehended.

It is the total failure of the security forces to track down the killers that points to the culpability of the South African Police Force and elements of the Defence Force in this destabilization, as well as the connivance of the Government.

The victims on the ground have the perception that those security forces are part and parcel of the killings.

My experience and that of my comrades in the ANC [African National Congress] is that the De Klerk government shows no will at all, of wanting to adequately deal with this crucial problem.

28· 1· 94   Rockey
404 / 1227

Students Task force   648-5575
                                  (Aziz)
Women task force.

religious groups·
                    28· 1· 94
legislation on land reform, industrial policy
housing
                        ^^
            2· 1· 94·

The entire country was deeply shocked by the murder of
so many children in Mitchell's Plain.
Last Sunday I sent a telegram of sympathy to the
bereaved families which we distributed to the mass
media.
In spite of my tight schedule I will spend the rest
of the day visiting the bereaved families to give them
support. Children are our most precious possession, it is
an indescribable tragedy that they should die under
such tragic circumstances

From a personal file, January 1994, see page 349.

The entire country was deeply shocked by the murder of so many children in Mitchell's Plain.[14]

Last Sunday I sent a telegram of sympathy to the bereaved families which we distributed to the mass media.

In spite of my tight schedule I will spend the rest of the day visiting the bereaved families to give them support. Children are our most precious possession; it is an undesirable tragedy that they should die under such tragic circumstances.

45. FROM A PERSONAL FILE

1.
Share developments in democratic forces.

2.
Our problem is to face the very 1st democratic elections with 17 million voters who have never voted before.

3.
Illiteracy rate of 67% and 63% of our voters are rural based.

4.
Our problem is how to access people and introduce voters to education on how to vote.

5.
We are contesting this election with the NP [National Party] which has already 150 election offices. We have none save our regional offices.

---

14. Nineteen boys had been murdered by a serial killer in Mitchell's Plain, Cape Town.

6.

NP is one of the most efficient and well-organised political parties in the country.

7.

Enjoy mass support – opinion polls indicate that we would emerge as majority party. But decisive thing is to be able to carry voters to the voting booth.

46. FROM A NOTEBOOK, c.1994

1.

Personalise political experience

2.

Contrast between first visit and 2 later visits.
Prisoner facing the unknown
To persuade 25 comrades to leave prison . . .

3.

Death of my mother and eldest son
Natural causes, accident
Refused permission to attend burials

4.

Failure to thank those who helped me during early '40s

5.

Hoped I would find them alive on my return. They all went.
Thought world itself was dying.

6.

Harassment of my family
Zami and children

Psychological persecution –
<u>Adverse news about wife</u>

7.
Relations between prisoners and warders very bad
But furious arguments among warders – Sgt Opperman.

8.
Unity among prisoners – ANC, PAC, APDUSA – Makwetu, Pokela, Eddie, Neville, Saths Cooper, Walter, Govan, Kathy, Peake, Dennis Brutus – cowards – heroes.[15]

9.
Opportunity to stand back and reflect.

10.
Kramat, plays, Antigone.
Ability to read biographies and newspapers, to exchange views with others.

11.
Negotiations – meeting with PW Botha[16]

12.
Meeting with De Klerk on 9.2.89

13.
Pollsmoor and Victor Verster

15. Clarence Makwetu, John Nyathi Pokela, Edward (Eddie) Daniels, Dr Neville Alexander, Sathasivan (Saths) Cooper, Walter Sisulu, Govan Mbeki, Ahmed Kathrada, George Peake, Dennis Brutus, see People, Places and Events.
16. Pieter Willem (P W) Botha, see People, Places and Events.

I was receiving intelligence reports to the effect that the right-wing Afrikaners had decided to stop the forthcoming elections by violence. To be on the safe side the president of an organisation must carefully check the accuracy of such reports. I did so, and when I discovered that they were accurate I decided to act.

I flew down to the Wilderness, the retirement home of former president PW Botha, [and] reminded him of the communiqué we jointly issued when I was still in prison in July 1989. In that communiqué we pledged to work together for peace in our country. I informed him that peace was now threatened by the right wing and asked him to intervene. He was co-operative and confirmed that Afrikaners were deter-mined to stop the elections. But he added that he did not want to discuss the matter with me alone, and suggested that I bring President FW de Klerk, Ferdi Hartzenberg and the General [Constand Viljoen].[17]

I proposed that we should also include the leader of the extreme Afrikaner right wing, Eugene Terre'Blanche, on the grounds that he was a reckless demagogue who could attract larger crowds than President De Klerk.[18] On this issue the former president was so negative that I dropped the subject.

I returned to Johannesburg and immediately telephoned President De Klerk and informed him of Botha's invitation. He was as hostile to the whole idea of us meeting the former president as the latter was towards Terre'Blanche. I then approached the progressive Afrikaner theologian, Professor Johan Heyns, to bring together the general, Hartzenberg,

17. Ferdinand Hartzenberg (1936–). Originally a National Party politician, but helped to form the right-wing Conservative Party in 1982. Constand Viljoen (1933–). Former head of the apartheid-era defence force and leader of Freedom Front.
18. Eugène Ney Terre'Blanche (1941–2010). Founder of the far-right Afrikaner Weerstandsbeweging (or AWB) which was committed to the creation of a Boer/Afrikaner republic.

Terre'Blanche and myself.[19] Terre'Blanche was uncompromising and rejected any meeting with me, a communist, as he said.

I then met the General and Hartzenberg and asked whether it was true that they were preparing to stop the elections by violent means. The General was frank and admitted that this was correct and that Afrikaners were arming, and that a bloody civil war was facing the country. I was shaken but pretended that I was supremely confident of the victory of the liberation movement. I told them that they would give us a hard time since they were better trained militarily than us, commanded more devastating weaponry and because of their resources, they knew the country better than us. But I warned that at the end of that reckless gamble they would be crushed. We were on the verge of an historic victory after we had inflicted a mortal blow to white supremacy. I pointed out this was not due to their consent; it was in spite of their opposition. I added that we had a just cause, numbers and support of the international community. They had none of these. I appealed to them to stop their plans and to join the negotiations at the World Trade Centre.

48. FROM THE UNPUBLISHED SEQUEL TO HIS AUTOBIOGRAPHY

My installation as the first democratically elected President of the Republic of South Africa was imposed on me much against my advice.

As the date of the general elections approached, three senior ANC [African National Congress] leaders informed me that they had consulted widely within the organisation, and that the unanimous decision was that I should stand as President if we won the election. This, they said, was what they would propose at the first meeting of our parliamentary caucus.

---

19. Johan Adam Heyns (1928–94). Theologian of the Dutch Reformed Church.

I advised against the decision on the grounds that I would turn seventy-six that year, that it would be wise to get a far younger person, male or female, who had been out of prison, met heads of state and government, attended meetings of world and regional organisations, who had kept abreast of national and international developments, who could, as far as was possible, foresee the future course of such developments.

I pointed out that I had always admired men and women who used their talents to serve the community, and who were highly respected and admired for their efforts and sacrifices, even though they held no office whatsoever in government or society. The combination of talent and humility, of being able to be at home with both the poor and the wealthy, the weak and the mighty, ordinary people and royalty, young and old, men and women with a common touch, irrespective of their race or background, are admired by humankind all over the globe . . .

I urged the three senior leaders that I would prefer to serve without holding any position in the organisation or government. One of them, however, put me flat on the carpet. He reminded me that I had always advocated the importance of collective leadership, and that as long as we scrupulously served that principle we could never go wrong. He bluntly asked whether I was now reflecting what I had consistently preached. Although that principle was never intended to exclude a strong defence of what one firmly believed in, I decided to accept their proposal.

I, however, made it clear that I would serve for one term only. Although my statement seemed to have caught them unawares, they replied that I should leave that matter to the organisation. I did not want any uncertainty on this question. Shortly after I became President I publicly announced that I would serve one term only and would not seek re-election.

49. FROM THE UNPUBLISHED SEQUEL TO HIS AUTOBIOGRAPHY

On voting day, an elderly African lady from the Northern Transvaal, as it was then known, told the election official at the polling station that she wanted to vote for the boy who came from jail. Although she mentioned some name, she did not know to which organisation he belonged. After interrogation, the polling station was able to sort out the problem to her satisfaction.

50. FROM THE UNPUBLISHED SEQUEL TO HIS AUTOBIOGRAPHY

The fighters of Umkhonto we Sizwe (MK) displayed unrivalled courage and infiltrated the country, attacked government installations, and clashed with apartheid forces . . . now and again, putting them to flight.

Other freedom fighters worked inside the country either above or underground, urging the masses to rise and resist all forms of oppression and exploitation. They braved the brutality of the regime regardless of what happened to themselves. For liberation they were ready to pay the highest price.

Still others languished in apartheid jails, fearlessly asserting their right to be treated as human beings in their own motherland. They literally dug themselves in[to] the lion's den, demonstrating once again, the universal principle that the freedom flame cannot be smothered by evil men.

Suddenly in April 1994 the same fire-eaters who had mastered the art of resistance, and who had worked relentlessly for the total destruction of white supremacy, without any previous training and experience in governance, were entrusted with the awesome task of governing the most advanced and wealthy country on the African continent.

The unprecedented challenge was to restore the human dignity of all our people by removing all forms of racial

First Session of Parliament
25. 5. 94

Mr de Klerk's statement
Die NP is willig om sy taak te doen.
① Die tema van die toespraak van die president
Issues of minorities will be fully addressed.
self beskikking: Local govt can provide
room for self- govt.
Indicate progress in negotiating.

Kader Asmal.
All of us are here for the first time
notion of inclusiveness
RDP way of dealing with the past

Mr Marais.
Congratulates Sibusiso Bengu.
Persuasion will be used.

Coming from different backgrounds NB

Theywe Mkhitso.
In Xhosa: nabalela u Mongameli

Chief Buthelezi:
OR, Zeph, Sabelo — President
also Deputy- President.
Thank everybody who has contributed to success of this day.
State of Emergency

Mandela's notes from his first session of parliament as president of South Africa,
25 May 1994.

discrimination, introducing the principle of equality in every sphere of our lives.

This was the momentous challenge facing our pioneers in democratic government. This was the major rubicon to cross for the former freedom fighters who had preached ungovernability, boycott and sanctions. Now the former terrorist had the task of uniting South Africa, of implementing the core principle of the Freedom Charter which declares that South Africa belongs to all its people, black and white.

51. FROM THE UNPUBLISHED SEQUEL TO HIS AUTOBIOGRAPHY

Good leaders fully appreciate that the removal of tensions in society, of whatever nature, puts creative thinkers on centre stage by creating an ideal environment for men and women of vision to influence society. Extremists, on the other hand, thrive on tension and mutual suspicion. Clear thinking and good planning was never their weapon.

52. FROM THE UNPUBLISHED SEQUEL TO HIS AUTOBIOGRAPHY

The apartheid regime had put law and order in disrepute. The human rights of the majority of the population were ruthlessly suppressed, there was detention without trial, torture and murder of political activists, open criticism of the Appeal Court judges who were independent and gave judgement against the regime, and the packing of the judiciary with conservative lawyers. The police, especially the Security Branch, were [a] law unto themselves. Because of this crude practice, and out of my own convictions, I exploited every opportunity to promote respect for the law and the judiciary . . . in the new SA there is nobody, not even the President, [who] is above the law . . . the rule of law generally and in particular the judiciary should be respected.

The President and two Deputy-Presidents, the Ministers of Defence and of Safety and Security, Generals Georg Meiring and Van der Merwe should be briefed by the National Intelligence Service at the earliest possible convenience on the following issues.

1) Were any documents containing intelligence material destroyed or intelligence information wiped off from computers during the period 1 February 1990 and 31 May 1994?
    a) If so, what [were] the . . . full particulars of such material or information
    b) The dates of such destruction or wiping off
    c) The name or names of the persons who authorized such destruction or wiping off.

2) Does the State Security Council and its structures, like the Joint Management Committees, still exist?

    a) If so, who are the members of such State Security Council and Joint Management Committees?
    b) If not the exact details of when they were dismantled
    c) A list of members before they were dismantled
    d) The purpose of the State Security Council
    e) What happened to its funds and equipment

3) A list of the organisations on which a list of the agents . . . who penetrated organisations or institutions spied upon.

4) Does the Civilian Cooperation Bureau still exist? A detailed explanation of its structure and personnel must be furnished.

   a) If not, when was it dismantled?
      What happened to its funds and other equipment?

5) Does the Directorate of Covert Collection still exist?
   a) If so, who are its members?
   b) It not, when was it dissolved?
   c) What happened to its funds and equipment

6) The original copy of the Report of General Pierre Steyn must be supplied.
   a) Precisely for what criminal acts were several senior officers of the army dismissed or asked to resign as a result of that report?

      Who is responsible for politically motivated violence which has led to the murder of close to 20,000 people?

      Is it alleged that the parties responsible for politically motivated violence were also responsible for the death of freedom fighters like Neil Aggett, [Rick] Turner, Imam Haroon, Ahmed Timol, David Webster, [Matthew] Goniwe and others, Griffiths and Victoria Mxenge; Pebco 3; Bheki Mlangeni

7) Does the Vlakplaas Unit continue to exist[20]
   Who were its members and [what] has happened to them.
   What was or is its purpose before, if it continued [or]
   dismantled what happened to its funds and equipment.

8) Detailed information on the operations of hit squads in the
   country. Is this correct? What were they paid according to
   Goldstone Report members of the V [Vlakplaas] Unit

54. FROM A NOTEBOOK

Mood of confidence and hope
(Middelburg)

Various sources have made encouraging assessment of the
performance of govt.

Review of 1995 and outlook for 1996 positive – media

Hope for future continues to be the dominant mood.

Completed or completing process of planning and visible
delivery and speeding up change.

Transformed local govt where people are governed

Business confidence grown – SA started experience a net out-
flow of capital in 1985; Continued for period of 9½ years up
to 1994 –

R51,7 billion left the country.

....

20. 'The Vlakplaas Unit', a division of the counter-insurgency unit of the South African Police, was
responsible for the torture and deaths of many anti-apartheid activists.

Situation changed dramatically after 10 May 1994. Net capital inflow experienced –

From middle of 1994 to end of 1995 net capital inflow estimated at R30 billion.

By end of 1995 Reserve Bank had repaid all its short term foreign loans.
Public confidence growing
63% = 66%
Breaking into areas once far beyond reach

55. FROM A PERSONAL FILE, c.1996

Trail of blood in Tvl since July 1990 or 1991
Sebokeng ±32
Krugersdorp – 36
Sebokeng – 200
Soweto and JHB – 45 + 9
Meeting with De Klerk over Sebokeng 1990 –
He never issued any condolence.
No arrest.
800,000

56. FROM A NOTEBOOK

1) Phone Ted
2) Kofi Annan
3) Jakes Gerwel[21]
4) Oprah Winfrey
5) Elastic socks

....

21. G J (Jakes) Gerwel, see People, Places and Events.

Mum Gra's [Graça Machel] worldwide travels have been a source of concern to me for some time now, and it will be a real relief when her contract with Unicef expires at the end of the year, when she will be able to devote her outstanding abilities to the people, especially the children of Mozambique.

She returned to SA [South Africa] . . . on /8/96 where she and her colleagues were finalizing their report to the UNO [United Nations Organization].[22] She lived with us, as usual, until 8/96 when she left for Mozambique. I cannot describe my joy and happiness to receive the love and warmth of such a humble but gracious and brilliant lady.

But modern inventions enable us to remain in contact even when she is abroad. It gives me unbelievable comfort and satisfaction to know that there [is] somebody somewhere in the universe on whom I can rely especially on matters where my political comrades cannot provide me.

58. FROM A PERSONAL FILE

As usual after 9 pm granddaughter Rochelle sits on my bed after giving me my eye treatment. I expect a few kind words from her before she kisses me 'goodnight'. Instead she drops a bomb. 'Granddad,' she says, 'I must give you a report which will leave [you] completely devastated. It is not the type of thing you expect from me . . . as a result I will leave home immediately and settle elsewhere. You have always stressed the importance of education generally and specifically with regard to myself and the Thembu Royal House, whose performance in this regard has always been less than mediocre. You have given me full support in this regard. You will always be in my thoughts

22. In 1994 Machel was appointed by the United Nations to lead a study on the impact of armed conflict on children.

Grandpa. But I am leaving home to settle elsewhere.' Although courteous throughout, she spoke fearlessly and clearly.

I was stunned and could not believe it was my own grandchild who was tearing my heart apart. She has always been most meticulous in looking after me, taking off my shoes and socks before I retired to bed, telling me beautiful stories, enquiring what time I wanted my breakfast the following morning.

59. FROM A PERSONAL FILE – DRAFT NOTES ON ST VALENTINE'S DAY IN ANSWER TO A SCHOOLGIRL'S ENQUIRY INTO WHAT THE DAY MEANS TO HIM

Age and a conservative cultural background do not make it easy for me to discuss in public such intimate feelings or emotions. This is specially the case when the question is asked by one young enough to be a grandchild. It might well be that if one attempted a definition which departs from that which appears in the standard dictionaries, and bearing in mind the main forms of civilization of the world, they may be as many definitions as there are human beings.

I would hope that the average individual experiences one of the highest levels of emotional attachments satisfaction and happiness when in love . . .

It will probably shock many people to discover how colossally ignorant I am about simple things the ordinary person takes for granted. Having been born and grown up in a rural environment with parents who could neither read nor write, one hardly ever heard about Valentine's Day.

Moving to the cities one was gradually drawn into mainstream politics, and there was little room for upgrading oneself with information on such issues. Only during the last five years did I receive Valentines cards and gifts. But one must naturally develop enormous respect for those who bring happiness to others anonymously far from the limelight.

Unfortunately my tight programme does not allow me to find time to celebrate Valentine's Day either today or in the future.

Many of today's younger generation are independent and clear thinkers with their own set of values. It would be . . . most presumptious for a man of 78 to advise them on how to handle relationships. Moreover, this is not a question of [advice] but of social conditions. Give the younger generation opportunities for education and better their lives, they will glitter with excellence.

I would think that people who subscribe to the same values, who share a common vision and who accept each others' integrity have laid a basis for a good relationship. But to this there will be a wide range of notable exceptions.

60. FROM A NOTEBOOK, c.1996 ABOUT PLANS TO DEVELOP ROBBEN
    ISLAND INTO A MUSEUM

Robben Island
Dpt [Department] of Art, Culture etc
Independent structure
Beyond range of ordinary
Human desire to exploit
Tourists destruction
Museum must be a source of
Inspiration not money
Special Board of Trustees

61. FROM A NOTEBOOK

1.
Engagement elsewhere: wish well

2.

Ireland has been in limelight throughout
its history

3.

Never difficult to identify who started trouble.
But we soon reach stage where neither party is
altogether wrong or right.

4.

Indictment of Irish leaders that they are not capable
of solving their own affairs.

62. FROM A PRESIDENTIAL DIARY

Monday 29.12.97: Left Qunu for C.T. [Cape Town] but cancelled attendance to Franklin Sonn's daughter's wedding because of severe sciatica attack on right leg.[23]

30.12.97: bridal couple instead of arriving at 7 am for break-fast as arranged only came at 8.45 am. Their photographer from Rapport [newspaper] had to leave. Spanish couple left Ysterplaat [Air Force Base] at 10 am reaching Maputo at 12.15. Stayed at the nearest Govt [Government] Guest House to Gra's [Graça Machel's] residence.

31.12.97: Remained upstairs immobilized by severe sciatica. Visited by Comrade Presid[ent]. Joachim Chissano and informs me of the house arrest of K.K. [Kenneth Kaunda] and conditions of house arrest.[24]

....

23. Franklin Sonn (1939–). Member of the ANC. South Africa's ambassador to the USA 1995–98.
24. Kenneth (K K) Kaunda (1924–). President of Zambia, 1964–91. He was placed under house arrest for five months.

Had dinner with Gra, and chdn [children] and watched passing of the old year and fire display from Polana Hotel.

1.1.98: Could not make family lunch and had to have lunch with Zina in my private quarters. Wished Zindzi and Rochelle Happy New Year. Theron and physiotherapist

2.1.98: P.M. M

1.1.98: Nothing special – refused to return to S.Q.

4.1.98: H.C. [high commissioner] came
Dr Hugo, Theron have lunch with Gra. Gave me 2 injections and returned

5.1.98: Argument with Judy, Gra over WM [Winnie Mandela]. I said I do not want to have relationship in which there are certain areas in which we cannot share. She's part of your history.

6.1.98: H.C. in Moz [Mozambique] wants another 4 yr contract.

7.1.98: Met for 15 minutes my friend Jeremy Anderson, former Parks Director of the Mpumalanga Game Reserves. Congratulate Arap Moi on his inauguration as President of Kenya.

Telephoned Chief Antonio Fernandez from Maputo to Washington to wish him Merry Christmas and a Happy New Year. He points out that he has attempted to contact me several times from Washington, but was unable to reach me. It sometimes pains me when dependable friends who have shared resources with us when we were all alone in our fight against apartheid, but who are regarded by the staff as mere strangers bent on disturbing the President.

19.1.98: Called on 9th floor Shell House and was informed that security was against my occupying an office on this floor and recommended that I go back to 10th floor.[25] I flatly turned down their recommendation. Secretary-General Kgalema [Motlanthe] agreed with me.[26] Also had a discussion with outgoing acting S.G [Secretary General] Cheryl Carolus on the above matter when I explained that I will attend.[27]

22.1.98: King Letsie III and I, in the presence of President Masire of Botswana, launch the Lesotho Highlands Water Project. But had to leave without taking lunch because of weather conditions.

23.1.98: Visited the Acting Queen of Western Pondoland and the Queen Mother to pay my respects, arranged with Colleen Ross to admit future King Ndamase Mangaliso to Kearsney College.[28]

24.1.98: Inspected Mr Zeka's house which is on sale for R950,000. and asked for details of the bond.

24.1.98: Met Chief Bangilizwe, Dalaguba, Zwelodumo, Chief Sandile Mgudlwa, Chief Khawudle, Chief Silimela, and Chief Mnqanqeni.

25. Shell House was the headquarters of the ANC in central Johannesburg.
26. Kgalema Petrus Motlanthe (1949–). Leading member of the ANC. Interim President of South Africa, September 2008 – May 2009. Deputy President of South Africa, 2009–.
27. Cheryl Carolus (1958–). Politician. Member of ANC. South Africa's High Commissioner to London.
28. Queen Bongolethu Ndamase, mother of Ndamase Ndamase, the current ruler of a section of the AbaThembu.

24.1.98: Instructed Georg Meiring to dispatch helicopter to Tanzania.

24.1.98: Lunch with King Buyelekhaya and the Queen.[29]

24.1.98: Took call from President Clinton

25.1.98: Took call from President Museveni

63. FROM A NOTEBOOK

I was somewhat uncomfortable about the festivities at Qunu on New Year's Day. On Christmas Day we had more than 1 000 children from the surrounding villages and about 100 adults. We had slaughtered 11 sheep, one of which was donated by Zwelibanzi Dalindyebo, King of the T[h]embus and an ox from Zwelithini ka Zulu, King of the Zulus. The crowd was in a joyful mood and they ate all the meat except the skin and horns.

On previous occasions my guests on New Year are normally less than those at Christmas. But on this occasion I had slaughtered only 12 sheep in the belief that this would be more than enough. You can imagine my discomfort when more people than at Christmas [arrived] and when some children who had walked kilometres to Qunu complained that they had not eaten. Next time I will not be caught unprepared.

Visited by Thandizulu Sigcau, King of the Pondos. In accordance with custom, I slaughtered a sheep for him, and gave him a second provision. He was not altogether in agreement with the suggestion made by his brother, Vulindlela Ndamase, King of Western Pondoland, to the effect that the King[s] should be members of the House of Traditional Leaders

29. Buyelekhaya Dalindyebo. Heir to the AbaThembu royal throne. Queen Noluntu Dalindyebo. Junior wife of King Buyelekhaya Dalindyebo.

in their respective areas. I then suggested that I would prefer to be guided by them on the topic. I proposed they should meet to take a common position.

Also visited by Queen Cleopatra Dalindyebo, in the company of Chief Nokwale Balizulu, the ruling chief over our area. Drunkenness amongst Thembu Chiefs.

64. FROM A NOTEBOOK

How far are we in developing common data base
Checking corruption
Qualification of analysts
Many illegal flights
Travelling abroad on regular basis

65. FROM A NOTEBOOK

1.

We pass through this world but once and opportunities you miss will never be available to you again.

2.

Fix your aims and objects in life and, as a general rule, as far as possible never deviate from it.

3.

The ANC [African National Congress] understood this principle very well.

4.

In early 50s already we invited all S.As [South Africans] to send demands for a people's charter.

5.

We also invited leaders of all political parties of that day to join us in preparing for a Congress of the People. NP [National Party], Liberal Party.

6.

Adopted basic policy – Freedom Charter which proclaimed that SA belongs to all of us.

7.

1961 called for Convention of the People.

8.

1984 ANC approached President Botha – meeting between ANC and NP.
Overthrow of white supremacy the work of the liberation movement – ANC, PAC, Azapo [Azanian People's Organisation] in varying degrees.[30]
Transformation also collective effort.

9.

Initiative of ANC has changed situation. Polecat to a miracle

10.

Development programmes – Black and white
Doors of World opened.

....

30. The Azanian People's Organisation, founded in 1978, was inspired by the Black Consciousness Movement and merged three banned organisations: the Black People's Convention (BPC), the South African Students' Organisation (SASO) and the Black Community Programmes (BCP).

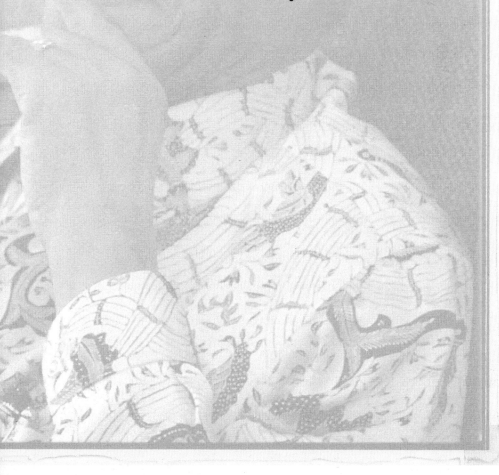

CHAPTER THIRTEEN

Away

Discussion with President George W Bush
White House   12 November 2001

How much time have I got?

Compliments on manner in which he
has handled important issues:
Meeting various Heads of States.
especially Presidents Mbeki & Obasanjo
2.

Afghanistan.
my press statement.
No pulling out before BL is flushed out.
Civilian casualties unfortunate, but that
happens in every war.
3.
Palestine — Almost 30 years of fruitless
efforts.
my Proposal
Arafat affair unfortunate

From a notebook, see pages 390–391.

[Yasser] Arafat . . . was also visiting Egypt and I met him after meeting [President Hosni] Mubarak. Mubarak – I met him straight from the airport; I went to his palace and he received me well and we had dinner there, after I had briefed him about our situation and thanked him and the people of Egypt for their support. We had dinner, then I went to my hotel, and the following day I met Arafat.

That was a very hairy experience I had there because we had to address a meeting in a *hall* and we [were] escorted by the police to the meeting. But the crowd was frighteningly large and I realised what was going to happen. I said to the police officer, they should bring reinforcements and open a way so that we could walk through. They tried; they collected some policemen, more than they had given us, to escort us. Then the officer in charge said I must come out. I said, 'No, let members of my entourage go in first,' because I was afraid that the crowd was *so* big that if I went in first, there might be, you know, a rush, and pandemonium, and my delegation, you see, will not be able to make it because what the police were concentrating on was me, around me, you know; even cutting off my delegation. Then [the officer] tried to get my delegation, but a few steps away, he came back [and] says, 'No, you can come now.' So I came out. In spite of the cordon that they had formed, the crowd just *broke* through. You know, I lost one of my shoes as a result of the pandemonium. It had to be brought inside when I was in the hall . . . and I [was] separated [from] Winnie. They pushed her out . . .

They want to *touch*, they want to shake hands, and some of them, you know, can be very selfish . . . the members of the public. They catch you and they don't want . . . to release you and other people are struggling to hold you . . . '*Oh*, I have been wanting to see you for a long time; what a day for me to catch your hand!' And he's holding you . . . You know, my hair was ruffled . . . and they *stepped* on my heel and [my] shoe came [off]. For about *ten minutes* they were looking for Winnie, and eventually they got her in. She was so angry with me; she didn't talk the whole day! 'Why do you leave me?' I said, 'What choice did I have?' I was pushed left and right, and the soldiers themselves now, the police, were pushing me to make me escape from the crowd. I never even got a chance of addressing them because they wouldn't keep quiet: shouting, you know: 'Mandela!' . . . That type of thing, in admiration, you know. We tried to say, 'Well, look I've come here to *speak* to you.' They wouldn't what-you-call, they wouldn't give me a chance. And then I said, 'Well, then I'm going away.' Then some little order . . . but once I started, then they started [shouting] again. So we decided to go upstairs to the balcony . . . and be able to address them from [there], but it just didn't help. I . . . never [saw] such a *rowdy* meeting. *Rowdy* because of enthusiasm, because of *love*, you know. I never delivered the address. I tried several times . . . I had to abandon it.

2. FROM A CONVERSATION WITH RICHARD STENGEL ABOUT HIS
    VISIT TO THE UNITED STATES

Oh, but the Americans were very warm and *very* enthusiastic . . . It was of course very exciting to land in New York, which is a city I have heard and read about since I was an adolescent . . . I found, of course, our representative in the United States Miss Lindi Mabuza . . . accompanied by Thabo Mbeki, the head of the Department of International Affairs, Thomas Nkobi, the Treasurer General, Barbara Masekela who is now the head of the president's office and . . . several others. We were then escorted by security to our hotel.

. . . I can't remember . . . when the ticker tape took place . . . the sequence of events . . . That [ticker tape parade] was the most exciting experience I had in the United States of America . . . I knew that there was widespread interest in the anti-apartheid struggle in South Africa, in the United States of America, but to see that reflected in the conduct of the people when I arrived in New York was something very encouraging, very inspiring. The excitement of the people, the remarks they made which indicated unwavering solidarity with our struggle – in the street, in buildings, offices and residential . . . flats – it was just amazing; it swept me from my feet completely . . . To know that you are the object of such goodwill makes one humble indeed. And that is how I felt.

3. FROM A CONVERSATION WITH RICHARD STENGEL ABOUT HIS VISIT TO THE UNITED NATIONS

But I then spoke, but during the session our people had to send me home because we have a lot of friends in the United Nations and they came to shake hands with me, and I can't shake hands sitting, you know? With diplomats and especially ladies – diplomats who are ladies – and when somebody comes you see I get up and I – I instinctively get up and shake hands. Now Thabo Mbeki and Frene Ginwala, members of our delegation, appealed to me to remain seated.[1] I say, 'But I can't do that; when somebody comes to see me I must stand up and shake hands' but they say, 'You are disturbing the conference.' I say, 'Well stop them from coming to greet me. If you allow [them] to come and greet me, I have no alternative; I must stand.' Then

1. Frene Ginwala (1932–). Journalist and politician. Speaker of the National Assembly of South Africa, 1994–2000.

they said, 'No, you go home. Go to, go to your hotel. It's better for you to remain there instead of disturbing the conference here' and that is how I left. [*laughs*] Yes. And they say, 'You stay there until the conference is over, until this [United Nations] Security Council is over.' And that's what happened. [*chuckles*]

4. FROM A CONVERSATION WITH RICHARD STENGEL ABOUT HIS
   SENSE OF THE AMERICAN SECURITY

American security is very professional, highly professional . . . They brief you on how to move [and they tell you] that the most dangerous moment is when you leave any place to [go to] your car and when you leave the car to [go to] your place. And they insist . . . on a swift movement . . . When you travel from one place to the other you are surrounded by security. It's difficult to stop and talk to people as one would like when you visit a new place . . . [to] find out how they think and what their views [are] on a wide variety of issues. But security both . . . here and in the States won't allow you to do that. Therefore, it's very difficult to assess and to be alive to the differences in the various regions that you visit.

5. FROM A CONVERSATION WITH RICHARD STENGEL ABOUT
   PRESIDENT CLINTON'S INAUGURATION

I have not seen such people gathered together in one place except [at] the Zion Christian Church in April last year where there were more than a million people . . . In this, what-you-call, place where they held the inauguration it's a little hill . . . and then you can see the people going *down* to the valley, choking the streets . . . There was the platform, the stage . . . And then the whole ceremony started. It was done with a precision which was absolutely impressive . . . The capacity to organise such a big event was enormous . . . I couldn't concentrate because of the warmth of the people coming to greet [me] and sometimes obscuring [my] sight of what was going on at the stage . . . So security, in order to protect me, also stood in front of me and even blocked my seeing the, what-you-call, the dais you see? . . . I was tremendously impressed by the warmth of the people towards the ANC [African National Congress] . . . I thought that people like Oliver [Tambo] and . . . others had done remarkable work in bringing the ANC to the notice of the people, to the notice of the Americans. Because . . . of the work that had been done by the organisation . . . people were so aware of who I was. And although it interfered with my . . . following the proceedings. But nevertheless I liked that, you see, because it was an expression of warmth and kindness and love. And then the speech of Clinton covered almost everything. It was global [and] very brief . . . He said what was necessary; I admired that. And then of course the way he admired Bush. It was clear now that the fight was over and . . . Americans were grouping together . . . to face their common problems . . . I thought that was a great vision.

[In the] . . . evening, there [were] dances and I went to one of them, and then I was told that I and Mr Kweisi Mfume, the chairperson of the Congressional Black . . . Caucus will meet Clinton in a holding room . . .[2] We went there, shook hands with him and [had] a number of exchanges; not much because he was on his feet . . . After that he then went into the hall. There was a band playing; he took the saxophone and played. And we all danced, we all jived, you know. [It] was very moving, very moving indeed . . . That informality on his part was also tremendous. To have a president, you know, who is so close to the people. He *has* a common touch and that

2. Kweisi Mfume (1948–). Chairman of the National Association for the Advancement of Colored People.

tremendously impressed me. With all his dignity, but nevertheless that common touch.

6. FROM A CONVERSATION WITH RICHARD STENGEL ABOUT THE
    1990 CONCERT AT WEMBLEY STADIUM IN LONDON

I wanted to see Tracy Chapman and the Manhattan Brothers . . . I have always been intrigued by that young lady, and I was sitting in a box . . . when she came on the stage I was really excited and she then started playing . . . I was beginning to enjoy the music when . . . I was told that Neil Kinnock was here to see me and I had to come out. I was keen to see Kinnock because the Labour Party and its leader Neil Kinnock had been a *strong* pillar in our struggle, in the anti-apartheid struggle. They had demanded my release, and they had welcomed me when I reached London. They were very good and I was happy to meet him . . . but I regretted missing Tracy Chapman. But after I had seen Neil Kinnock then I went back to my seat [and] the Manhattan Brothers . . . came on the stage. Man, they evoked *such* memories of the fifties . . . Then I heard that the Russian ambassador . . . was there to see me. *Two* events . . . which I . . . looked forward to, I couldn't see. At the end of the concert . . . I went to see all the stars and shook hands with them . . . I really enjoyed myself, but of course the security was interfering. [They] didn't want me to be there for a long time . . . so I had just enough time to shake hands with [the performers] and to congratulate them. And of course I addressed the crowd itself.

7. FROM A CONVERSATION WITH RICHARD STENGEL
    ABOUT NATIONALISATION

There was already a *furious* reaction in South Africa to the statement I made from prison where I said nationalisation was still our policy; we had not changed . . . Of course there was a reaction from the business community, and that reaction . . . set one thinking because one thing that is important is . . . [to] have the support of *business* . . . When I came out [of prison] we concentrated on explaining to business why we adopted the policy of nationalisation and, of course, American businessmen . . . put a lot of pressure . . . on us to . . . reconsider the question of nationalisation . . . From the point of view of encouraging investment in South Africa, one had to think seriously about the matter . . .

The decisive moment . . . was when I attended the World Economic Forum in Davos, Switzerland, where I . . . met the major industrial leaders of the world . . . who made it a point . . . to express their views very candidly on the question of nationalisation, and I realised, as never before, that if we want investments we will have to review nationalisation without removing it altogether from our policy . . . we had to remove the fear of business that . . . their assets will be nationalised.

8. CONVERSATION WITH RICHARD STENGEL ABOUT HIS TRIP
   TO CANADA

STENGEL: In Canada you were received by Mr Mulroney?[3]
MANDELA: Yes, that's right, and in Canada I addressed a meeting . . . and a lady then asked me a question as I was walking out. Brian Mulroney had given me five million dollars, and . . . this lady . . . [asked], 'Mr Mandela, this five million dollars that you got from Mr Mulroney, are you going to use it for murdering people? As you have been doing?' Now I wanted to respond to her peacefully and in a serious way, but before I knew [it] she was thrown out. They pushed her, you know, and she fell . . . I tried to stop the thing but I was late and so they hustled me out. She turned out to . . . [have] been a member of

----

3. Brian Mulroney (1939–). Prime minister of Canada, 1984–93.

the PAC [Pan Africanist Congress] . . . And the way she looked at me and [said], 'Mandela, this five million you got from Mr Mulroney, are you going to use it for *murdering* your people?' [*laughs*] . . . Oh, gee whiz! They treated her very roughly.

9. FROM A CONVERSATION WITH RICHARD STENGEL ABOUT
    GOOSE BAY

In Canada, at a place called Goose Bay, we stopped there to refill before we crossed over to Dublin, and as I was walking to the airport building I saw some people just outside the fence of the airport and I asked . . . the official who was taking us to the airport building, 'Now who are those?' He says, '. . . those are Eskimos.' Now I had never seen an Eskimo and I had always thought of them as people who are catching . . . polar bears and seals . . . I thought I should go and see these people . . . And I was grateful that I did that because these were young people in their teens, late teens . . . And as I chatted to them I was *amazed* to find out that these were high school children. They knew – they had heard that we were going to land and refill and . . . *I* was very happy to meet them and was tremendously impressed because they knew about the release; they watched the release and also they knew one or two meetings which I had addressed. And it was the *most* fascinating conversation, precisely because it was *shocking*. I was *rudely* shocked, awakened to the fact that my knowledge of the Eskimo community was very backward because I never imagined that [they] were [at] schools . . . and [that] they were just like ourselves. I never imagined that. Although I was in the struggle, the freedom struggle, I should have . . . know[n] that people *anywhere*, throughout the world, change from their less advanced positions . . .

I enjoyed that conversation very much, but the result . . . is that I caught . . . pneumonia . . . I [had come] from Oakland

and the temperature there was about 40 degrees, [and] flew non-stop from Oakland to Goose Bay . . . [where] the temperature was minus 15 degrees and you could see patches of snow . . . [From] the change of climate . . . and standing outside . . . in the cold (although I had an overcoat), by the time I went to the airport building I had already caught a cold. And the airport building was warm; there was a fire and the manager was a lady – Eskimo lady – but very advanced, you know, very highly cultured person, and who told me about one of her friends in the Canadian Embassy in South Africa. And then there was another Eskimo, a male, who was the assistant to the lady. He was also very impressive and he said, 'Well, according to our custom I must welcome you with music.' And he explained. He took an instrument. It was a guitar, but traditional – the woodwork, you know, showed it was traditional. And even the strings, you see, were not arranged in the same way as Western guitars are arranged. Then he explained; he said, 'Well, I'm going to . . . This song with which I'm going to welcome you shows the night.' And then he started the music. The tone is a dull one, and dragging the notes, but very sombre, and then later there was a change in the mood: becoming brighter, at first hardly noticeable. Then as he continued to play the song this cheerful note became dominant and then it became brighter and brighter and even his facial appearance was changing, you know, in tune with the music, until he reached, you know, the peak where the music was very *bright*, you know, and very *lively*, and that is how he welcomed us.

10. FROM A CONVERSATION WITH RICHARD STENGEL ABOUT
    CONTRACTING PNEUMONIA

It was in Ireland that the cold got me. I had telephoned my family doctor Dr Nthato Motlana and Dr Gecelter, the chap

. . . [who] helped in the operation on me. I had asked them to meet me in Dublin because I was not feeling well and I thought I should be seen by the people who had been treating me, you know? They saw me and they said . . . that there was nothing serious . . . I was [also] treated by the . . . prime minister's doctor in Dublin, and then . . . addressed the joint session in the Parliament . . . Then we proceeded to London. I was recovering, but [as] I came out of the hotel, I was not aware that it was raining . . . and Winnie said to me, 'Please let's go back for your coat' . . . I didn't want to be late for the British prime minister and . . . I said, 'No, let's go; we'll be late if we go back.' So when I got into the car a few drops caught me. And that made it worse . . . *Now* the pneumonia became very serious . . . As I was going out I met a group of youngsters, again in their teens, and they wanted autographs, so . . . I said, 'Look I'm in a hurry. When I come back I'll give it to you.' And they said, 'What time?' I said, 'Sometime in the afternoon.' And . . . I forgot about the thing. When I was coming back I was also rushing for another appointment and I found them . . . still waiting. They were there in the morning about nine o'clock . . . [and at] four o'clock they were still waiting. So I say, 'Well, gentlemen, I am sorry; I am rushing for an appointment.' They say, 'You promised; you gave us your word . . . your word of honour. We've have waited for you. Sign!' . . . When they said I had . . . pledged my honour I found it very difficult so I signed each one . . . and as I was signing, one of our chaps . . . said, 'No, sign [only] one.' But the children had waited there for the whole day . . . so I signed everything they gave me. [Someone] said to me, 'No, they are going to sell the others, the other autographs.' [*laughs*] That's what they do. They hunt for autographs, you see, and then they go round and say, 'Look, do you want the autograph of so and so? Here it is.' Five . . . pounds, something like that. So they . . . must have made some money [*laughs*] . . .

I met [with] Mrs Thatcher . . . for . . . close to three hours, and naturally we discussed the question of sanctions and the general political situation in South Africa. She was interested in our relations with [Mangosuthu] Buthelezi . . . I made *no impression whatsoever* on the question of sanctions . . . [I said] to her that 'We are an oppressed community and we need to do something . . . to put pressure on the regime to change its policies, and the only pressure of a formidable nature that we could exert is that of sanctions.' I *couldn't* make any impression. But she was charming and then I had a private lunch with her . . . She was very warm, you know; she was just the opposite of what I was told. Yes. And in fact I had then to ask to be excused because I had to attend another appointment . . . But . . . she herself was very generous about her time, and I was also tremendously impressed by her . . . I was impressed by her *strength* of character – really an iron lady . . .

I made this statement in Ireland that *in* South Africa we have decided to *speak* to the regime, to the enemy, and we regard this as consistent with the guidelines laid by the United Nations . . . that member states must try and resolve their problems through peaceful means. And I urged the IRA [Irish Republican Army] and the British government to . . . resolve their problems peacefully, and I was then asked this question in the House of Commons, and I repeated what I said. [*chuckles*] But the chap who actually raised this question and criticised me for having made this suggestion . . . was jeered, booed by other MPs . . . He was booed. Some said, '*Nonsense*', '*Rubbish*!' [*chuckles*]

11. FROM A CONVERSATION WITH RICHARD STENGEL ABOUT QUEEN BEATRIX AND QUEEN ELIZABETH II

I found the Dutch queen *very* interesting, very intelligent, well-informed, very confident, very accessible you know? There was no *rigid* protocol . . . I spent a very lovely time with her and I was just rather amazed by the amount of information that she had, and her keenness to discuss world problems . . . Very fine lady indeed.

[Queen Elizabeth] is one of the longest reigning monarchs and she is a fine lady. When you talk to her, she has a wonderful sense of humour . . . I watched her during the Commonwealth Conference in Harare in 1991, I think. Dr Mahathir, the prime minister of Malaysia was asked to propose a toast and . . . he said that, 'Well, we used to be under the British Empire and Queen Elizabeth was there and we had a sultan who did not rule and we had a viceroy and advisors whose advice *had* to be accepted. We are members of a Commonwealth where the wealth is not common' . . . She was enjoying *all* these jokes, you know . . . Thereafter I had an opportunity of speaking to her . . . She was just sparkling and completely at ease. I thought she was a great lady, also very sharp. Very sharp. There may be a great deal of formality around her, but . . . as an individual [she] is a very simple person, very plain. I formed a good impression of her.

12. FROM A CONVERSATION WITH RICHARD STENGEL ABOUT HIS
    TRIP TO FRANCE

[I] was received by [President] François Mitterrand in grand style . . . It's a . . . misconception to think that socialists act like rascals, you know? . . . The arrangement was that I should approach from one side of the square and he would approach from another and we would meet in the middle of the square . . . He was there with Danielle [his wife] and I was there with Winnie and it was raining. It was very difficult weather conditions, but he had . . . his raincoat; I had [mine] . . . We met in the middle, shook hands; then we went to something like a tent and met there, exchanged views. I briefed him about the situation in the country and then we went for dinner . . .

We were given one of the executive jets from Paris to Geneva. The weather was very bad and . . . people were very anxious and I thought I should make a joke . . . I said, 'If anything happens to my wife I'll sue these chaps.' People didn't see the joke; they were very much worried because of the bumps and so on, you see. Because if something happened to the plane we will all die so I wouldn't have an opportunity of instituting an action . . . They were so anxious that they didn't catch the joke.

13. A CONVERSATION WITH RICHARD STENGEL

MANDELA: Gee whiz; the Pope is also an outstanding person.[4] Humble, *very* humble. And I had an audience with him for about thirty minutes, if I'm not mistaken. Then the others, the rest of the delegation were called, and he gave us medals and prayed for us . . . I was impressed, you know, because when I was in jail I read a story . . . he had a holiday in the Alps . . . and . . . was then walking with one of his colleagues and he suddenly stopped and he says, 'By the way, this is Nelson Mandela's birthday today.' There was that story . . . He just said, 'Do you remember it's Nelson Mandela's birthday today?'
STENGEL: Oh, the Pope said that?
MANDELA: The Pope said that; he remembered that. And so he is a man who appears to take more than an ordinary superficial interest in our affairs in South Africa . . . He received us *very* well . . . I briefed him on the situation and he then *made* the statement that he fully supports the struggle against apartheid and he wished us well and strength . . . *Yes*, he's a linguist, man!

---

4. Pope John Paul II (1920–2005).

He's a *linguist*. Did you know that he also plays the guitar, you know? . . . He's quite a wonderful chap. [*laughs*] And then the most *widely* travelled pope. The *most* widely travelled pope . . . I met Prime Minister Andreotti . . . Prime Minister Andreotti and I also met the president . . .[5] How can I forget the name of the president? [*laughs*]

14. FROM A CONVERSATION WITH RICHARD STENGEL

In another country – I won't mention it by name because people can be very sensitive in Africa – in another country, we [got] the impression, both in prison and when I came out, that that is a democratic country, because there are elections, or so we thought . . . So I am well received there, treated as a head of state and so on, and at the *banquet* in the evening, I complimented the president for having made it possible for democracy to be introduced in this country and for the fact that he allows the people to determine who should form the government. But whilst I was talking, I saw some people . . . smiling sarcastically . . . [*laughs*] And so I asked one of our guys, 'What is the position here?' He says, 'Well, you said very nice things but did you know how many people are in prison here, for no other reason except that they oppose the government, by *peaceful* methods? They want to challenge them in elections and because [the government] fears them, they have put them in jail.' [*laughs*] Very difficult . . . [Now] when I go to a country, I make it a point . . . [first] to read some tract about that country, the *broad* features of their political system, you know, and the problems that they have.

---

5. Francesco Cossiga (1928–2010). President of the Italian Republic, 1985–92.

15. FROM A CONVERSATION WITH RICHARD STENGEL ABOUT MEETING FIDEL CASTRO

Castro is a very striking chap . . . We addressed a meeting together. What is the name of that town, man? A crowd like that in a small country? It was a fantastic crowd; I think there were about 300,000 people. Everyone *seated* on chairs. He spoke about three hours without a piece of paper, quoted figures, and he showed that America was bankrupt, you know? And *not* a single person left except to go to the toilet and come back . . . I was tremendously impressed by Castro and also by his humility – very humble chap, you know? When . . . I [was] driving with him through the city, he just sat down and folded his arms, and I was the person who was waving to the crowd . . . After speaking, we . . . went into the crowd; he was greeting everybody . . . I noticed that he will greet . . . a white person, then he goes to greet somebody who's dark. I don't know whether that was purely accidental or deliberate. [He was] very warm, talked to them for some time . . . I then realised that this enthusiasm and waving was not really for me as we were driving through the city; it was directed to Castro . . . Nobody bothered about me at all [*laughs*] . . . I was tremendously impressed by him.

16. FROM A CONVERSATION WITH RICHARD STENGEL ABOUT VISITING KENYA, UGANDA AND MOZAMBIQUE

In both Uganda and Kenya I found the climate . . . very interesting . . . In Uganda the . . . soil is so rich that you can literally throw anything down – a seed – and it will grow. They are self-sufficient in . . . things like fruits . . . and a number of [other] agricultural products . . . [In] Kenya I found that they could plant mealies [maize] throughout the year . . . They had three, what-you-call, three stages of mealies growing: one ripe, the other just about to be ripe . . . the other one still just above the ground . . . which indicated how good their climate is from the point of view of agriculture . . . In South Africa . . . except [for] those farms, you see, where there is . . . sufficient irrigation, mealies is planted once a year. But we were *well* received in all these countries . . . I met [President] Chissano in Mozambique, in Maputo. It was clear that the war had damaged the economy of the country. They were going through a very hard time, but I thought Chissano was handling the problems very well. And I also met Mrs Graça Machel, the wife of the late president of Mozambique, and I was very happy. I was meeting her for the first time. A very impressive woman and striking personality. I spent about three days in Maputo. The day we were leaving there was a bomb scare which came from South Africa . . . There was [supposed to be] a bomb [on] that plane . . . We had to be taken out of the plane, they had to search [it] and our luggage had to be kept back. They had to go through it to search it properly and to send it the following day . . . When we came back there was tight security at the airport because these alarmists had also made a threat that they would deal with me when I come back. But nothing happened.

17. FROM A NOTEBOOK

Discussion with President George W Bush
White House   12 November 2001.

How much time have I got?

1.

Compliments on manner in which he has handled important issues

Meeting various Heads of States especially Presidents Mbeki and Obasanjo

2.

Afghanistan

My press statement.

No pulling out before B.L. [Osama bin Laden] is flushed out.

Civilian casualties unfortunate, but that happens in every war.

3.

Palestine – Almost 30 years of fruitless efforts.

My proposal

Arafat affair unfortunate

4.

Burundi increase in funding[6]

5.

Lockerbie[7]

6. In 1999, Mandela was appointed by the United Nations secretary-general as chief mediator of peace negotiations to bring an end to the civil war in Burundi between the Tutsis and the Hutus.

7. Following the 1988 Lockerbie bombing of Pan Am Flight 103, in which 270 people were killed, Mandela mediated with Libyan leader Colonel Muammar Gaddafi to surrender Abdelbaset Ali Mohmed al Megrahi and his co-accused to the United Nations.

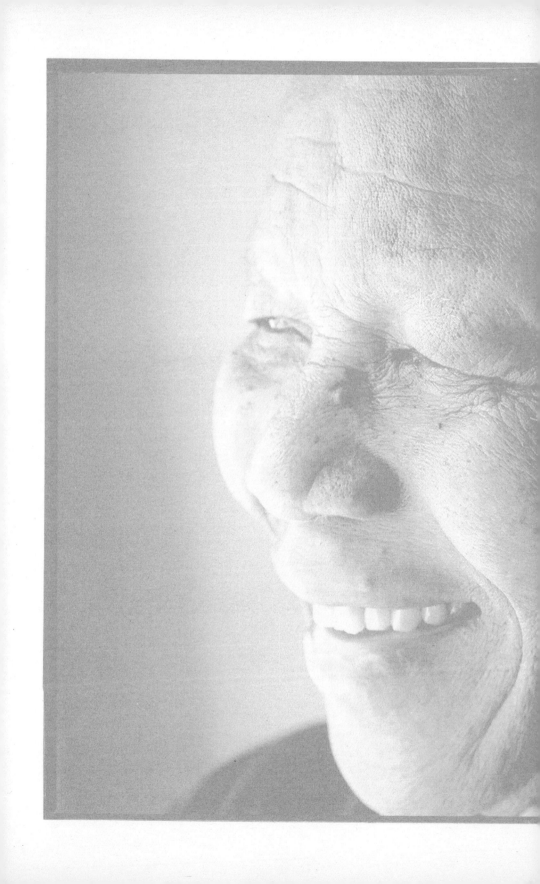

CHAPTER FOURTEEN

Home

'The plundering of indigenous land, exploitation of its mineral wealth and other raw materials, confinement of its people to specific areas, and the restriction of their movement have, with notable exceptions, been the cornerstones of colonialism throughout the land.'

··

Excerpt from the unpublished sequel to his autobiography, see page 395.

The plundering of indigenous land, exploitation of its mineral wealth and other raw materials, confinement of its people to specific areas, and the restriction of their movement have, with notable exceptions, been the cornerstones of colonialism throughout the land.

This was the form British colonialism took in South Africa, so much so, that after the passing of the Land Act of 1913 by the South African government, a white minority of barely 15 per cent of the country's population owned about 87 per cent of the land, while the black majority – Africans, Coloureds and Indians – occupied less than 13 per cent. They were forced to live in squalor and poverty or to seek employment on white farms, in the mines and urban areas.

When the Nationalist Party came to power in 1948, Afrikaners acted with unbelievable cruelty and sought to rob blacks even of these meager rights to land they still possessed.

Communities large and small, who had occupied areas from time immemorial, where their ancestors and beloved ones were buried, were mercilessly uprooted and thrown into the open veld, [left] there to fend for themselves. And this was done by a white community led by an educated but infamous clergy[man] and his successors who used their skills and religion to commit various atrocities against the black majority which God forbade. Yet they hypocritically claimed that their evil schemes were inspired by God.

(Quote: Sol Plaatje on the The Land Act of 1913)

2. CONVERSATION WITH AHMED KATHRADA ABOUT THE PRESSURE OF BEING RECOGNISED

MANDELA: Oh, by the way, did I tell you that one day I walked from Lower Houghton to Michael's house? Michael Harmel and Eli Weinberg?[1]

KATHRADA: In those days?

MANDELA: . . . No, I say I walked last Sunday. I walked from Lower Houghton right up to their houses, their old houses.

KATHRADA: Gee whiz.

MANDELA: And, but of course Michael's house was owned by somebody else, but I was able to make it out to find it.

KATHRADA: The Weinberg house is still there.

MANDELA: No, it's still there.

KATHRADA: Sheila is still there.[2]

MANDELA: And Sheila came whilst I was there because there was – there were doubts because it's now fenced in a different way, you know, with poles . . .

KATHRADA: Ja.

MANDELA: . . . and so on. And, but I was sure this was the house and then whilst I was still there some old lady came and said, 'No, that's the former house of Michael Harmel', and then Sheila also joined us.

KATHRADA: Oh.

MANDELA: Mmmhh.

KATHRADA: I hope you were there with your security.

MANDELA: . . . Yes . . . the police were there and security.

KATHRADA: Oh. Is it far from there?

MANDELA: I took about a little over an hour to reach it.

KATHRADA: It's quite a distance, man.

---

1. Eli Weinberg, see People, Places and Events.
2. Sheila Weinberg (1945–2004). Anti-apartheid activist. Member of the ANC and Gauteng Legislature. Daughter of Eli Weinberg.

MANDELA: Quite a distance. But I was walking really very slowly, not in a hurry.

KATHRADA: But doesn't it attract a lot of attention?

MANDELA: Ooh Christ! Don't say that, don't say that.

KATHRADA: Ah.

MANDELA: You know, it's a difficult life, this one.

KATHRADA: Ja.

MANDELA: Not being able to do what you want.

KATHRADA: Ja, it's very . . .

MANDELA: Because walks are something I like. It's difficult now. It's better here . . . in Westbrook because the yard itself is . . .

KATHRADA: It's very big, yes.

3. CONVERSATION WITH AHMED KATHRADA ABOUT INDIVIDUAL POLICE OFFICERS

KATHRADA: You know the day we went to Howick?

MANDELA: Aha.

KATHRADA: That colonel who was there . . . *he* told me that Van Wyk is farming. He even told me where he was, but I forget now.

MANDELA: Is that so?

KATHRADA: Mmm.

MANDELA: Well you know that he made very good statements.

KATHRADA: Ja, in the *Sunday Times*?

MANDELA: Mmm.

KATHRADA: Where he said that he would be prepared to serve under Mandela.

MANDELA: That's right, yes.

KATHRADA: He'd be 'honoured' to serve . . .

MANDELA: Mmhh. It's good to see these chaps. Dirker died, hey?

KATHRADA: *No*, he's very much alive . . . Some, some journalist went to see him

MANDELA: Is that so?

KATHRADA: And he [Dirker] said, 'Look are you a member of the AWB [Afrikaner Weerstandsbeweging]?' Dirker said. [The journalist] said no . . . [Dirker said,] 'Then I don't want to speak to you'.

MANDELA: He's AWB?

KATHRADA: Ja. Well Dirker would be, man.

MANDELA: That's true.

KATHRADA: He . . . is in Oudtshoorn. You know he comes from Oudtshoorn . . .

MANDELA: Is he also farming? Or . . .

KATHRADA: I don't know if he's farming but he's in Oudtshoorn . . . That chap was a very crude fellow.

MANDELA: Gee whiz. And what happened to Kruger? Do you know?

KATHRADA: Nothing at all. I haven't heard at all.

MANDELA: No, that's one chap I want to see, man.

KATHRADA: Ja. Now that was a very decent chap.

MANDELA: Absolutely.

KATHRADA: Ja. It would be good, you see, if one day one can get hold of some of these old special branch fellows; they'll tell us who's where . . .

MANDELA: *Who* can we get, man? Because, you know, it's such an act of generosity . . . to say to these fellows, can we have a *braai* [barbecue]?

KATHRADA: Exactly. That, that's just going through my mind now. If we could think of some little function where we invite these chaps, police, warders, you know? If we can get hold of them, it'll be a very nice gesture.

MANDELA: Absolutely, man . . . And, if you remind me, you know, on Wednesday, I can ask [General] Van der Merwe . . .

to come and see me and to give him this task to trace these people, you know? . . .

KATHRADA: Well that would be a very good thing.

MANDELA: Yes. Oh, I am sure Dirker would come.

KATHRADA: Of course, now he would come . . .

MANDELA: And old Van Wyk. What about the beast, Swanepoel. Is he still alive?

KATHRADA: Yes . . . I don't know if you still remember. There was an invasion of the Israeli Embassy in Fox Street? In 1967, [19]68.

MANDELA: Oh, I see, I see, yes. That's right.

KATHRADA: There was a siege.

MANDELA: Yes, that's right, yes.

KATHRADA: Where some people invaded . . . [And] occupied it . . . and then there was some shoot-out or . . .

MANDELA: That's right, yes. I remember that.

KATHRADA: . . . Swanepoel was in charge of [the police operation] and this person was sentenced to twenty years or something. Now [he] is released and he went to visit Swanepoel and Swanepoel says . . . he became one of the family . . . visited often, and now, he was wondering, he hasn't visited him for a long time, what's happened to . . . this chap . . .

MANDELA: Man, that would be very good to call these chaps.

KATHRADA: Ja, even Swanepoel. Why not?

MANDELA: Yes, yes . . .

KATHRADA: But we must think about it because there's a lot of hostility towards Swanepoel, hey?

MANDELA: Yes.

KATHRADA: Then of course there is also hostility against other police who tortured . . . our people.

MANDELA: Yes . . .

KATHRADA: A chap like Mac [Maharaj], for instance. I don't know if he'll ever agree to [come], because Swanepoel . . .

MANDELA: Tortured him?

KATHRADA: Ja . . . Andimba [Toivo ja Toivo], very badly too.[3]

MANDELA: Mmm.

KATHRADA: Zeph [Mothopeng].[4]

MANDELA: Yes.

KATHRADA: A lot of people were tortured by him.

MANDELA: Mmm.

4. CONVERSATION WITH AHMED KATHRADA ABOUT
   EXAGGERATION

KATHRADA: Aha. OK. Then, page 156 [of *Long Walk to Freedom* draft] . . . 'Now the South African security forces would know precisely where I was, which is precisely what we wanted.' Now, in a later part of this chapter you are talking of your trip to England, where you did not want people to know.

MANDELA: No, that's – that is an exaggeration . . . That is what we wanted. We never wanted that.

KATHRADA: Aha.

MANDELA: Just take that out.

KATHRADA: OK.

MANDELA: You see, the question of dramatising things, even when they are not correct . . .

KATHRADA: Aha.

MANDELA: . . . is a typical American thing.

5. CONVERSATION WITH AHMED KATHRADA ABOUT
   PERSONAL ISSUES

KATHRADA: Then [page] 115 [of *Long Walk to Freedom* draft]: 'How did Winnie react to your declaration that you wanted

---

3. Herman Andimba Toivo ja Toivo (1924–). Namibian freedom fighter, a South West African People's Organisation (SWAPO) leader and political prisoner.
4. Zephania Lekoame Mothopeng (1913–90). Political activist. President of the PAC.

to marry her – you wanted her to marry you? Must have been quite astounding?'

MANDELA: No, I told them that I don't want to be dealing with personal issues.

KATHRADA: Ah.

MANDELA: Say that I'm not answering that question.

KATHRADA: Ah.

MANDELA: I've told them.

KATHRADA: OK.

MANDELA: Or just say I can't remember.

KATHRADA: Ah.

MANDELA: And I wouldn't like the matter to be taken further because they might put [it in] their own words.

KATHRADA: Then last question: 'How had your family reacted to your divorce and remarriage?'

MANDELA: No, I'm not answering that.

KATHRADA: Again, hey?

MANDELA: Mmm. I'm not answering that question.

6. FROM A PERSONAL FILE – NOTES AT A MEETING IN ARUSHA,
    TANZANIA, DURING THE BURUNDI PEACE PROCESS,
    16 JANUARY 2000

Few of the parties negotiating, if any, seem to have learnt the art of compromise. The inflexibility of certain parties will inevitably make it difficult to secure the compromises necessary for a workable agreement . . . There is a deeply entrenched perception, which is shared even by some highly experienced and impartial political analysts, that the real problem in Burundi is the lack of a dynamic leadership which understands the importance of national unity, of peace and reconciliation, a leadership with vision and which is moved by the slaughter of innocent civilians.

I do not know whether this perception is accurate or not. I will decide the question as we continue together to seek a formula for peace and stability. I believe that all of you are capable of rising to expectations and to meet the enormous challenges facing your country. The fact that you have emerged as leaders of your country, whatever mistakes you committed and weaknesses revealed in your thinking and actions, proves that you are all opinion makers who are worried over the tragic events that have led to the slaughter of thousands of your people.

But the failure to agree on many core issues, the numerous splits in your political organisations, the lack of a sense of urgency, in a situation which requires bold initiatives, is undoubtedly an indictment against all of you . . . Compromise is the art of leadership and you compromise with your adversary, not with your friend. It would seem from a study of your situation that all of you have been posturing, inflexible, concentrating on manouevering to discredit or weaken your rivals. Hardly any one of you has concentrated on drawing attention to those issues that unite you and your people.

Studying the latest history of your country, you seem to be totally unaware of the fundamental principles which ought to motivate every leader.

    a)   That there are good men and women in all communities. In particular there are good men and women among the Hutus, Tutsis and the Twa; that the duty of a real leader is to identify those good men and women and give them tasks of serving the community.

    b)   That a true leader must work hard to ease tensions, especially when dealing with sensitive and complicated issues. Extremists normally thrive when there is tension, and pure emotion tends to supercede rational thinking.

c) A real leader uses every issue, no matter how serious and sensitive, to ensure that at the end of the debate we should emerge stronger and more united than ever before.

d) In every dispute you eventually reach a point where neither party is altogether right or altogether wrong. When compromise is the only alternative for those who seriously want peace and stability.

7. FROM THE UNPUBLISHED SEQUEL TO HIS AUTOBIOGRAPHY

Draft.

16.10.98
The Presidential Years.
Chapter One.

Men and women, all over the world, right down the centuries, come and go.

Some leave nothing behind, not even their names. It would seem that they never existed at all.

Others do leave something behind: the haunting memory of the evil deeds they committed against other people; gross violation[s] of human rights, not only limited to oppression and exploitation of ethnic minorities or vice versa, but who even resort to genocide in order to maintain their horrendous policies.

The moral decay of some communities in various parts of the world reveals itself among others in the use of the name of God to justify the maintenance of actions which are condemned by the entire world as crimes against humanity.

Among the multitude of those who have throughout history committed themselves to the struggle for justice in all its implications, are some of those who have commanded

Draft.   16. 10. 98

The Presidential Years.

Chapter One.

Men and women, all over the world, right
down the centuries, come and go.

Some leave nothing behind, not even their
names. It would seem that they never
existed at all.

Others do leave something behind: the haunting
memory of the evil deeds they committed against
other people; gross violation of human
rights, not only limited to oppression and
exploitation but of ethnic minorities or
vice versa, but who even resort to genocide in
order to maintain their horrendous
policies.

The moral decay of some communities
in various parts of the world reveals itself among others
in the use of the name of God to justify
the maintenance of actions which are
condemned by the entire world as crimes
against humanity.

Among the multitude of those who have
throughout history committed themselves to
the struggle for justice in all its upheavals,
are some of those who have commanded

....

From the unpublished sequel to his autobiography, see pages 403, 406.

invincible liberation armies who waged stirring operations and sacrificed enormously in order to free their people from the yoke of oppression, and to better their lives by creating jobs, building houses, schools, hospitals, introducing electricity, and bringing water clean and healthy water to people especially in the rural areas. Their aim was to remove the gap between the rich and the poor, the educated and uneducated, the healthy and those afflicted by preventable diseases.

Indeed when reactionary regimes were ultimately toppled, the liberators tried to the best of their ability and within the limits of their resources to carry out these noble objectives and to introduce clean government free of all forms of corruption. Almost every member of the oppressed group was full of hope that their cherished dreams would at last be realised, that they would in due course regain the human dignity denied to them for decades and even centuries.

But history never stops to play tricks even with seasoned and world famous freedom fighters. Frequently in history erstwhile revolutionaries have easily succumbed to greed, and the tendency to divert public resources for

From the unpublished sequel to his autobiography, see page 406.

invincible liberation armies who waged stirring operations and sacrificed enormously in order to free their people from the yoke of oppression, to better their lives by creating jobs, building houses, schools, hospitals, introducing electricity, and bringing clean and healthy water to people especially in the rural areas. Their aim was to remove the gap between the rich and the poor, the educated and uneducated, the healthy and those afflicted by preventable diseases.

Indeed when reactionary regimes were ultimately toppled, the liberators tried to the best of their ability and within the limits of their resources to carry out these noble objectives and to introduce clean government free of all forms of corruption. Almost every member of the oppressed group was full of hope that their cherished dreams would at last be realised, that they would in due course regain the human dignity denied to them for decades and even centuries.

But history never stops to play tricks even with seasoned and world famous freedom fighters. Frequently erstwhile revolutionaries have easily succumbed to greed, and the tendency to divert public resources for personal enrichment ultimately overwhelmed them. By amassing vast personal wealth, and by betraying the noble objectives which made them famous, they virtually deserted the masses of the people and joined the former oppressors, who enriched themselves by mercilessly robbing the poorest of the poor.

There is universal respect and even admiration for those who are humble and simple by nature, and who have absolute confidence in all human beings irrespective of their social status. These are men and women, known and unknown, who have declared total war against all forms of gross violation of human rights wherever in the world such excesses occur.

They are generally optimistic, believing that, in every community in the world, there are good men and women who personal enrichment ultimately overwhelmed them. By amassing vast personal wealth, and by betraying the noble objectives which made them famous, they virtually deserted the masses of the people and joined the former oppressors, who enriched themselves by mercilessly robbing the poorest of the poor.

There is universal respect, and even admiration, for those who are humble and simple by nature, and who have absolute confidence in all human beings irrespective of their social status. These are men and women, known and unknown, who have declared total war against all forms of gross violation of human rights wherever in the world such excesses occur.

They are generally optimistic, believing that, in every community in the world, there are good men and women who believe in peace as the most powerful weapon in the search for lasting solutions. The actual situation on the ground may justify the use of violence which even good men and women may find it difficult to avoid. But even in such

....

From the unpublished sequel to his autobiography, see pages 406, 409.

cases The use of force would be an exceptional measure whose primary aim is to create the necessary environment for peaceful solutions. It is such good men and women who are the hope of the world. Their efforts and achievements are recognised far beyond the borders of their countries, beyond the grave, even. ~~beyond the grave~~. They become immortal.

My general impression, after reading several autobiographies, is that an autobiography is not merely a catalogue of events and experiences in which a person has been involved, but that it also serves as some blueprint on which others may well model their own lives.

This book has no such pretensions as it has nothing to leave behind. As a young man I was the combined all the weaknesses, errors and indiscretions of a country boy; whose range of vision and experience was influenced mainly by events in the area in which I grew up and the colleges to which I was sent. I was relied on arrogance in order to hide my weakness as an adult my comrades raised me from and obscurely other fellow prisoners, with some significant exceptions, from obscurity to either a devil or a foggy hero. enigma, although the aura of being one of the worlds longest serving prisoners never totally evaporated.

....

From the unpublished sequel to his autobiography, see pages 409–410.

> 5.
>
> One issue that deeply worried me in prison was the false image I unwittingly projected to the outside world; of being regarded as a saint. I never was one even on the basis of an earthly definition of a saint as a sinner who keeps on trying.

From the unpublished sequel to his autobiography, see page 410.

believe in peace as the most powerful weapon in the search for lasting solutions. The actual situation on the ground may justify the use of violence which even good men and women may find it difficult to avoid. But even in such cases the use of force would be an exceptional measure whose primary aim is to create the necessary environment for peaceful solutions. It is such good men and women who are the hope of the world. Their efforts and achievements are recognised beyond the grave, even far beyond the borders of their countries, they become immortal.

My general impression, after reading several auto-biographies, is that an autobiography is not merely a catalogue of events and experiences in which a person has been involved, but that it also serves as some blueprint on which others may well model their own lives.

This book has no such pretentions as it has nothing to leave behind. As a young man I . . . combined all the weaknesses, errors and indiscretions of a country boy, whose range of vision and experience was influenced mainly by events in the area in which I grew up and the colleges to which I was sent. I relied on arrogance in order to hide my weaknesses. As an adult my comrades raised me and other fellow prisoners, with some significant exceptions, from obscurity to either a bogey or enigma, although the aura of being one of the world's longest serving prisoners never totally evaporated.

One issue that deeply worried me in prison was the false image that I unwittingly projected to the outside world; of being regarded as a saint. I never was one, even on the basis of an earthly definition of a saint as a sinner who keeps on trying.

Supplementary Information

APPENDIX A

....

Timeline

1918: Rolihlahla Mandela is born on 18 July at Mvezo in the Transkei to Nosekeni Fanny and Nkosi Mphakanyiswa Gadla Mandela.

1925: Attends primary school near the village of Qunu. His teacher gives him the name 'Nelson'.

1930: Following the death of his father, Mandela is entrusted to the care of Chief Jongintaba Dalindyebo, the regent of the Thembu people. He goes to live with him in Mqhekezweni at The Great Place.

1934: Undergoes the traditional circumcision ritual, initiating him into manhood. He attends Clarkebury Boarding Institute in Engcobo.

1937: Attends Healdtown, a Wesleyan College in Fort Beaufort.

1939: Enrols at the University College of Fort Hare, Alice, the only black university in South Africa. Meets Oliver Tambo.

1940: Expelled from Fort Hare for embarking on protest action.

1941: Escapes an arranged marriage and moves to Johannesburg where he finds work in the gold mines as a night watchman. Meets Walter Sisulu, who finds him employment as an articled clerk at the law firm Witkin, Sidelsky and Eidelman.

1942: Continues studying for his Bachelor of Arts degree (BA) by correspondence through the UNISA (University of South Africa). Begins to attend ANC (African National Congress) meetings informally.

1943: Graduates with a BA and enrols for a Bachelor of Laws degree (LLB) at the University of the Witwatersrand.

1944: Co-founds the ANCYL (ANC Youth League). Marries Evelyn Ntoko Mase and they have four children: Thembekile (1945–69); Makaziwe (1947), who died at nine months old; Makgatho (1950–2005); and Makaziwe (1954).

1948: Elected national secretary of the ANCYL, and onto the Transvaal National Executive of the ANC.

1951: Elected president of the ANCYL.

1952: Elected ANC president of the Transvaal province and is automatically a deputy president of the ANC. Public spokesperson and national volunteer-in-chief of the Defiance Campaign, which begins on 26 June 1952. He is arrested on a number of occasions and spends several days in jail. He is convicted with nineteen others under the Suppression of Communism Act and sentenced to nine months' imprisonment with hard labour, suspended for two years, and also receives the first in a series of banning orders preventing him from participating in any political activity. With Oliver Tambo he opens Mandela and Tambo, South Africa's first African law partnership.

1953: Devises the M-Plan for the ANC's future underground operations.

1955: The Freedom Charter is adopted at the Congress of the People in Kliptown. Mandela, along with other banned comrades, watches the proceedings in secret, from the roof of a nearby shop.

1956: Arrested and charged with treason along with 155 members of the Congress Alliance. The trial continues for four and a half years.

1958: Divorces Evelyn Mase. Marries Nomzamo Winifred Madikizela and they have two daughters: Zenani (1959) and Zindziswa (1960).

1960: Following the Sharpeville Massacre on 21 March, the government declares a state of emergency and Mandela is detained. On 8 April, the ANC and PAC (Pan Africanist Congress) are banned.

1961: Acquitted in the last group of twenty-eight in the 1956 Treason Trial; all the other accused had charges withdrawn at different stages of the trial. In March, Mandela appears at the All-in African Congress in Pietermaritzburg as the main speaker and demands a national convention to draw up a new constitution for South Africa. In April, he goes underground. In June, the armed wing of the ANC, Umkhonto we Sizwe (MK), is formed with Mandela as its first commander-in-chief, and launched on 16 December with a series of explosions.

1962: In January, Mandela departs South Africa to undergo military training and to garner support for the ANC. He leaves the country clandestinely through Botswana (then Bechuanaland) and re-enters South Africa from there in July. He receives military training in Ethiopia and in Morocco, close to the border of Algeria. In total he visits twelve African states, and also spends two weeks in London, UK, with Oliver Tambo. On 5 August he is arrested near Howick in KwaZulu-Natal, and is sentenced to five years' imprisonment on 7 November for leaving the country without a passport and inciting workers to strike.

1963: Mandela is transferred to Robben Island Prison on 27 May, before being suddenly returned to Pretoria Central Prison two weeks later. On 11 July, police raid Liliesleaf Farm in Rivonia and arrest almost all of the High Command of MK. In October, Mandela is put on trial for sabotage with nine others in what becomes known as the Rivonia Trial. James Kantor has charges withdrawn and Rusty Bernstein is acquitted.

....

1964: In March, James Kantor has charges withdrawn. In June, Rusty Bernstein is acquitted, but Mandela, Walter Sisulu, Ahmed Kathrada, Govan Mbeki, Raymond Mhlaba, Denis Goldberg, Andrew Mlangeni and Elias Motsoaledi are convicted and sentenced to life imprisonment. All except Goldberg, who serves his sentence in Pretoria, are taken to Robben Island Prison.

....

1968: Mandela's mother dies on 26 September. His request to attend her funeral is refused.

....

1969: Mandela's eldest son, Madiba Thembekile (Thembi), is killed in a car accident on 13 July. Mandela's letter to the prison authorities requesting permission to attend his funeral is ignored.

....

1975: Begins writing his autobiography in secret. Sisulu and Kathrada review the manuscript and make comments. Mac Maharaj and Laloo Chiba transcribe it into tiny handwriting, and Chiba conceals it inside Maharaj's exercise books. It is smuggled out by Maharaj when he is released in 1976.

....

1982: Mandela along with Walter Sisulu, Raymond Mhlaba, Andrew Mlangeni and, later, Ahmed Kathrada are sent to Pollsmoor Prison. They share a large communal cell on the top floor of a cell block.

....

1984: Rejects an offer by his nephew K D Matanzima, the president of the so-called independent state (or bantustan) of Transkei, to be released into the Transkei.

....

1985: Rejects President P W Botha's offer to release him if he renounces violence as a political strategy. On 10 February his statement of rejection is read out to a rally in Soweto by his daughter, Zindzi. In November, Mandela undergoes prostate surgery in the Volks Hospital. He is visited in hospital by the minister of justice, Kobie Coetsee. On his return to prison he is held alone. Begins exploratory talks with members of the government over the creation of conditions for negotiations with the ANC.

....

1988: A twelve-hour pop concert to celebrate Mandela's seventieth birthday, held at Wembley Stadium, London, UK, is broadcast to sixty-seven countries. Contracts tuberculosis and is admitted to Tygerberg Hospital, then Constantiaberg Medi-Clinic. He is discharged in December, and moved to Victor Verster Prison, near Paarl.

....

1989: Graduates with an LLB degree through the University of South Africa.

1990: The ANC is unbanned on 2 February. Mandela is released from prison on 11 February.

1991: Elected ANC president at the first ANC national conference in South Africa since its banning in 1960.

1993: Awarded the Nobel Peace Prize with President F W de Klerk.

1994: Votes for the first time in his life in South Africa's first democratic elections on 27 April. On 9 May he is elected first president of a democratic South Africa, and on 10 May he is inaugurated as president in Pretoria. His autobiography, *Long Walk to Freedom*, is published.

1996: Divorces Winnie Mandela.

1998: Marries Graça Machel on his eightieth birthday.

1999: Steps down after one term as president.

2001: Diagnosed with prostate cancer.

2004: Announces he is stepping down from public life.

2005: Makgatho, Mandela's second-born son, dies in January. Mandela publicly announces that his son has died of AIDS complications.

2006: Publishes *Mandela: The Authorised Portrait*.

2007: Witnesses the installation of grandson Mandla Mandela as chief of the Mvezo Traditional Council.

2008: Turns ninety years old. Asks the emerging generations to continue the fight for social justice.

2009: Mandela's birthday, 18 July, is endorsed by the United Nations as International Nelson Mandela Day.

2010: His great-granddaughter, Zenani Mandela, is killed in a car accident in June.

2011: Hospitalised for a lung infection.

2012: Hospitalised for an abdominal complaint. Post presidential office closed. Celebrates his ninety-fourth birthday.

APPENDIX B

....

Map of South Africa, *c*.1996

Province	City/town/village	Description
Eastern Cape	Mvezo	Mandela's birthplace.
	Qunu	Village Mandela lived as a child and built a home after his release from prison.
	Mqhekezweni	The Great Place where Mandela moved to when he was around the age of nine.
	Engcobo	Clarkebury Boarding Institute where Mandela obtained his junior certificate.
	Fort Beaufort	Attended college at Healdtown.
	Alice	Attended University College of Fort Hare.
Gauteng	Johannesburg	Moved to Johannesburg in April 1941. Lived in Alexandra and Soweto before his imprisonment. Lived in Soweto and Houghton upon his release. Lived in Houghton through his presidency and retirement.
	Kliptown	The Freedom Charter was adopted by the Congress of the People, 1955.
	Pretoria	Pretoria Central Prison, 1962–63, 1963–64. Location of his trial in 1962 and the Rivonia Trial. Inaugurated as president, May 1994. Offices at the Union Buildings while president, 1994–99.
	Sharpeville	Sharpeville Massacre, 21 March 1960.
	Rivonia	Liliesleaf Farm, the underground safe house.
KwaZulu-Natal	Pietermaritzburg	All-In African Conference, 22 March 1961.
	Howick	Arrested, 5 August 1962.
Western Cape	Robben Island	Imprisoned on Robben Island for two weeks from May 1963, and for eighteen years from 13 June 1964 to 30 March 1982.
	Cape Town	Imprisoned at Pollsmoor Prison, March 1982 to August 1988. Treated at Tygerberg Hospital, 1988. Treated at Constantiaberg Medi-Clinic, 1988. Office and home while president, 1994–99.
	Paarl	Held at Victor Verster Prison, December 1988 to 11 February 1990.

Map of Africa, *c.*1962

Map showing the route taken by Nelson Mandela during his trip to Africa and London, UK, in 1962. He visited twelve African states, during which time he met with political leaders in an effort to elicit political and economic support for MK and underwent military training in Morocco and Ethiopia. He also spent two weeks in London with Oliver Tambo.

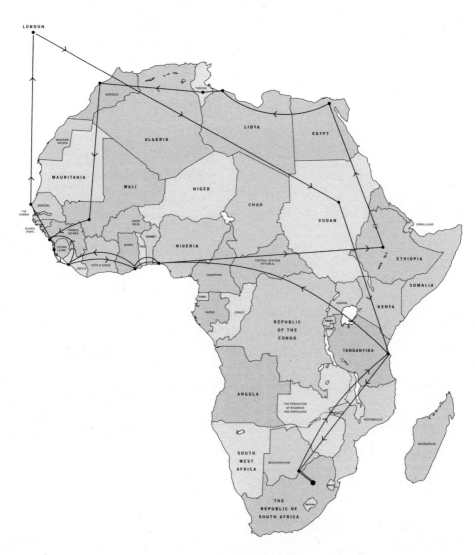

Countries visited in order (with specific cities where known)

Bechuanaland (Lobatse, Kasane)	Arrived 11 January 1962
Tanganyika (Mbeya, Dar es Salam)	Arrived 21 January 1962
Nigeria (Lagos)	Arrived 25 January 1962
Ethiopia (Addis Ababa)	Arrived 30 January 1962
Egypt (Cairo)	Arrived 12 February 1962
Libya (Tripoli)	Arrived 25 February 1962
Tunisia (Tunis)	Arrived 27 February 1962
Morocco (Casablanca, Rabat, Oujda)	Arrived 6 March 1962
Mali (Bamako)	Arrived 28 March 1962
French Guinea (Conakry)	Arrived 12 April 1962
Sierra Leone (Freetown)	Arrived 16 April 1962
Liberia (Monrovia)	Arrived 19 April 1962
Ghana (Accra)	Arrived 27 April 1962
Nigeria (Lagos)	Arrived 17 May 1962
Ghana (Accra)	Arrived 27 May 1962 (45-minute stopover)
Liberia (Monrovia)	Arrived 27 May 1962
French Guinea (Conakry)	Arrived 28 May 1962
Senegal (Dakar)	Arrived 1 June 1962
United Kingdom (London)	Arrived 7 June 1962
Sudan (Khartoum)	Arrived 19 June 1962
Ethiopia (Addis Ababa)	Arrived 26 June 1962
Sudan (Khartoum)	Arrived 1962, exact date unknown
Tanganyika (Dar es Salam, Mbeya)	Arrived 1962, exact date unknown
Bechuanaland (Kanye, Lobatse)	Arrived 1962, exact date unknown

APPENDIX C

Abbreviations for Organisations

AAC	All-African Convention
ANC	African National Congress (SANNC before 1923)
ANCWL	African National Congress Women's League
ANCYL	African National Congress Youth League
APDUSA	African People's Democratic Union of Southern Africa
COD	Congress of Democrats
COSATU	Congress of South African Trade Unions
CPC	Coloured People's Congress
CPSA	Communist Party of South Africa (SACP after 1953)
FEDSAW	Federation of South African Women
IFP	Inkatha Freedom Party
MK	Umkhonto we Sizwe
NEUF	Non-European United Front
NEUM	Non-European Unity Movement
NIC	Natal Indian Congress
PAC	Pan Africanist Congress
SACP	South African Communist Party (CPSA before 1953)
SACTU	South African Congress of Trade Unions
SAIC	South African Indian Congress
SANNC	South African Native Natal Congress (ANC after 1923)
TIC	Transvaal Indian Congress
UDF	United Democratic Front

APPENDIX D

People, Places and Events

Abdurahman, Abdullah

(1872–1940). Medical doctor, politician and anti-apartheid activist. Father of Cissie Gool. First black person to be elected to the Cape Town City Council and the Cape Provincial Council. President of the African Political Organisation (APO). Posthumously awarded the Order for Meritorious Service: Class 1 (Gold) by Mandela in 1999, for his work against racial oppression.

African National Congress (ANC)

Established as the South African Native National Congress (SANNC) in 1912. Renamed African National Congress (ANC) in 1923. Following the Sharpeville Massacre in March 1960, the ANC was banned by the South African government and went underground until the ban was lifted in 1990. Its military wing, Umkhonto we Sizwe (MK), was established in 1961, with Mandela as commander-in-chief. The ANC became South Africa's governing party after the nation's first democratic elections on 27 April 1994.

African National Congress Women's League (ANCWL)

Established in 1948. Actively involved in the 1952 Defiance Campaign and the anti-pass campaigns.

African National Congress Youth League (ANCYL)

Founded in 1944 by Nelson Mandela, Anton Lembede, Walter Sisulu, A P Mda and Oliver Tambo as a reaction to the ANC's more conservative outlook. Its activities included civil disobedience and strikes in protest against the apartheid system. Many members left and formed the Pan Africanist Congress (PAC) in 1959. Banned between 1960 and 1990.

African People's Democratic Union of Southern Africa (APDUSA)

Formed in 1961 to champion the rights of the oppressed rural peasant classes and urban working classes and to politically educate them. Affiliated to the Non-European Unity Movement (NEUM) and the All-African Convention (AAC). Led by Tabata Isaac Bangani.

Alexander, Dr Neville

(1936–2012). Academic, political and anti-apartheid activist. Founder of the National Liberation Front (NLF) against the apartheid government. Convicted of sabotage in 1962 and imprisoned on Robben Island for ten years. Awarded the Lingua Pax Prize for his contribution to the promotion of multilingualism in post-apartheid South Africa, 2008.

Asvat, Dr Zainab
(1923–). Anti-apartheid activist. Imprisoned for her participation in the 1946 Passive Resistance Campaign. One of the first women to be elected to the executive of the Transvaal Indian Congress (TIC) in 1946. She was banned for five years in 1963, and when it expired she went to London on an exit permit. Her father, Ebrahim Asvat, participated in Gandhi's passive resistance campaigns. He was elected chairperson of the Transvaal British Indian Association in 1918.

Autshumao (spelt by Mandela as Autshumayo)
(d. 1663). Khoikhoi leader. Learnt English and Dutch and worked as an interpreter during the Dutch settlement of the Cape of Good Hope in 1652. He and two of his followers were banished by Jan van Riebeeck to Robben Island in 1658 after waging war with the Dutch settlers. He was one of the first people to be imprisoned on Robben Island and the only person to ever successfully escape.

Barnard, Dr Lukas (Niël)
(1949–). Academic. Professor of political studies at the University of the Orange Free State, 1978. Head of South Africa's Intelligence Service, 1980–92. Held clandestine meetings with Mandela in prison in preparation for his subsequent release and rise to political power. This included facilitating meetings between Mandela and Presidents P W Botha and, later, F W de Klerk. Director-general Western Cape Provincial Administration, 1996–2001.

Bernstein (née Schwarz), Hilda
(1915–2006). Author, artist and anti-apartheid and women's rights activist. City Councillor in Johannesburg from 1943 to 1946. The only communist to be elected to public office, on a 'whites only' vote. Married Lionel (Rusty) Bernstein. Founding member of the Federation of South African Women (FEDSAW), the first nonracial women's organisation in South Africa, in 1956, and the South African Peace Council. Member of the ANC's Women's League. Following the Rivonia Trial in 1964, she escaped on foot to Botswana, before relocating to London, UK. Awarded the Order of Luthuli in Silver in 2004 for her contribution to the attainment of gender equality and a free and democratic society in South Africa.

Bernstein, Lionel (Rusty)
(1920–2002). Architect and anti-apartheid activist. Leading member of the Communist Party of South Africa (CPSA). Founding member and leader of the Congress of Democrats (COD), one of the participating organisations in the 1955 Congress of the People at which the Freedom Charter was adopted. Defendant in the 1956 Treason Trial. After being acquitted in the Rivonia Trial he and his wife, Hilda, went into exile

(they crossed into neighbouring Botswana on foot). He remained a leading member of the ANC, whilst practising as an architect.

Bizos, George
(1928–). Greek-born human rights lawyer. Member and co-founder of the National Council of Lawyers for Human Rights. Committee member of the ANC's Legal and Constitutional Committee. Legal advisor for Convention for a Democratic South Africa (CODESA). Defence lawyer in the Rivonia Trial. Also acted for high-profile anti-apartheid activists, including the families of Steve Biko, Chris Hani and the Cradock Four in the Truth and Reconciliation Commission. Appointed by Mandela to South Africa's Judicial Services Commission.

Black Consciousness Movement
Anti-apartheid movement targeting black youth and workers. Promoted pride in black identity. It emerged in the mid 1960s as a reaction to the political vacuum created by the continued banning and imprisonment of members of the ANC and the PAC. Had its origins in the South African Students Organisation (SASO) led by Steve Biko, who founded the movement.

Botha, Pieter Willem (P W)
(1916–2006). Prime minister of South Africa, 1978–84. First executive state president, 1984–89. Leader of South Africa's National Party. Advocate of the apartheid system. In 1985, Mandela rejected Botha's offer to release him on the condition that he rejected violence. Botha refused to testify at the Truth and Reconciliation Commission in 1998 about apartheid crimes.

Brutus, Dennis
(1924–2009). Educator and anti-apartheid and human rights activist. Co-founder and president of the South African Non-Racial Olympic Committee (SANROC), which persuaded Olympic committees from other countries to suspend South Africa from the 1964 and 1968 Olympic Games, and to subsequently expel the country from the Olympic movement in 1970. He was sentenced to eighteen months' hard labour in 1963 for breaking his banning order. Part of his sentence was spent on Robben Island. He fled South Africa in 1966.

Buthelezi, Mangosuthu
(1928–). South African politician and Zulu prince. Member of the ANC until the relationship deteriorated in 1979. Founder and president of the Inkatha Freedom Party (IFP) in 1975. Chief Minister of KwaZulu. Appointed South African Minister of Home Affairs, 1994–2004, and acted as president several times during Mandela's presidency.

Cachalia (née Asvat), Amina
(1930–2013). Anti-apartheid and women's rights activist. Member of the ANC and TIC. Co-founder and treasurer of FEDSAW. Founder of Women's Progressive Union.

Married Yusuf Cachalia. Banning orders from 1963 to 1978 prevented her from attending social gatherings or political meetings, entering any place of education or publishing house and leaving the magisterial district of Johannesburg.

Cachalia, Ismail Ahmad (Maulvi)

(1908–2003). Anti-apartheid activist. Leading member of the SAIC, TIC and ANC. Key participant in the 1946 Passive Resistance Campaign. Deputy volunteer-in-chief to Mandela in the 1952 Defiance Campaign, and amongst the twenty accused in the Defiance Campaign Trial. Went to the Bandung Conference in 1955 with Moses Kotane. Fled to Botswana in 1964 and set up ANC offices in New Delhi. His father Ahmad Mohamed Cachalia was a close associate of Gandhi's and was chairperson of the Transvaal British Indian Association, 1908–18.

Cachalia, Yusuf

(1915–95). Political activist. Secretary of the South African Indian Congress (SAIC). Brother of Maulvi Cachalia. Husband of Amina Cachalia. Served a nine-month suspended sentence following his involvement in the 1952 Defiance Campaign. Banned continuously from 1953.

Chiba, Isu (Laloo)

(1930–). Anti-apartheid activist. Member of the SACP and TIC. Platoon commander of MK. Tortured by the South African security police causing him to lose the hearing in one of his ears. Member of MK's Second National High Command, for which he was sentenced to eighteen years' imprisonment, which he served on Robben Island. Assisted in transcribing Mandela's autobiographical manuscript in prison. Released in 1982. Member of the United Democratic Front (UDF). MP, 1994–2004. Received the Order of Luthuli in Silver in 2004 for his lifetime contribution to the struggle for a nonracial, non-sexist, just and democratic South Africa.

Coetsee, Hendrik (Kobie)

(1931–2000). South African politician, lawyer, administrator and negotiator. Deputy Minister for Defence and National Intelligence, 1978. Minister of Justice, 1980. Held meetings with Mandela from 1985 about creating the conditions for talks between the National Party and the ANC. Elected President of the Senate following South Africa's first democratic elections in 1994.

Communist Party South Africa (CPSA)

(*See* South African Communist Party.)

Congress Alliance

Established in the 1950s and made up of the ANC, SAIC, COD and the South African Coloured People's Organisation (later the CPC). When SACTU was established in 1955, it became the fifth member of the Alliance. It was instrumental in organising the Congress of the People and mobilising clauses for inclusion in the Freedom Charter.

Congress of the People

The Congress of the People was the culmination of a year-long campaign where members of the Congress Alliance visited homes across the length and breadth of South Africa recording people's demands for a free South Africa, which were included in the Freedom Charter. Held 25–26 June 1955 in Kliptown, Johannesburg, it was attended by 3,000 delegates. The Freedom Charter was adopted on the second day of the Congress.

Cooper, Sathasivan (Saths)

(1950–). Psychologist and anti-apartheid activist. Proponent of Black Consciousness. Secretary of the Black People's Convention, 1972. Banned and restricted to the Durban magisterial district for five years in 1973. Convicted for assaulting a policeman during a strike in 1973. Sentenced to ten years' imprisonment in 1974 for helping to organise rallies that celebrated the victory of the Mozambican Liberation Movement. He was released on 20 December 1982. Elected vice-president of the Azanian People's Organisation (AZAPO) in 1983.

Dadoo, Dr Yusuf

(1909–83). Medical doctor, anti-apartheid activist and orator. President of SAIC. Deputy to Oliver Tambo on the Revolutionary Council of MK. Chairman of the SACP, 1972–1983. Leading member of the ANC. First jailed in 1940 for anti-war activities, and then for six months during the 1946 Passive Resistance Campaign. Was among the twenty accused in the 1952 Defiance Campaign Trial. He went underground during the 1960 State of Emergency, and into exile to escape arrest. Awarded the ANC's highest honour, Isitwalandwe Seaparankoe, in 1955 at the Congress of the People.

Dalindyebo, Chief Jongintaba

(d. 1942). Chief and regent of the Thembu people. Became Mandela's guardian following his father's death. Mandela went to live with him at The Great Place at Mqhekezweni when he was nine years old.

Dalindyebo, King Sabata Jonguhlanga

(1928–1986). Paramount chief of the Transkei, 1954–80. Leader of the Democratic Progressive Party. Nephew of Chief Jongintaba Dalindyebo. Fled to Zambia in 1980 after being convicted of violating the dignity of President Matanzima of the Transkei.

Daniels, Edward (Eddie; Mandela calls him 'Danie')

(1928–). Political activist. Member of the Liberal Party of South Africa. Member of the African Resistance Movement which sabotaged non-human targets as a statement against the government. Served a fifteen-year sentence in Robben Island Prison where he was held in B section with Mandela. He was banned immediately after his release in 1979. Received the Order of Luthuli in Silver from the South African government in 2005.

de Klerk, Frederik Willem (F W)

(1936–). Lawyer. President of South Africa, 1989–94. Leader of the National Party, 1989–97. In February 1990 he unbanned the ANC and other organisations and released Mandela from prison. Deputy president with Thabo Mbeki under Mandela from 1994 to 1996. Leader of New National Party, 1997. Awarded the Prince of Asturias Award in 1992 and the Nobel Peace Prize in 1993 with Nelson Mandela, for his role in the peaceful end to apartheid.

Defiance Campaign Against Unjust Laws

Initiated by the ANC in December 1951, and launched with the SAIC on 26 June 1952, against six apartheid laws. The Campaign involved individuals breaking racist laws such as entering premises reserved for 'whites only', breaking curfews and courting arrest. Mandela was appointed national volunteer-in-chief and Maulvi Cachalia as his deputy. Over 8,500 volunteers were imprisoned for their participation in the Defiance Campaign.

Dube, John Langalibalele

(1871–1946). Educator, publisher, editor, writer and political activist. First president general of the SANNC (renamed as the ANC in 1923) established in 1912. Established the Zulu Christian Industrial School at Ohlange. Established the first Zulu/English newspaper *Ilanga lase Natal* (*Sun of Natal*) in 1904. Opponent of the 1913 Land Act. Member of the executive of the AAC, 1935. Mandela voted at the Ohlange school in 1994 for the first time in his life, and then visited Dube's grave to report that South Africa was now free.

Federation of South African Women (FEDSAW)

Established 17 April 1954 in Johannesburg as a national, nonracial women's organisation. Instrumental in the anti-pass campaigns which culminated in a historic march of 20,000 women on 9 August 1956 (now celebrated as Women's Day in South Africa) to the South African government's Union Buildings in Pretoria.

First, Ruth

(1925–82). Academic, journalist and anti-apartheid and women's rights activist. Married Joe Slovo, 1949. Met Mandela while attending the University of the Witwatersrand. Arrested, charged and then acquitted in the Treason Trial. Fled to Swaziland with her children during the 1960 State of Emergency. Detained in solitary confinement for ninety days in 1963 and fled to the UK on her release. Lived in exile in Mozambique from 1977 and was killed by a parcel bomb there on 17 August 1982.

Fischer, Abram (Bram)

(1908–75). Lawyer and political and anti-apartheid activist. Leader of the CPSA. Member of the COD. Charged with incitement for his involvement in the African Mine Workers' Strike for better wages in 1946. Successfully defended Mandela and other leading ANC members in the Treason Trial. Led the defence in the Rivonia Trial, 1963–64. Continually subjected to banning orders and in 1966 he was sentenced to life imprisonment for violating the Suppression of Communism Act and conspiring to commit sabotage. Awarded the Lenin Peace Prize in 1967.

Fischer (née Krige), Susanna Johanna (Molly)

(1908–64). Teacher and anti-apartheid activist. Member of the CPSA and FEDSAW. Married Bram Fischer, 1937. In 1955 she was banned from three organisations and forced to resign from her position as secretary of the South African Society for Peace and Friendship with the Soviet Union. Detained in the 1960 State of Emergency. She died in a car accident in 1964 en route to Cape Town with her husband to attend her daughter's twenty-first birthday party.

Freedom Charter

A statement of the principles of the Congress Alliance, adopted at the Congress of the People in Kliptown, Soweto, on 26 June 1955. The Congress Alliance rallied thousands of volunteers across South Africa to record the demands of the people. The Freedom Charter espoused equal rights for all South Africans regardless of race, land reform, improved working and living conditions, the fair distribution of wealth, compulsory education and fairer laws. The Freedom Charter was a powerful tool used in the fight against apartheid.

Gerwel, G J (Jakes)

(1946–). Academic. Director-general in the office of President Mandela, 1994–99. Secretary of the cabinet in the Government of National Unity, 1994–99. Chancellor of Rhodes University. Distinguished Professor in the humanities, University of the Western Cape. Chairman of the Nelson Mandela Foundation.

Goldberg, Denis

(1933–). Anti-apartheid and political activist. Member of the SACP. Co-founder and leader of the COD. Technical officer in MK. Arrested at Rivonia in 1963 and subsequently served a life sentence in Pretoria Local Prison. On his release in 1985 he went into exile in the UK and represented the ANC at the Anti-Apartheid Committee of the United Nations. Founded Community HEART in 1995 to help poor black South Africans. Returned to South Africa in 2002 and was appointed special advisor to Minister of Water Affairs and Forestry Ronnie Kasrils.

Gool, Zainunnisa (Cissie)

(1897–1963). Lawyer and anti-apartheid activist. Daughter of Abdullah Abdurahman. Founder and first president of the National Liberation League (NLL) and president of the Non-European United Front (NEUF) in the 1940s. Arrested and charged for her involvement in the 1946 Passive Resistance Campaign, and banned in 1954. In 1962, she was the first black woman to graduate from law school in South Africa and to be called to the Cape Bar. Posthumously awarded the Order of Luthuli in Silver by the South African government for her outstanding contribution to the struggle for liberation and for the ideals of a just, non-racist and democratic South Africa.

Hani, Thembisile (Chris)

(1942–93). Anti-apartheid and political activist. Member of the ANCYL from the age of fifteen. He also joined the SACP. Member and eventually head of MK. He was active in the ANC underground in the Eastern and Western Capes, and eventually went into exile, where he rose through the ranks of MK. Returned to South Africa in 1990. General secretary of the SACP from 1991. Assassinated outside his home in Johannesburg in 1993 by Janusz Waluś. Posthumously awarded the ANC's highest honour, Isitwalandwe Seaparankoe, in 2008.

Harmel, Michael

(1915–74). Journalist, intellectual, trade unionist and anti-apartheid activist. Leading member of the SACP and editor of *The African Communist*. Member of MK. Assisted in the establishment of the South African Congress of Trade Unions (SACTU). Co-founder of the COD. Continuously banned. The SACP asked him to go into exile in 1962, where he played a prominent role in the SACP, ANC and MK.

Hepple, Bob

(1934–). Lawyer, academic and anti-apartheid activist. Member of the COD and SACTU. Represented Mandela in 1962 following his arrest for leaving the country illegally and for inciting workers to strike. Arrested at Liliesleaf Farm in 1963, but the charges were dropped on the condition that he appeared as a state witness. He subsequently fled South Africa. Knighted in 2004.

Hodgson, Jack

(1910–77). Anti-apartheid activist. Member of the SACP. National secretary of the Springbok Legion, an anti-fascist organisation for World War II veterans. Co-founder and first secretary of the COD. Co-founder of MK. Assisted in the training of MK recruits. Banned by the apartheid government. Charged in the Treason Trial. Listed as a co-conspirator in the indictment of the Rivonia Trial.

Jabavu, Davidson Don Tengo

(1885–1959). Academic, poet and political and anti-apartheid activist. Son of John Tengo Jabavu. First black professor at the University College of Fort Hare, Alice. President of the AAC, established in 1935, in opposition to segregationist legislation. Educator and co-founder of the SANNC (renamed as the ANC in 1923).

Jabavu, John Tengo

(1859–1921). Academic, writer, newspaper editor and political activist. Father of Davidson Don Tengo Jabavu. Established the first black-owned newspaper, *Imvo Zabantsundu* (*Black Opinion*), in 1884. Assisted in the establishment of the South African Native College (University of Fort Hare) in 1916. Posthumously awarded the Order of Luthuli in Gold.

Joseph (née Fennell), Helen

(1905–92). Teacher, social worker and anti-apartheid and women's rights activist.

Founding member of the COD. National secretary of FEDSAW. Leading organiser of the Women's March of 20,000 women to Pretoria's Union Buildings. An accused in the 1956 Treason Trial. Placed under house arrest in 1962. Helped care for Zindzi and Zeni Mandela when their parents were both imprisoned. Awarded the ANC's highest honour, Isitwalandwe Seaparankoe, in 1992.

Kantor, James

(1927–75). Lawyer. Despite not being a member of the ANC or MK, he was put on trial at Rivonia, possibly due to the fact that his brother-in-law and business partner was Harold Wolpe who had been arrested at Liliesleaf Farm. Was later acquitted and fled South Africa.

Kathrada, Ahmed Mohamed (Kathy)

(1929–). Anti-apartheid activist, politician, political prisoner and MP. Leading member of the ANC and of the SACP. Founding member of the Transvaal Indian Volunteer Corps and its successor, the Transvaal Indian Youth Congress. Imprisoned for one month in 1946 for his participation in the SAIC's Passive Resistance Campaign against the Asiatic Land Tenure and Indian Representation Act. Convicted for his participation in the 1952 Defiance Campaign. Banned in 1954. Co-organiser of the Congress of the People and a member of the Congress Alliance General Purpose Committee. Detained during the 1960 State of Emergency. One of the last twenty-eight accused in the Treason Trial acquitted in 1961. Placed under house arrest in 1962. Arrested at Liliesleaf Farm in July 1963 and charged with sabotage in the Rivonia Trial. Imprisoned on Robben Island, 1964–82, then Pollsmoor Prison until his release on 15 October 1989. MP from 1994, after South Africa's first democratic elections, and served as political advisor to President Mandela. Chairperson of the Robben Island Council, 1994–2006. Awarded Isitwalandwe Seaparankoe, the ANC's highest honour, in 1992; the Pravasi Bharatiya Samman Award from the President of India, and several honorary doctorates.

Khoikhoi

Original inhabitants of South Africa. The Khoikhoi were pastoral people who depended on their cattle and sheep for subsistence.

Kotane, Moses

(1905–78). Anti-apartheid and political activist. Secretary general of the SACP, 1939–78. Treasurer general of the ANC, 1963–73. Defendant in the 1956 Treason Trial. One of the twenty accused in the Defiance Campaign trial. In 1955 he attended the Bandung Conference in Indonesia. Detained in the 1960 State of Emergency, then placed under house arrest. He went into exile in 1963. Awarded the ANC's highest honour, Isitwalandwe Seaparankoe, in 1975.

Kruger, James (Jimmy)

(1917–87). Politician. Minister of Justice and Police, 1974–79. President of the Senate, 1979–80. Member of the National Party. Infamously remarked that Steve Biko's death in detention in 1977 left him 'cold'.

Luthuli, Chief Albert John Mvumbi

(1898–1967). Teacher, anti-apartheid activist and minister of religion. Chief of Groutville Reserve. President-general of the ANC, 1952–67. From 1953 he was confined to his home by government bans. Defendant in the 1956 Treason Trial. Sentenced to six months (suspended) in 1960 after publicly burning his passbook and calling for a national day of mourning following the Sharpeville Massacre. Awarded the Nobel Peace Prize in 1960 for his non-violent role in the struggle against apartheid. Awarded the ANC's highest honour, Isitwalandwe Seaparankoe, in 1955 at the Congress of the People.

Machel, Graça (née Simbine)

(1945–) Mozambican teacher, human rights activist, international advocate for women's and children's rights, and politician. Married Nelson Mandela, July 1998. Widow of Mozambican president Samora Machel (d. 1986). Member of the Mozambican Liberation Front (FRELIMO) which fought for and won independence from Portugal in 1976. Mozambican Minister for Education and Culture after independence. Among numerous awards she has received the United Nations' Nansen Medal in recognition of her long-standing humanitarian work, particularly on behalf of refugee children.

Madikizela-Mandela, Nomzamo Winifred (Winnie)

(1936–). Social worker and anti-apartheid and women's rights activist. Member of the ANC. Married to Nelson Mandela, 1958–96 (separated 1992). Mother of Zenani and Zindziswa Mandela. First qualified black medical social worker at the Baragwanath Hospital in Johannesburg. Held in solitary confinement for seventeen months in 1969. Placed under house arrest from 1970 and subjected to a series of banning orders from 1962 to 1987. Established the Black Women's Federation, 1975, and the Black Parents' Association, 1976, in response to the Soweto Uprising. President of the ANC Women's League, 1993–2003. ANC MP.

Maharaj, Satyandranath (Mac)

(1935–). Academic, politician, political and anti-apartheid activist, political prisoner and MP. Leading member of the ANC, SACP and MK. Convicted of sabotage in 1964 and sentenced to twelve years' imprisonment which he served on Robben Island. Helped to secretly transcribe Mandela's autobiography, *Long Walk to Freedom*, and smuggled it out of prison when he was released in 1976. Commanded Operation Vulindlela (Vula), an ANC underground operation to establish an internal underground leadership. Maharaj served on the secretariat of CODESA. Minister of Transport, 1994–99. Envoy to President Jacob Zuma.

Maki

(*See* Mandela, Makaziwe.)

Makwetu, Clarence

(1928–). Political and anti-apartheid activist and political prisoner. Member of the

ANCYL. Co-founder and later president of the PAC, 1990–96. Charged with furthering the aims of the PAC in 1963 and sentenced to five years' imprisonment. Following his release from Robben Island he was escorted to the Transkei, but was banished by his cousin K D Matanzima in 1979. First president of the Pan Africanist Movement (PAM), the front organisation of the PAC, 1989. MP following the 1994 democratic elections. Recipient of the Order of Luthuli in Silver.

Mandela, Evelyn Ntoko
(*See* Mase, Evelyn Ntoko.)

Mandela, Madiba Thembekile (Thembi)
(1945–69). Mandela's eldest son to his first wife, Evelyn. Died in a car accident.

Mandela, Makaziwe
(1947). Mandela's first-born daughter to his first wife, Evelyn. Died at nine months old.

Mandela, Makaziwe (Maki)
(1954–). Mandela's second-born daughter to his first wife, Evelyn.

Mandela, Makgatho (Kgatho)
(1950–2005). Mandela's second-born son to his first wife, Evelyn. Lawyer. Died of AIDS complications on 6 January 2005 in Johannesburg following the death of his second wife, Zondi Mandela, who died from pneumonia as a complication of AIDS in July 2003.

Mandela, Nkosi Mphakanyiswa Gadla
(d. 1927). Chief, counsellor and advisor. Descendant of the Ixhiba house. Mandela's father. Deprived of his chieftainship following a dispute with a local white magistrate.

Mandela, Nosekeni Fanny
(d. 1968). Mandela's mother. Third wife of Nkosi Mphakanyiswa Gadla Mandela.

Mandela, Winnie
(*See* Madikizela-Mandela, Nomzamo Winifred.)

Mandela, Zenani (Zeni)
(1959–). Mandela's first-born daughter to his second wife, Winnie.

Mandela, Zindziswa (Zindzi)
(1960–). Mandela's second-born daughter to his second wife, Winnie.

Marks, John Beaver (J B)
(1903–1972). Political and anti-apartheid activist and trade unionist. President of the ANC in the Transvaal. Chair of the SACP. Banned under the Suppression of

Communism Act. President of the Transvaal Council of Non-European Trade Unions. President of the African Mine Workers Union (AMWU). Organised the 1946 African Mine Workers' Strike. Deployed by the ANC to join the headquarters of the External Mission in Tanzania, 1963.

Mase, Evelyn Ntoko
(1922–2004). Nurse. Married to Nelson Mandela, 1944–57. Mother to Madiba Thembekile (1945–69), Makaziwe (1947) who died at nine months old, Makgatho (1950–2005) and Makaziwe (1954–). Cousin of Walter Sisulu who first introduced her to Mandela. Married a retired Sowetan businessman, Simon Rakeepile, in 1998.

Matanzima, Kaiser Daliwonga (K D)
(1915–2003). Thembu chief and politician. Mandela's nephew. Member of the United Transkei Territorial Council, 1955, and an executive member of the Transkei Territorial Authority, 1956. Chief Minister of the Transkei, 1963. Established and led the Transkeian National Independence Party with his brother George Matanzima. First prime minister of the Transkei Bantustan when it gained nominal independence in 1976. State president of the Transkei, 1979–86.

Matthews, Professor Zachariah Keodirelang (Z K)
(1901–1968). Academic, politician, anti-apartheid activist. Member of the ANC. First black South African to obtain a BA degree at a South African institution, 1923. First black South African to obtain an LLB degree in South Africa, 1930. Conceptualised the Congress of the People and the Freedom Charter. Following the Sharpeville Massacre, with Chief Albert Luthuli he organised a 'stay-away', a national day of mourning, on 28 March 1960. In 1965 he retired to Botswana, and became its ambassador to the USA.

Mbeki, Archibald Mvuyelwa Govan (clan name, Zizi)
(1910–2001). Historian and anti-apartheid activist. Leading member of the ANC and the SACP. Served on the High Command of MK. Father of Thabo Mbeki (president of South Africa, 1999–2008). Convicted in the Rivonia Trial and sentenced to life imprisonment. Released from Robben Island Prison, 1987. Served in South Africa's post-apartheid Senate, 1994–1997, as deputy president of the Senate, and its successor, the National Council of Provinces, 1997–99. Awarded the ANC's highest honour, Isitwalandwe Seaparankoe, in 1980.

Mbeki, Mvuyelwa Thabo
(1942–). Politician and anti-apartheid activist. President of South Africa, 1999–2008. Deputy president, 1994–99. Son of Govan Mbeki. Joined the ANCYL in 1956 at the age of fourteen. Left South Africa with other students in 1962. He quickly rose through the ranks of the ANC in exile, and underwent military training in the Soviet Union. He worked closely with O R Tambo and led the ANC delegation that held secret talks with the South African government, participating in all subsequent interactions with the South African government. He served as president of the ANC, 1997–2007.

Meer, Professor Fatima

(1928–2010). Writer, academic and anti-apartheid and women's rights activist. Married Ismail Meer, 1950. Established Student Passive Resistance Committee in support of the 1946 Passive Resistance Campaign against apartheid. Founding member of FEDSAW. First black woman to be appointed as a lecturer at a white South African university (University of Natal), 1956. Banned from 1953 and escaped an assassination attempt. She embraced the Black Consciousness ideology. Founded the Institute of Black Research (IBR), 1975. First president of the Black Women's Federation, established in 1975. Author of *Higher Than Hope* (published 1988), the first authorised biography of Mandela.

Mhlaba, Raymond (clan name, Ndobe)

(1920–2005). Anti-apartheid activist, politician, diplomat and political prisoner. Leading member of ANC and SACP. Commander-in-chief of MK. Arrested in 1963 at Rivonia and sentenced to life imprisonment at the Rivonia Trial. Imprisoned on Robben Island until he was transferred to Pollsmoor Prison in 1982. Released in 1989. He was involved in the negotiations with the National Party government leading to the democratisation of South Africa. Member of the ANC National Executive Committee, 1991. Premier of the Eastern Cape, 1994. South African High Commissioner to Uganda, 1997. Awarded the ANC's highest honour, Isitwalandwe Seaparankoe, in 1992.

MK

(*See* Umkhonto we Sizwe.)

Mkwayi, Wilton Zimasile (clan name, Mbona; nickname, Bri Bri)

(1923–2004). Trade unionist, political activist and political prisoner. Member of the ANC and SACTU. Union organiser for African Textile Workers in Port Elizabeth. Volunteer in the 1952 Defiance Campaign, and later active in the campaign for the Congress of the People. Escaped during the 1956 Treason Trial and went to Lesotho. Joined Umkhonto we Sizwe and had military training in the People's Republic of China. Became MK's commander-in-chief after the arrests at Liliesleaf Farm. Convicted and sentenced to life in what became known as the 'Little Rivonia Trial'. He served his sentence on Robben Island. Released October 1989. Elected to the Senate in the National Parliament in 1994, then deployed to the Eastern Cape Provincial Legislature, where he served until his retirement from public life in 1999. Awarded the ANC's highest honour, Isitwalandwe Seaparankoe, in 1992.

Mlangeni, Andrew Mokete (clan name, Motlokwa; nickname, Mpandla)

(1926–). Anti-apartheid activist, political prisoner and MP. Member of the ANCYL, ANC and MK. Convicted at the Rivonia Trial in 1963 and sentenced to life imprisonment. Served eighteen years on Robben Island and was transferred to Pollsmoor Prison in 1982. Awarded the ANC's highest honour, Isitwalandwe Seaparankoe, in 1992.

Mompati, Ruth Segomotsi

(1925–). Anti-apartheid and women's rights activist, MP, ambassador and mayor. Typist for Mandela and Oliver Tambo at their law practice in Johannesburg, 1953–61. Member of the ANC. Head of the women's division of the ANC in Tanzania. Head of the ANC's Board of Religious Affairs. Founding member of FEDSAW. South African ambassador to Switzerland, 1996–2000. Mayor of Vryburg/Naledi, North West Province.

Moolla, Moosa Mohamed (Mosie)

(1934–). Anti-apartheid activist and diplomat. Member of the Transvaal Indian Youth Congress (TIYC) and TIC. Full-time employee of the National Action Council for the Congress of the People. Among the last thirty accused in the 1956–61 Treason Trial. Detained and held in solitary confinement under the ninety-day law, 1963. Was re-detained but managed to escape by bribing a young guard, Johannes Greeff, and fled across the border to Tanzania. In 1972 he became the ANC's chief representative in India. In November 1989 he was appointed the ANC representative to the World Peace Council. From 1990, he worked in the ANC's Department of International Affairs in South Africa. He was the first South African ambassador to Iran, and then high commissioner to Pakistan until his retirement in 2004.

Moroka, Dr James Sebe

(1892–1985). Medical doctor, politician and anti-apartheid activist. President of the ANC, 1949–52. Convicted in the Defiance Campaign Trial in 1952. During the trial he appointed his own lawyer, disassociated himself from the ANC and pleaded for mitigation. As a consequence he was not re-elected president of the ANC, and was replaced by Chief Luthuli.

Motsoaledi, Elias (clan name, Mokoni)

(1924–94). Trade unionist, anti-apartheid activist and political prisoner. Member of the ANC, SACP and Council of Non-European Trade Unions (CNETU). Banned after the 1952 Defiance Campaign. Helped to establish SACTU in 1955. Imprisoned for four months during the 1960 State of Emergency and detained again under the ninety-day detention laws of 1963. Sentenced to life imprisonment at the Rivonia Trial and imprisoned on Robben Island from 1964 to 1989. Elected to the ANC's National Executive Committee following his release. Awarded the ANC's highest honour, Isitwalandwe Seaparankoe, in 1992.

Naicker, Dr Gangathura Mohambry (Monty)

(1910–78). Medical doctor, politician and anti-apartheid activist. Co-founder and first chairperson of the Anti-Segregation Council. President of the Natal Indian Congress (NIC), 1945–63. Signatory of the 'Doctor's Pact' of March 1947, a statement of cooperation between the ANC, TIC and NIC, which was also signed by Dr Albert Xuma (president of the ANC) and Dr Yusuf Dadoo (president of the TIC).

Nair, Billy

(1929–2008). Politician, anti-apartheid activist, political prisoner and MP. Member of the ANC, NIC, SACP, SACTU and MK. Charged with sabotage in 1963 and imprisoned on Robben Island for twenty years. Joined the UDF on his release. Arrested in 1990 and accused of being part of Operation Vula. MP in the new democratic South Africa.

National Party

Conservative South African political party established in Bloemfontein in 1914 by Afrikaner nationalists. Governing party of South Africa, June 1948 to May 1994. Enforced apartheid, a system of legal racial segregation that favoured minority rule by the white population. Disbanded in 2004.

Ndobe

(*See* Mhlaba, Raymond)

Ngoyi, Lilian Masediba

(1911–80). Politician, anti-apartheid and women's rights activist, and orator. Leading member of the ANC. First woman elected to the ANC Executive Committee, 1956. President of the ANC Women's League. President of FEDSAW, 1956. Led the Women's March against pass laws, 1956. Charged and acquitted in the Treason Trial. Detained in the 1960 State of Emergency. Detained and held in solitary confinement for seventy-one days in 1963 under the ninety-day detention law. Continuously subjected to banning orders. Awarded the ANC's highest honour, Isitwalandwe Seaparankoe, in 1982.

Nokwe, Philemon Pearce Dumasile (Duma)

(1927–78). Lawyer and political activist. Member of the ANCYL. Leading member of the ANC. Secretary of the ANCYL, 1953–58. Participated in the Defiance Campaign. Prevented from teaching, he studied law and became the first black lawyer to be admitted to the Transvaal Supreme Court. However he could not practise as he was an accused in the 1956–61 Treason Trial. He was elected secretary general at the ANC's annual conference in 1958, a post he held until 1969. He was ordered by the ANC to flee into exile, and he left the country in 1963 with Moses Kotane. He helped establish the ANC in exile, lobbying at many international forums.

Nzo, Alfred Baphetuxolo

(1925–2000). Leading member of the ANCYL and ANC. Participant in the 1952 Defiance Campaign, and the Congress of the People. In 1962, Nzo was placed under twenty-four-hour house arrest, and in 1963 he was detained for 238 days. After his release the ANC ordered him to leave the country. He represented the ANC in various countries including Egypt, India, Zambia and Tanzania. He succeeded Duma Nokwe as secretary general in 1969, and held this post until the first legal ANC conference in South Africa in 1991. He was part of the ANC delegation that participated in talks with the De Klerk government after 1990. Appointed Minister of Foreign Affairs in the newly democratic South Africa, 1994. Received a number of awards including the Order of Luthuli in Gold, 2003.

OR
(*See* Tambo, Oliver.)

Pan Africanist Congress (PAC)
Breakaway organisation of the ANC founded in 1959 by Robert Sobukwe, who championed the philosophy of 'Africa for Africans'. The PAC's campaigns included a nationwide protest against pass laws, ten days before the ANC was to start its own campaign. It culminated in the Sharpeville Massacre on 21 March 1960, in which police shot dead sixty-nine unarmed protestors. Banned, along with the ANC, in April 1960. Unbanned on 2 February 1990.

Peake, George
(1922–). Political activist, founding member and national chairperson of the South African Coloured People's Organisation (later the CPC), 1953. Charged and acquitted in the Treason Trial. Subjected to banning orders and detained for five months in the 1960 State of Emergency. Cape Town city councillor from March 1961 until he was charged with sabotage and imprisoned for two years in 1962. Fled South Africa in 1964.

Plaatje, Solomon Tshekisho (Sol)
(1876–1932). Author, journalist, linguist, newspaper editor and political publicist, and human rights activist. Member of the African People's Organisation. First secretary general of the SANNC (renamed as the ANC in 1923), 1912. First black South African to write a novel in English (*Mhudi*, published 1913). Established the first Setswana/English weekly, *Koranta ea Becoana* (*Newspaper of the Tswana*), 1901, and *Tsala ea Becoana* (*The Friend of the People*), 1910. Member of the SANNC deputation that appealed to the British Government against the Land Act of 1913, which severely restricted the rights of Africans to own or occupy land.

Pokela, John Nyathi
(1922–85). Anti-apartheid activist. Member of the ANCYL. Co-founder and leading member of the PAC. Sentenced to thirteen years' imprisonment in 1966 for his participation in Poqo, the PAC's armed wing. President of the PAC from 1981.

Pollsmoor Maximum Security Prison
Prison in the suburb of Tokai, Cape Town. Mandela was moved there along with Walter Sisulu, Raymond Mhlaba, Andrew Mlangeni and, later, Ahmed Kathrada in 1982.

Qunu
Rural village in South Africa's Eastern Cape Province where Mandela lived after his family moved from his birth place of Mvezo.

Radebe, Gaur

(1908–*c*.1968). Political and anti-apartheid activist. Mandela's colleague at Witkin, Sidelsky and Eidelman who encouraged him to attend ANC and SACP meetings. Member of the ANC. Co-founder of the African Mine Workers Union, 1941. Assisted in organising the Alexandra bus boycotts, 1943–44. Assisted Selope Thema in the formation of the National-Minded Bloc, a conservative wing of the ANC which opposed its alliance with the SACP. Leading member of the PAC after it was formed in 1959.

Resha, Robert

(1920–1973). Political and anti-apartheid activist. Leading member of the ANCYL and the ANC. Acting president of the ANCYL, 1954–55. Participated in the Defiance Campaign. Active in the campaign against the forced removal of people from Sophiatown. Acquitted in 1961 with the last group of twenty-eight in the 1955 Treason Trial. He left the country soon after and played a leading role in the exiled ANC, representing it at many forums, including the United Nations. He accompanied Mandela to Oujda, Morocco, during his trip to Africa in 1962, and represented the ANC in an independent Algeria.

Rivonia Trial

Trial between 1963 and 1964 in which ten leading members of the Congress Alliance were charged with sabotage and faced the death penalty. Named after the suburb of Rivonia, Johannesburg, where six members of the MK High Command were arrested at their hideout, Liliesleaf Farm, on 11 July 1963. Incriminating documents, including a proposal for a guerrilla insurgency named Operation Mayibuye, were seized. Mandela, who was already serving a sentence for incitement and leaving South Africa illegally, was implicated, and his notes on guerrilla warfare and his diary from his trip through Africa in 1962 were also seized. Rather than being cross-examined as a witness, Mandela made a statement from the dock on 20 April 1964. This became his famous 'I am prepared to die' speech. On 11 June 1964 eight of the accused were convicted by Justice Qartus de Wet at the Palace of Justice in Pretoria, and the next day were sentenced to life imprisonment.

Robben Island

Island situated in Table Bay, seven kilometres off the coast of Cape Town, measuring approximately 3.3 kilometres long and 1.9 kilometres wide. Has predominantly been used as a place of banishment and imprisonment, particularly for political prisoners, since Dutch settlement in the seventeenth century. Three men who later became South African presidents have been imprisoned there: Nelson Mandela (1964–82), Kgalema Motlanthe (1977–87) and Jacob Zuma (1963–73). Now a World Heritage Site and museum.

Sampson, Anthony

(1926–2004). Writer and journalist. Mandela's biographer for *Mandela: The*

Authorised Biography (published 1999). Edited the South African magazine *Drum*, a leading magazine for an urban black South African readership, in Johannesburg in the 1950s.

Sharpeville Massacre

Confrontation in the township of Sharpeville, Gauteng Province. On 21 March 1960, sixty-nine unarmed anti-pass protestors were shot dead by police and over 180 were injured. The PAC-organised demonstration attracted between 5,000 and 7,000 protesters. This day is now commemorated annually in South Africa as a public holiday: Human Rights Day.

Sidelsky, Lazar

(1911–2002). Member of the Law Society of the Transvaal. Employed Mandela as an articled clerk at his legal practice, Witkin, Sidelsky and Eidelman, in Johannesburg in 1942. Granted mortgages for Africans at a time when few firms were prepared to do so.

Sikhakhane, Joyce

(1943–). Journalist and anti-apartheid activist. Wrote about the families of political prisoners, including Albertina Sisulu and Winnie Mandela, which resulted in her being arrested under the Protection Against Communism Act, then re-detained under the Terrorism Act and forced to spend eighteen months in solitary confinement. Banned on her release. She fled South Africa in 1973. Employed by the Department of Intelligence in the democratic South Africa.

Sisulu (née Thethiwe), Nontsikelelo (Ntsiki) Albertina

(1918–2011). Nurse, midwife, anti-apartheid and women's rights activist, and MP. Leading ANC member. Married Walter Sisulu, whom she met through her nursing friend, Evelyn Mase (Mandela's first wife), 1944. Member of the ANCWL and FEDSAW. Played a leading role in the 1956 women's anti-pass protest. The first woman to be arrested under the General Laws Amendment Act, 1963, during which time she was held in solitary confinement for ninety days. Continually subjected to banning orders and police harassment from 1963. She was elected as one of the three presidents of the UDF at its formation in August 1983. In 1985 she was charged with fifteen other UDF and trade union leaders for treason in what became known as the Pietermaritzburg Treason Trial. MP from 1994 until she retired in 1999. President of the World Peace Council, 1993–96. Recipient of the South African Women for Women Woman of Distinction Award 2003, in recognition of her courageous lifelong struggle for human rights and dignity.

Sisulu, Walter Ulyate Max (clan names, Xhamela and Tyhopho)

(1912–2003). Anti-apartheid activist and political prisoner. Husband of Albertina Sisulu. Met Mandela in 1941 and introduced him to Lazar Sidelsky who employed him as an articled clerk. Leader of the ANC, and generally considered to be the 'father of the struggle'. Co-founder of the ANCYL in 1944. Arrested and charged under the Suppression of Communism Act for playing a leading role in the 1952 Defiance Campaign. Arrested and later acquitted in the 1956 Treason Trial. Continually served with banning orders and placed under house arrest following the banning of the ANC and PAC. Helped established MK, and served on its High Command. Went underground in 1963 and hid at Liliesleaf Farm, in Rivonia, where he was arrested on 11 July 1963. Found guilty of sabotage at the Rivonia Trial, and sentenced to life imprisonment on 12 June 1964. He served his sentence on Robben Island and at Pollsmoor Prison. Released on 15 October 1989. One of the ANC negotiating team with the apartheid government to end white rule. Awarded the ANC's highest honour, Isitwalandwe Seaparankoe, in 1992.

Skota, Mweli

(c.1880s). Clerk, journalist, court interpreter, businessman and newspaper publisher. Leading member of SANNC (later renamed ANC). Founder and editor of *Abantu-Batho*, the ANC newspaper. Member of the AAC.

Slovo, Joe

(1926–95). Anti-apartheid activist. Married Ruth First, 1949. Leading member of the ANC and the CPSA. Commander of MK. Joined the CPSA in 1942 and studied law at the University of the Witwatersrand where he met Mandela and was active in student politics. He helped establish the COD, and was accused in the 1956 Treason Trial. Detained for six months during the 1960 State of Emergency. He assisted in setting up MK. Went into exile from 1963 to 1990 and lived in the UK, Angola, Mozambique and Zambia. General secretary of the SACP, 1986. Chief of staff of MK. Participated in the multi-party negotiations to end white rule. Minister of Housing in Mandela's government from 1994. Awarded the ANC's highest honour, Isitwalandwe Seaparankoe, in 1994.

Sobukwe, Robert Mangaliso

(1924–78). Lawyer, anti-apartheid activist and political prisoner. Member of the ANCYL and the ANC until he formed the PAC based on the vision of 'Africa for Africans'. Editor of the *Africanist* newspaper. Arrested and detained following the Sharpeville Massacre in 1960. Convicted of incitement and sentenced to three years' imprisonment. Before he was released, the General Law Amendment Act No. 37 of 1963 was passed, which allowed for people already convicted of political offences to have their imprisonment renewed – this later became known as the 'Sobukwe Clause' – which resulted in him spending another six years on Robben Island. He was released in 1969 and joined his family in Kimberley, where he remained under twelve-hour house arrest and was restricted from participating in any political activity as a result of a banning order that had been imposed on the PAC. While in prison he studied law, and he established his own law firm in 1975.

South African Communist Party (SACP)

Established in 1921 as the Communist Party of South Africa (CPSA), to oppose imperialism and racist domination. Changed its name to the South African Communist Party

(SACP) in 1953 following its banning in 1950. The SACP was only legalised in 1990. The SACP forms one-third of the Tripartite Alliance with the ANC and COSATU.

South African Indian Congress (SAIC)

Founded in 1923 to oppose discriminatory laws. It comprised the Cape, Natal and Transvaal Indian Congresses. Initially a conservative organisation whose actions were limited to petitions and deputations to authorities, a more radical leadership that favoured militant non-violent resistance came to power in the 1940s under the leadership of Yusuf Dadoo and Monty Naicker.

State of Emergency, 1960

Declared on 30 March 1960 as a response to the Sharpeville Massacre. Characterised by mass arrests and the imprisonment of most African leaders. On 8 April 1960 the ANC and PAC were banned under the Unlawful Organisations Act.

Stengel, Richard

Editor and author. Collaborated with Mandela on his autobiography, *Long Walk to Freedom* (published 1994). Co-producer of the documentary *Mandela*, 1996. Editor of *Time* magazine.

Suppression of Communism Act, No. 44, 1950

Act passed 26 June 1950, in which the state banned the SACP and any activities it deemed communist, defining 'communism' in such broad terms that anyone protesting against apartheid would be in breach of the act.

Suzman, Helen

(1917–2009). Academic, politician, anti-apartheid activist and MP. Professor of Economic History, University of Witwatersrand. Founded a branch of the United Party at University of Witwatersrand in response to the apartheid state's racist policies. MP for the United Party, 1953–59, then later the anti-apartheid Progressive Federal Party (1961–74). The only opposition political leader who was permitted to visit Robben Island.

Tambo (née Tshukudu), Adelaide Frances

(1929–2007). Nurse, community worker and anti-apartheid and women's rights activist. Married Oliver Tambo, 1956. Member of the ANCYL. Participated in the Women's March, 1956. Recipient of numerous awards including the Order of Simon of Cyrene, July 1997, the highest order given by the Anglican Church for distinguished service by lay people; and the Order of the Baobab in Gold, 2002.

Tambo, Oliver Reginald (O R)

(1917–93). Lawyer, politician and anti-apartheid activist. Leading member of the ANC and founder member of the ANCYL. Co-founder, with Mandela, of South Africa's first African legal practice. Became secretary general of the ANC after Walter Sisulu was banned, and deputy president of the ANC, 1958. Served with a five-year banning order, 1959. Left South Africa during the 1960s to manage the external activities of the ANC and to mobilise opposition against apartheid. Established military training camps outside South Africa. Initiated the Free Mandela Campaign in the 1980s. Lived in exile in London, UK, until 1990. Acting president of the ANC, 1967, after the death of Chief Albert Luthuli. Was elected president in 1969 at the Morogoro Conference, a post he held until 1991 when he became the ANC's national chairperson. Awarded the ANC's highest honour, Isitwalandwe Seaparankoe, in 1992.

Thema, Selope

(1886–1955). Journalist and political activist. Leading member of the ANC. Secretary of the deputation to the Versailles Peace Conference and the British government, 1919.

Treason Trial

(1956–61). The Treason Trial was the apartheid government's attempt to quell the power of the Congress Alliance. In early morning raids on 5 December 1956, 156 individuals were arrested and charged with high treason. By the end of the trial in March 1961 all the accused either had the charges withdrawn or, in the case of the last twenty-eight accused including Mandela, were acquitted.

Tshwete, Steve Vukile

(1938–2002). Anti-apartheid activist, political prisoner, politician and MP. Member of the ANC and MK. Imprisoned on Robben Island, 1964–78, for being a member of a banned organisation. Served on the ANC Executive Committee, 1988, and participated in the talks about talks at Groote Schuur in 1990. Minister of Sport and Recreation, 1994–99. Promoted the de-racialisation of South African sport. Minister of Safety and Security, 1999–2002.

Turok, Ben

(1927–). Academic, trade unionist, political and anti-apartheid activist, and MP. Member of the CPSA and ANC. Leading member of the South African COD involved in organising the Congress of the People, 1955. Founding member of MK. Arrested and later acquitted in the Treason Trial. Represented Africans of the Western Cape on the Cape Provincial Council, 1957. Escaped into exile in 1966.

Tutu, Archbishop Desmond

(1931–). Archbishop Emeritus and anti-apartheid and human rights activist. Bishop of Lesotho, 1976–78. First black general secretary of the South African Council of Churches, 1978. Following the 1994 election, he chaired the Truth and Reconciliation Commission to investigate apartheid-era crimes. Recipient of the 1984 Nobel Peace Prize for seeking a non-violent end to apartheid; the Albert Schweitzer Prize for Humanitarianism, 1986; and the Gandhi Peace Prize, 2005.

Tyhopho
(*See* Sisulu, Walter)

Umkhonto we Sizwe (MK)
Umkhonto we Sizwe, meaning 'spear of the nation', was founded in 1961 and is commonly known by the abbreviation MK. Nelson Mandela was its first commander–in-chief. It became the military wing of the ANC. After the 1994 elections MK was disbanded and its soldiers incorporated into the newly formed South African National Defence Force (SANDF) with soldiers from the apartheid South African Defence Force, Bantustan defence forces, IFP's self-protection units and Azanian People's Liberation Army (APLA), the military wing of the PAC.

Verwoerd, Dr Hendrik Frensch
(1901–66). Prime minister of South Africa, 1958–66. Minister of Native Affairs, 1950–58. National Party politician. Widely considered the architect of apartheid, he advocated a system of 'separate development'. Under his leadership South Africa became a republic on 31 May 1961. Assassinated in parliament by Dimitri Tsafendas.

Victor Verster Prison
Low-security prison located between Paarl and Franschhoek in the Western Cape. Mandela was transferred there in 1988, and lived in a private house inside the prison compound. There is a statue of Mandela just outside the prison gates. Now named Drakenstein Correctional Centre.

Vorster, Balthazar Johannes (B J)
(1915–83). Prime minister of South Africa, 1966–78. President of South Africa, 1978–79.

Weinberg, Eli
(1908–81). Trade unionist, photographer and political activist. Member of the SACP. Continuously subjected to banning orders from 1953 onwards. Detained for three months in 1960 during the State of Emergency and again in September 1964. Sentenced to five years' imprisonment after being found guilty of being a member of the Central Committee of the SACP. Fled South Africa in 1976 on the instruction of the ANC.

Xhamela
(*See* Sisulu, Walter)

Zami
(*See* Madikizela-Mandela, Nomzamo Winifred)

Zeni
(*See* Mandela, Zenani)

Zindzi
(*See* Mandela, Zindziswa)

SELECT BIBLIOGRAPHY

Books:
Davenport, Rodney and Christopher Saunders, *South Africa: A Modern History*, 5th ed., Macmillan Press, London, 2000

Kathrada, Ahmed, *Memoirs*, Zebra Press, Cape Town, 2004

Mandela, Nelson, *Long Walk to Freedom*, Little, Brown and Company, London, 1994

Meer, Fatima, *Higher Than Hope*, Skotaville Publishers, Johannesburg, 1988

Nelson Mandela Foundation, *A Prisoner in the Garden: Opening Nelson Mandela's Prison Archive*, Penguin, 2005

Nicol, Mike, *Mandela: The Authorised Portrait*, PQ Blackwell, Auckland, 2006

Sampson, Anthony, *Mandela: The Authorised Biography*, HarperCollins Publishers, London, 2000

Sisulu, Elinor, *Walter and Albertina Sisulu: In Our Lifetime*, David Philip Publishers, Cape Town, 2002

Websites:
www.justice.gov.za/trc
www.nelsonmandela.org
www.robben-island.org.za
www.sahistory.org.za

443

ACKNOWLEDGEMENTS

We are grateful to Zindzi Mandela for permission to reproduce her poem 'A Tree Was Chopped Down', and for her support of the Nelson Mandela Centre of Memory and Dialogue.

We thank President Barack Obama for his generous foreword, and Ambassador Donald Gips for facilitating liaison with the President.

We acknowledge the importance to this book of the two sound archives created by Ahmed Kathrada and Richard Stengel, both of which were lodged by their creators with the Centre of Memory and Dialogue after the book had been conceived.

The photographic images for the book have been made with skill and great patience by Matthew Willman, with the exception of the following: pp. xxiv–1 (rural scene) and pp. 4–5 (young Thembu initiates) – McGregor Museum, Kimberley, Duggan-Cronin Collection; pp. 20–21 (Mandela formal portraits), pp. 58–59 (Mandela burning his pass) and p. 110 (Mandela in candlewick bedspread) – Eli Weinberg; pp. 28–29 (crowd at Drill Hall gates) – Museum Africa, Times Media Collection; pp. 32–33 (Orlando township) – Leon Levson; pp. 84–85 (Mandela in London, UK) – Mary Benson; pp. 110–111 (*Rand Daily Mail*) – Avusa Publications; pp. 110–111 (Cato Manor protest) – Laurie Bloomfield; pp. 130–131 (prisoners in courtyard) – UWC-Robben Island Museum, Mayibuye Archives, Cloete Breytenbach; pp. 264–265 (Mandela's desk, Robben Island) and pp. 206–207 (Mandela in prison garden) – South African National Archives, courtesy Nelson Mandela Foundation; pp. 126–127 (barbed-wire fence, Robben Island) and pp. 156–157 (Mandela's cell on Robben Island) – Matthew Willman; pp. 240–241 (Mandela revisiting Robben Island prison cell) – Corbis, David Turnley; pp. 318–319 (F W de Klerk and Mandela at National Peace Convention, Johannesburg) – Rodger Bosch; pp. 322–323 (1994 election day queue) – *Argus News*; pp. 372–373 (Mandela in print shirt) – PQ Blackwell; pp. 392–393 (Mandela close-up) – Nelson Mandela Foundation.

We are indebted to the following repositories for providing access to materials: Mandela House Museum, South African National Archives, University of Fort Hare and University of the Witwatersrand (Historical Papers).

For assistance and support we thank Zahira Adams, Jon Butler, Eric Chinski, Diana and Kate Couzens, Achmat Dangor, Lee Davies, Imani Media, Zelda la Grange, Molly Loate, Winnie Madikizela-Mandela, Zenani Mandela, Zindzi Mandela, Rochelle Mtirara, Judge Thumba Pillay, Natalie Skomolo, Wendy Smith, Jack Swart, Ivan Vladislavic and Gerrit Wagener.

For Nelson Mandela Foundation Centre of Memory and Dialogue: Verne Harris, Sahm Venter, Ahmed Kathrada, Tim Couzens, Sello Hatang, Razia Saleh, Lucia Raadschelders, Zanele Riba and Boniswa Nyati.

For originating publisher PQ Blackwell: Geoff Blackwell, Ruth Hobday, Bill Phillips, Cameron Gibb, Rachel Clare, Dayna Stanley, Sarah Anderson, Jonny Geller, Betsy Robbins, Kate Cooper and Sloan Harris.

INDEX

....

Page numbers in **bold** indicate imagery or maps. Page numbers in *italics* refer to interviews or conversations with Nelson Mandela (NM). Titles of poems and songs are in single quotes; films, books, plays and album titles are *italicised*, and writers and artists noted in brackets. Common names, customary titles and clan names are included, in brackets, where possible.